ROUTLEDGE LIBRARY EDITIONS:
DEVELOPMENT

AFRICA AND EUROPE

AFRICA AND EUROPE

From Partition To Interdependence
Or Dependence?

Edited by
AMADU SESAY

Volume 84

Routledge
Taylor & Francis Group

LONDON AND NEW YORK

First published in 1986

This edition first published in 2011
by Routledge
2 Park Square, Milton Park, Abingdon, Oxon, OX14 4RN

Simultaneously published in the USA and Canada
by Routledge
270 Madison Avenue, New York, NY 10016

Routledge is an imprint of the Taylor & Francis Group, an informa business

© 1986 Amadu Sesay

British Library Cataloguing in Publication Data
A catalogue record for this book is available from the British Library

ISBN 13: 978-0-415-58414-2 (Set)
eISBN 13: 978-0-203-84035-1 (Set)
ISBN 13: 978-0-415-60144-3 (Volume 84)
eISBN 13: 978-0-203-83573-9 (Volume 84)

Publisher's Note
The publisher has gone to great lengths to ensure the quality of this reprint but
points out that some imperfections in the original copies may be apparent.

Disclaimer
The publisher has made every effort to trace copyright holders and welcomes
correspondence from those they have been unable to contact.

AFRICA AND EUROPE

From Partition To Interdependence Or Dependence ?

Edited by Amadu Sesay

CROOM HELM
London • Sydney • Dover, New Hampshire

© 1986 Amadu Sesay,
Croom Helm Ltd, Provident House, Burrell Row,
Beckenham, Kent BR3 1AT
Croom Helm Australia Pty Ltd, Suite 4, 6th Floor,
64-76 Kippax Street, Surry Hills, NSW 2010, Australia

British Library Cataloguing in Publication Data

Africa and Europe: from partition to
    interdependence or dependence?
    1. Europe – Foreign relations – Africa
    2. Africa – Foreign relations – Europe
    I. Sesay, Amadu
    327'.094   D34.A35

    ISBN 0-7099-4406-3

Croom Helm, 51 Washington Street, Dover,
New Hampshire 03820, USA

Library of Congress Cataloging-in-Publication Data

Africa and Europe: from partition to interdependence
    or dependence?

    1. Africa–relations–Europe. 2. Europe–
relations–Africa. I. Sesay, Amadu.
DT38.9.E85A34   1986   303.4'826'04   86-6362
ISBN 0-7099-4406-3

CONTENTS

Preface

Abbreviations

A.   HISTORICAL PERSPECTIVES

1. Europe and Africa: Prelude to the
   Partition   1
   Sola Akinrinade and Toyin Falola.
2. Berlin and Afro-European Relations ... 21
   Sola Akinrinade and Toyin Falola.
3. Goodbye to Berlin? The Partition of
   Africa Reconsidered 34
   Dennis Austin.

b.   INDEPENDENCE AND AFTER

4. Britain and Anglophone Africa 52
   James Mayall.
5. France's Involvement in Sub-Saharan
   Africa: A Corollary to Middle Power
   Status in the International System ... 75
   Daniel C. Bach.
6. Portugal, Angola and Mozambique: The
   Trend of Future Relationships 86
   Fola Soremekun.
7. The Soviet Union, Angola and the Horn
   of Africa: New Patterns in Afro-
   European Relations 104
   James Mulira.

C.   STRATEGIC AND ECONOMIC RELATIONSHIPS

8. Africa's Strategic Relationship with
   Western Europe: The Dispensability
   Thesis 129

Contents

Jinmi Adisa and Adigun Agbaje.
9. The OAU's Response to European Military
Interventions in Africa 152
Amadu Sesay.
10. Africa and Europe: Collective
Dependence or Interdependence? 183
S.K.B. Asante.
11. The Dialectics of Regionalism:
EurAfrica and West Africa 222
Timothy M. Shaw

Notes on Contributors 246

Index 247

To the memory of my Father, a
percipient farmer who could tell
which seed would grow, when to sow
it, and where to sow it.

PREFACE

This collection has been brought together especially to mark the centenary of the Berlin Conference and the subsequent partition of Africa by the European powers between 1884 and 1885. That both events have had a profound impact on the continents of Africa and Europe and their peoples, and, indeed, the global system at large, has not been in doubt. The collection is therefore a modest contribution to the growing literature on Africa's pre-colonial, colonial and post-colonial relationships with Europe.

The idea of putting such a volume together was conceived in early 1984. In preparing it, I have had the assistance of various people, too many to name here individually. However, I would like to thank all the contributors for responding promptly to my request for chapters for the volume. Without their cooperation, the dream would not have come true. Secondly, I would like to thank the typists in the department for typing the manuscript; Mr. Amos Osagie and Mr. Eric Johnson. Finally, I would like to express my sincere gratitude to my wife and children for their usual love, understanding and encouragement.

Amadu Sesay,
Ile-Ife,
Nigeria.

ABBREVIATIONS

ACP	African, Caribbean and Pacific Countries.
ANC	African National Congress.
BC	Before Christ.
CBI	Confederation of British Industries.
CIA	Central Intelligence Agency.
CMS	Church Missionary Society.
EDF	European Development Fund.
EEC	European Economic Community.
ECOWAS	Economic Community of West African States.
FNLA	Front for the National Liberation of Angola.
GATT	General Agreement on Tariffs and Trade.
GNP	Gross National Product.
ICI	Imperial Chemical Industries.
IDA	International Development Agency.
IMF	International Monetary Fund.
ITUCNW	International Trade Union Committee of Negro Workers.
MPLA	Popular Movement for the Liberation of Angola.
NATO	North Atlantic Treaty Organisation.
NIEO	New International Economic Order.
OAU	Organisation of African Unity.
OECE	Organisation for Economic Cooperation and Development.
PMAC	Provisional Military Administrative Council.
SADCC	South Africa Development and Coordination Conferences.
SWAPO	South West Africa Peoples Organisation.
STABEX	Stabilisation of Exports.
UK	United Kingdom.
UN	United Nations.
UNCTAD	United Nations Conferences on Trade and Development.
UNITA	Union for the Total Independence of Angola.
USA	United States of America.
USSR	Union of Soviet Socialist Republics.

CHAPTER 1

AFRICA AND EUROPE: PRELUDE TO THE PARTITION

Sola Akinrinade and Toyin Falola

A.   EARLIEST CONTACTS AND THE SLAVE TRADE

The domination of parts of Africa by certain
European countries pre-dated the 1880s. The Romans
were the earliest significant European conquerors of
African peoples. The Roman contact was in the form
of military adventure, manifested in the attempt to
subjugate the famous African-based Empire of
Carthage. The enterprising Carthaginians had,
through hard work and ruthless suppression of
rivals, succeeded in establishing a commercial and
industrially viable state, with an equally viable
agricultural base. By the third century BC, the
rising state of the Romans, which had of necessity
accepted a subordinate position hitherto placed on
it by treaties with Carthage, demonstrated its
military power by challenging Carthage. The first of
the clashes was the First Punic war of 264-241 BC,
which resulted in a serious defeat for Carthage.
Rome again triumphed over Carthage despite the
military genius of Hannibal, the Carthaginian
leader, during the Second Punic War, 218-202 BC.
Carthage was finally destroyed by the Romans in 146
BC. Roman rule in North Africa later extended to
Egypt in the first century BC. In the process of
Roman rule in North Africa, many North Africans rose
to positions of eminence in the Roman Empire. Such
included Septimus Severus, who had the distinction
of being the first North African-born Roman
Emperor. It was also his son, Caracalla, who issued
the Caracalla Edict of 212, which gave Roman
citizenship to free men all over the Roman world.
The most famous, however, was Augustine, the fifth
century Bishop of the North African city of Hippo.
    Roman control over North Africa, however, began
to witness a steady decline from the third century.

1

This decline had, by the fifth century, allowed a group of European barbarians, the Vandals, to take over control of the western regions of North Africa without encountering many problems. The Vandals never succeeded in establishing an integrated administration. After about a century of Roman rule, the eastern Romans (the Byzantines) easily conquered and took over control of the North African state during the reign of Justinian in the mid-sixth century. The Byzantines equally found it difficult to consolidate the once extensive Roman holdings in North Africa into a single entity, neither could they secure the loyalty of the indigenous population.

The advent of the Muslim Arab invasions in the seventh century swept away traces of Roman rule in North Africa. Europeans gradually lost interest in Africa for some time. The re-awakening of European interest came with the activities of Portuguese mariners. The kingdom of Portugal had earlier conquered the North African kingdom of Morocco. In the military crew that won the victory over Morocco was Prince Henry, better known as Henry the Navigator. It was this man who, after observing the commercial position of North Africa, decided to divert the gold trade from the Atlantic coast towards Portugal. He then embarked on a voyage to discover a route to the Atlantic coast of Africa. Portuguese activities in Africa eventually extended to several parts of the continent, including the kingdom of Congo; the Gold Coast, where the fort known as Sao Jorge da Mina was built in spite of opposition from the Akan-speaking people in the area; the areas of present-day Angola, Mozambique and Benin. Many people were converted to Christianity by the Portuguese, especially in the Congo, where their king, Nzinga Kuwu, changed his name to Joao I after his baptism. Also, Mbemba Nzinga, one of Nzinga Kuwu's successors, changed his name to, and was better known as, Affonso I. It was Affonso I who made Christianity the state religion.[1]

Other European nations did not delay too long in following Portuguese steps in the newly-discovered African coasts. Spain and France were involved. Early clashes between Spain and Portugal led to the signing of the Treaty of Tordesillas of 1494, an agreement sanctified by various papal bulls.[2] But France expressed dissatisfaction with the arrangement, and it was rectified later. Thereafter, France penetrated into West Africa, establishing a base in Senegal. The Gold Coast area was a scene of active trade competition among rival European powers. The Dutch, after losing territories in Brazil to the Portuguese, sought bases in West Africa which would serve as a source of slave supply and they also conquered Portuguese territories in Angola. The British joined the race in the 1660s, with the foundation of the Company of Royal Adventurers to Africa. The company was succeeded in 1672 by the Royal African Company, which was replaced in 1750 by the Company of Merchants Trading in Africa. At various times other European countries had forts in the Gold Coast; such included the Swedes, the Danes and Brandenburgers. By the early eighteenth century there were about twenty-five major trading bases and an almost equal number of minor ones. These were later reduced to two, with the Dutch and the British as the principal occupiers. The eighteenth century European wars finally saw Britain as the major commercial force along the coastline.

The coming of these Europeans to various parts of Africa was occasioned by commercial motives. The whole idea behind the voyages of exploration that preceded the coming of the Europeans was to find an alternative sea route to India and to obtain luxury goods at the lowest possible price. The African land itself was not without its own goods which appealed to the Europeans. Such goods as gold, ivory, grain, spices and sugar were in high demand in Europe and even in India. Strategic points on the African coast, especially the West African coastline, were given such names as Grain Coast, Gold Coast, Ivory Coast, and so on. Side by side with these articles were exported slaves, and by the beginning of the sixteenth century the slave trade had begun to overshadow all other trades.

The continued maintenance of European positions on the African coastline was occasioned by the fact that the forts also served as suppliers of African slaves to the western world. The era of European slavery and slave trade in Africa was a major phase in Afro-European relations prior to partition. The slave trade which has been referred to as 'the most iniquitous of transactions in human history'[3] existed on a rather low scale before the Europeans came, and, contrary to the much vaunted propaganda that slavery was an integral part of the African society, not every society had a place for slaves; this was especially the case among the Masai, who were mainly interested in capturing cattle.[4] The emergence of Europeans on the scene marked a new phase in the African slave trade.

The beginning of European interest in African slave trade is often traced to 1441, when Gonzalves, one of the Portuguese explorers, captured a small groups of Africans and carted them away to Lisbon. Later, more and more Africans were taken to Portugal. Prince Henry's plan for the earlier set of Africans was to educate and use them to further 'civilise' their brethren back home in Africa. But his hope was not realised. By 1460, when Henry died, more than eight hundred Africans were exported to Portugal annually and were sold on arrival at the Lisbon dock as slaves. Henry did not approve of this trade, but after his death successive kings and princes supported it. Portugal maintained a lead in the West African slave trade throughout the fifteenth and for most of the sixteenth century, that is until other European nations began to pose determined opposition. Britain joined, first, through the activities of individuals like William Hawkins and Captain Windham, and later through chartered companies. Other countries joined and soon the Portuguese, the French, the Dutch, the Danes, the Germans, Swedes, Spaniards and the British were all involved in the trade in African slaves.

It should be realised, however, that the initial emphasis of trade was on gold, not on slaves. The 'discovery' of America in 1492 for the Spanish government by Christopher Columbus brought about drastic changes. When mineral deposits were found in Mexico and Peru, the aboriginal Red Indians were found incapable of, and insufficient for, working there. Recourse was made to the African slaves in Europe. The Spaniards then made an arrangement with the Portuguese, and an annual average of about 13,000 slaves was exported to Spanish holdings in the Americas. The development of interest by the French and the British in American possessions towards the end of the sixteenth century led to the sending out of explorers and the founding by the French of some colonies in North America. British colonies in North America were established in about the second decade of the seventeenth century. These British colonies were predominantly agricultural, and the consequent demand for labour boosted the supply of slaves, which up to then had been left in the hands of the Portuguese. With more mines being opened by the Spaniards and more plantations cultivated by the French and the British, the demand for slaves increased. Between 1530 and 1600 the annual average was 13,000 slaves.

This figure rose to 27,500 per annum throughout the seventeenth century and soared to an annual average of 70,000 in the eighteenth century. In the 1830s it was running at an all time high of 135,000 slaves per annum.[5]

The slave trade continued for almost three centuries, with an attitude of callous indifference until the conscience of religious and humanitarian groups was roused against it. But it was not until 1807 that the trade was declared illegal by the British Parliament. Even then, much remained to be done to wipe out this transatlantic trade. It was the humanitarian and philanthropic organisations, personified by such men as Granville Sharpe, William Wilberforce, Henry Curton, Charles Grant and Thomas Clarkson, that raised the agitation for abolition to an unprecedented height. They were actually involved in the Supreme Court judgement given by Justice Mansfield in 1772 which made slavery illegal on British soil and declared all slaves who set foot on English soil as emancipated. Again, their efforts in Britain and America aided the foundation of the colonies of Sierra Leone and Liberia, which acted as dumping grounds for liberated slaves. But the abolition of the slave trade could not be wholly attributed to the humanitarian factor. In fact, the arguments of the humanitarians themselves were drawn from the social and economic views prevalent at the time among scholars and politicians, that it would pay Britain better if the slave trade was abolished.

Such ideological and economic considerations were preached in the eighteenth century, when the doctrine of equality, fraternity and liberty of men became popularised. Montesquieu, the French political idealist, had preached the idea that bondage negates divine law. The American war of independence had advanced this view further and had asserted that all men were born equal. These political ideas had dominated the thinking of policy and decision-makers in France and Britain, and towards the end of the eighteenth century both countries were considering the possibility of setting free the slaves in bondage. The arguments advanced by a new wave of economists were also in favour of abolition. These men, including Adam Smith, Thomas Malthus and David Ricardo, criticised the false logic on which the old mercantilist idea that supported the slave trade was based. They advocated free trade, perfect competition and the distribution of wealth according to natural laws. Besides, there was also the industrial revolution which had started in Britain in the eighteenth century. The revolution transformed production by replacing labour with machinery, which meant an increasingly low need for slave labour on the farm and in the industries. It was then considered more economically wise to leave the would-be slaves on their lands in Africa to be taught how to produce large quantities of cotton, coffee, ground-nuts and palm oil for the market, whilst they would be encouraged to consume European-made goods. This appeared a valid reasoning to the politicians and economic advisers, and it was therefore no wonder that the cry for the abolition of the slave trade came from Britain.

The 1772 Mansfield judgement is generally regarded as the first effort to suppress the slave trade. However, it was only a judicial victory; it did not end the trade in slaves. The British Parliament legislated in 1807 that the slave trade was illegal for British subjects and extended this to cover the whole of the British Empire in 1833, having already attached the death penalty to the offence in 1824. Naval squadrons were set up and were empowered to search British ships on the Atlantic Ocean, free the captives and to punish any British citizen caught trading in slaves. But the fact that other countries participated in the trade ensured a continuance of the business, and African middlemen still persisted in marching captives to the coast. British efforts aimed at pressurising other European nations to stop the trade yielded results, as France outlawed the trade in 1818, and Brazil followed in 1825. But when the trade continued, Britain then sought the authority to search foreign ships to ascertain that they had no slaves aboard. This authority was granted by Spain and Portugal in 1817, Sweden in 1824, France in 1833, the United States in 1862 and the Netherlands in 1878. In addition, Britain signed a number of treaties that guaranteed the abolition with several European nations, including France in 1833, Spain in 1835, Portugal in 1842 and the United States in 1862. These efforts yielded some positive results, as about 130,000 slaves were released. However, during the same period (i.e. 1825-1865) up to 1.8 million slaves were exported. It was thus apparent that the steps would at best only reduce the number of slaves exported, not eradicate the trade itself.

The abolitionists changed tactics and adopted a positive policy towards abolition which was styled 'Christianity, Commerce and Colonisation'. It was an acceptance of the fact that the trade could be stopped only if attacked at the roots and that this could be done only through the provision of an alternative way of life that would render the slave trade less lucrative. It was also admitted that managing the long African coastline and policing the large number of communities would not be an easy task. This was the reasoning behind the founding of Sierra Leone by the abolitionists.

The Sierrra Leone colony was founded in 1787, handed over to the British Government in 1806 and made a Crown Colony in 1807. Liberia was founded by the American Colonisation Society in 1822, and a group of negroes who chose to leave the United States was deposited there. These two early colonial strongholds nurtured a breed of Africans who later went back to their homelands, especially southern Nigeria and Ghana, as the first generation of elites. They pioneered the development of western education, preached the gospel to the people and became vanguards for the European colonisation of Africa. Missionary societies were also established, notably the Baptist Missionary Society founded in 1792, the Church Missionary Society (1799), the British and Foreign Bible Society (1803) and the Methodist, to preach the gospel to Africans in their homelands. Later, it was found necessary to know more about the African hinterland; voyages of exploration were then sponsored into the African interior.

The final step in the abolition was the introduction of an alternative way of earning a living. This led to the promotion of 'legitimate trade'. Raw materials, especially palm oil, cotton, ground-nuts, coffee, etc., were cultivated on a large scale for external markets. This business eventually replaced the slave trade. In exchange, the Europeans brought their products, including clothes, cutlasses, knives, beer, matches, etc., for the Africans.

In spite of the negative impact of the slave trade, there were still pockets of resistance to the abolition of this obnoxious traffic. Apart from the Europeans who were involved and who naturally found abolition measures unpalatable, there were also elements of African resistance. This is because the majority of the African coastal kingdoms, even more than the European states, stood to be ruined by the suppression. Their economies were intricately intertwined with the slave trade, whilst the war lords became used to the act of catching and selling

7

slaves.

Other reasons account for the African resistance to the suppression of the trade. First, the alternative offered to the slave trade - 'legitimate trade' - was not immediately lucrative. None of the new cash products could bring in ready income as much as slaves. Cotton, upon which so many people based their hopes, did not flourish along the coast and was costly to produce. Secondly, African chiefs and elites who had benefited from the slave trade found it difficult to appreciate the British efforts to abolish the trade. In Bonny, for example, the British government so mismanaged the situation that the Bonny chief was antagonistic to the British authority there. Representatives of the British had negotiated four treaties with King Pepple of Bonny and had promised compensation in return for Bonny's abolition of the slave trade. However, in the end, Britain neither ratified the treaties nor paid any compensation to Pepple. When Pepple tried to force it to pay, he was quickly deported in 1854. But, finding that no one could efficiently hold Bonny together like him, Pepple was brought back in 1861. But the Bonny kingdom had by then been destroyed. Various other treaties were signed with coastal kings by the British but again the British never kept their own side of the bargain.

Thus, the abolition notwithstanding, the damage had already been done. First, there was vast depopulation of African territories and untold human suffering. The actual figure involved cannot be ascertained; many slaves died on the march to the coast and many more died on the voyage across the Atlantic - all of whom were never accounted for. A grave component of the demographic effect was the composition of those carried away - those exported were mainly men who could have helped in the economic development of their localities. Secondly, there was a general and widespread insecurity caused by the raids. Usually the majority of the slaves were procured through slave raids. Communities were attacked and houses set ablaze; fleeing inhabitants were caught and manacled; bloodshed, destruction and general panic gripped African territories. Under such conditions, no productive activity could be expected to take place. Furthermore, there was an increase in the amount of inter-state and inter-ethnic warfare. Captives of these wars who were hitherto used as household slaves were instantly committed for sale as slaves for export. Some writers have asserted that these inter-state wars led to the expansion of some coastal states: at best, this is only a half-truth. It must be realised that, though there was expansion, there was more importantly also large-scale destruction. The frontiers were always constantly being re-ordered, and more wars were fought over the flimsiest of causes. The introduction of firearms made the wars more bloody and total, and the strong drinks, like rum, taken by soldiers further goaded them into savage action. More importantly, the slave trade produced grave economic consequences for African land. There was a tremendous decline in the development of industries and of indigenous crafts. Those industries that manufactured beads, clothes, bronze, etc., were abandoned because of the general insecurity. Farming was done mainly at the subsistence level, since there was no demand for the surplus goods. Cash crop economy developed rather late because of the slave trade. It was not until the abolition of the slave trade that the Europeans began to promote the production of such cash crops as tobacco, sugar, coffee, rubber, etc. The examples of the decline of Benin, Dahomey and Asante are enough to demonstrate those states that diverted their energies from peaceful development of politics, arts and culture, to pre-occupation with predatory wars and wanton destruction in the process of capturing slaves.

But it was not all a bitter experience. The founding of Freetown (Sierra Leone) and Liberia in West Africa was a remarkable by-product of the slave trade. The settlements represent practical examples of the efforts of the philanthropists in trying to settle down the emancipated slaves in African homelands. But on the whole, the experience of slavery and the slave trade had paralysing effects on the African societies. The Europeans who came in the nineteenth century met societies in chaos and stagnation and concluded that African societies had always been like that, forgetting, however, that early Portuguese accounts of Benin, for example, spoke of the orderliness of, and the peaceful atmosphere in, the kingdom.

B. MISSIONARY ACTIVITIES

The Europeans believed that a clear knowledge of the hinterland was essential and necessary in order to suppress the slave trade and spread Christianity. They also wanted to justify the claim that they came to Africa to satisfy their scientific urge to know the unknown - the interior of Africa. European knowledge of Africa prior to this period was limited to the coast; whatever was known about the interior was only picked up and also distorted. One result of their exploration was that large areas of Africa became known to the Europeans, who were then able to estbalish trade and political links with those areas already explored. The Christian Missions were able to venture into the interior and the opening of churches and schools began. Exploration also popularised the claim that Africa was the "white man's grave" because many Europeans died in various expeditions.

Apart from preaching the gospel, the missionaries also paid particular attention to the development of western education in Africa. Elementary as well as teacher training schools were established. It is on record that by 1841 the Church Missionary Society (CMS) alone had opened twenty-one elementary schools in Sierra Leone and had founded two secondary schools. In 1827 the Mission established Fourah Bay College as a nursery school for the college being established for bright Sierra Leonean students at Islington, in England.

Furthermore, the missionary impact was felt in the agricultural sector. New crops were introduced by them; they set up plantations and experimental farms and educated farmers in the modern methods of production. An example was the Egba Cotton Board, promoted by the CMS in Abeokuta. It was the Mission that sampled all the products of western Yorubaland and came up with cotton for Egbaland. It was also the Mission that sent one of the returnee Egba to Britain to learn new methods of planting, harvesting and packing cotton for the market. Apart from cotton, the missions promoted the plantations of cocoa, palm oil and other cash crops along the African coastline, especially that of West Africa.

Their devotion to linguistic studies in Africa is another area in which the missionaries would also be remembered. As expected, the breeding place was Sierra Leone. This started when the Reverend Koelle arrived to head the Christian Institution and instructed all the missionaries being sent out by the CMS to engage in the translation of the scriptures to local languages. By 1880, most of the local languages could be written, and there were passages of the Bible written in Yoruba, Hausa, Igbo, Tenne, Twi, Ga, Ewa, Efik and others. Some of the missionaries established printing presses, like Henry Townsend's, which printed the Iwe Irohin.

Finally, the missions acted as vanguards of European colonial rule. By 1900 they had succeeded in producing a group of elites who not only mediated in the Euro-African disputes but whose views had also been slanted towards the side of the Europeans through a long period of exposure to indoctrination. For example, such missionaries as Bishop Phillips, James Johnson and Samuel Johnson, helped to secure the treaties that made Yorubaland a part of the Southern Nigerian Protectorate for the British.

C.   'LEGITIMATE' COMMERCE AND COLONIAL INTERESTS

The abolition of the slave trade did not put an end to European commercial activities in African territories. Two factors were responsible for the European decision to continue trading. First, they had invested a huge amount of money in ships, hulks and castles, and they could not bear the thought of losing the capital investment. Secondly, they found to their happiness that such articles as palm oil, ground-nuts, coffee, gum, rubber, cotton, timber and cocoa were in high demand in Europe. They thus began to promote the production of these cash crops and exported them, just as they did with slaves. 'Legitimate trade' was a carefully organised business enterprise, involving the growing of cash crops, the shipment of the produce, and the importation of manufactured goods. In addition, some small-scale mining and industrialisation also took place.
　　Like the missionary enterprise, the 'legitimate trade' removed people from the constant raids and panic and replaced with this an orderly and settled environment where agriculture and business could be actively pursued. Further the trade created in Africa another class of traders. There were always the long-distance traders, who engaged in trade with North Africa via the Sudanese middlemen, and chiefs who were strong enough to obtain slaves from the war-lords. These were stationed along the coastal areas. It was this second group of traders who soon changed from slave dealers to merchants in European finished products and marketers of raw materials. Included in this group of traders were those returnees who commanded enough capital and money to finance the trade. There were also some rich Africans who managed to make enough money to buy the means of transporting the articles of trade.
　　The coming of the multinational corporations to Africa could also be traced to this era of

'legitimate trade'. German, British, French and
other European companies came to Africa to trade.
They all had the military and economic backing of
their parent companies at home and operated in the
most ruthless way to outbid all competitors.
Sometimes the companies had to pool their resources
together and amalgamate so as to derive the maximum
benefit from the trade. An example was the Royal
Niger Company, which was chartered in 1886. Also,
'legitimate trade' introduced a cut-throat
competition among European traders and started the
drive to create spheres of interest for the
Europeans out of the coastal and hinterland areas of
Africa. This was the beginning of the scramble which
eventually led to the partition of Africa.

Finally, like the missionaries, the 'legitimate
traders' appealed to the rulers of the places with
which they traded for protection and assistance and
signed treaties of trade and friendship with them.
Such treaties not only guaranteed trade monopoly for
the traders; they also sealed the colonisation of
the areas. In fact, such rulers who resisted had
their domain attacked and forcibly annexed. It was
the treaties signed by Sir George Tubman Goldie, for
example, that guaranteed Nigeria for the British.

European presence in terms of acquisition of
territory pre-dated the 1880s, although territories
acquired before this period were not of much
significance. France, for example, had maintained a
foothold in Egypt for quite some time,[6] and in the
nineteenth century the French were active
principally in Senegal and Algeria.[7] In other parts
of Africa, European influence was equally not
serious, although its presence was registered in the
coastal areas. The British maintained Sierra Leone
as a colony and some small settlements in the Gambia.
They also held on to their forts along the Gold
Coast. The Dutch maintained their trading
settlements along the Gold Coast until these were
transferred to the British in 1872. The British also
annexed Lagos in 1861.[8] The French established their
presence along the coast between Senegal and the
Gold Coast and from 1849 developed Libreville on the
pattern of Freetown.[9] The Portuguese retained their
hold on Angola and Mozambique.[10] Although France
possessed minor colonial settlements on the north-
western coast of Madagascar, the great island of
Madagascar stayed out of European control, despite
the fact that French and British missionaries and
traders had at various times had considerable
influence in the area.[11]

European control remained limited to the coastal areas, but the urge to penetrate the hinterland and open it up for the purpose of commerce and missionary enterprise remained there. This urge became manifested in the attempts to trace the routes of the three great rivers - Niger, Nile and Congo. The activities of Mungo Park, Richard and John Lander, David Livingstone and Henry Morton Stanley, among others, adequately demonstrated the achievements of these major European explorers in various parts of Africa in the period before the 1880s. The interiors were then opened to the explorers and the routes of the major river systems were known. With the availability of this information to the Europeans, Africa was poised for the rush of the various European countries to gain territorial control of the continent.

But even with the discovery of the hinterland, European presence was kept to a minimum before 1880. The reasons for this included the lack of immunities against African diseases, a phenomenon which kept a high death rate among European adventurers into the hinterland, at least until 1857 when the use of quinine on a large scale began. Secondly, European attention was diverted to richer and more attractive areas. Moreover, some other European powers had acute internal problems which rendered them incapable of any long-term colonial activity. Among the major European powers, only Britain survived the nineteenth century without any revolution or major political strife. This situation put Britain in a leading position in the eventual race for European control of territories in Africa.

The decade of the 1880s did witness a significant change in the pace of European territorial acquisition in Africa. Apart from the traditional ones, new imperial powers also emerged, including Italy and Germany. Besides, there was also the individual involvement of King Leopold II of Belgium. Diverse reasons account for this upsurge of European interest, the most talked about being the economic motive of imperialism - the desire to acquire territories for the purpose of exploiting their raw materials and making them serve as dumping grounds of European manufactured goods. This explanation, well accepted by African scholars, is often denied by western authors. Among the alternative arguments proferred, a well-favoured one is that developed along the lines of strategic consideration. It argues that Africa had been left free by the great powers, especially by Britain, because the free trade policy pursued by the British had allowed their country to secure whatever interest it desired without necessarily exercising direct political control. Britain had only intervened directly in South Africa and annexed it in 1815 because of South Africa's location on the route to British India. This, however, does not explain French involvement in Algeria, which had no significant strategic advantage, but throws light on another reason for European involvement - the 'none-too-rational' reasons of national and dynastic prestige.

The activities of Britain have been associated with the upsurge of the general scramble. Britain, as noted above, had no pressing reason to secure direct political control which would involve responsibility and expense. But the British policy of commercial and cultural penetration depended very much on the continued presence of two vital conditions: (1) that the African states involved should be able to withstand the strains created by European commercial, financial and cultural impact; and (2) that Britain itself should be free from external interference so that the states should remain outside the political control of any other European nation. The moment these two conditions ceased to obtain marked the collapse of British policy. In those countries, especially Egypt and Zanzibar, which were most subject to European financial penetration, signs of internal collapse were apparent from 1870. But much more serious than these cracks in the African states was the emergence of other European states on the scene to challenge the British policy of informal influence in the continent.

The year 1870 ushered into Europe a new stability. The defeat of the French armies of Napoleon III by Prussian forces was followed by the proclamation of the German Reich with Bismarck, the 'iron and blood' man, as Chancellor. In the same year Italy completed the process of its unification when it took over control of Rome. But the new stability notwithstanding, Britain had little to fear from the emergent states: Bismarck was opposed to German colonialism, there was little to fear from any Italian colonial designs (which were insignificant at that time), and France, just defeated and in disrepair posed no threat.[12] But France achieved an unexpected stability in 1879, when the republicans took over control of government and almost immediately the country began to make her presence felt again in Africa. The new French situation was a welcome development to Bismarck, as he felt that the pursuit of colonies might serve to divert France's attention from Europe, and especially from its ambition to recover Alsace and Lorraine which had been seized by Germany after the Franco-Prussian war of 1870-71. In pursuit of this policy, Bismarck at the Berlin Congress of 1878, urged Britain to annex Cyprus and pressurised France into taking Tunis, a territory coveted by Italy in which 20,000 Italians were already settled. Tunis was occupied in 1881 by a French force, and in the face of obvious German support for France, Italy could not do anything.[13]

Apart from Tunis, the French also made advances in Senegal. But French adventures in Tunis and Senegal were not sufficient reason to warrant a general scramble, as these territories were far away from the British spheres of influence. It was rather developments in the Congo and Egypt that could be seen as the real beginning of the general movement towards partition. Indeed, the general scramble has been traced to the upsurge of activities in the Congo which had been precipitated by the adventures of Leopold II, the King of Belgium.[14] The Congo was an area of informal British predominance, but from 1876 the activities of Leopold II began to influence the course of events. Not satisfied with the constitutional restriction on his activities as the monarch in Belgium, Leopold began to dream of carving an empire for himself in Africa. Towards this end, he launched the International African Association, a body which he also headed. Designated as a humanitarian organisation, the Association had as its stated objective the further exploration and advancement of humanitarian concerns in Africa. The primary area of activity was supposed to be East Africa, as there were no competing claims by European powers in that region. Expeditions were despatched from 1877 in the interest of the Association rather than that of the Belgian government, which created stations along the trade routes to Lake Tanganyika and on the shores of the lake, as part of the scheme to reach the Arab-dominated regions of the Congo.

The discovery in 1877 of the course of the Congo river by Henry Morton Stanley affected the course of events in the Congo. Leopold seized the advantage of this discovery to divert his efforts towards the course of this waterway, which was unaffected by the rival claims of European powers.

15

Morton Stanley, who had been unable to interest
either the British public or private interests in
his development schemes for the Congo, now entered
the employ of Leopold II, with the initial task of
staking out claims for another organisation, a new
creation of the Belgium ruler, the International
Association of Congo. But it soon began to dawn on
other European countries that the Association was
anything but 'international', and Leopold soon began
to face challenges. The International African
Association had been created at a conference called
at Brussels by Leopold in 1876. This Brussels'
meeting had also created national branches of the
Association.[15] The French branch of the Association
had sponsored Pierre Savorgnan de Brazza in
exploring the hinterland of Gabon, which was a
French territory.[16] The information gathered through
the activities of de Brazza revealed clearly the
political ambitions of Leopold II. De Brazza, who
initially had been approached for his services by
Leopold, had been sent with the support of Jules
Ferry, the French Minister of Education at that
time, a man interested in colonial acquisition for
his country under the guise of a scientific mission.
De Brazza was able to penetrate the Congo river
above the area where Stanley was concluding
agreements with African rulers on behalf of
Leopold's association. Acting on his own initiative,
de Brazza concluded a treaty with an African leader
in the name of France in the area of present-day
Brazzaville. The Frenchman then went ahead and
concluded further treaties with other African rulers
and by 1882 he had already secured to France the
northern banks of the Congo and laid the basis for
the French colony of Gabon. Stanley and de Brazza
met on the latter's way back to the Atlantic coast
via the Congo, but no mention was made of de
Brazza's action. The treaties concluded by de Brazza
were presented to the government in France, and, as
a result of renewed interest in colonial
acquisition, the treaties were ratified. This
ratification opened a new chapter in the rush for
the acquisition of territories in Africa, as a
dangerous rivalry now ensued between France, a major
European power, and Leopold, at the head of an
essentially private organisation that had no locus
standi in international law.
    This event further roused into action other
European nations. The Portuguese, who had the
history of earlier activities in the Congo kingdom
to fall back upon, began to reassert their

jurisdiction in the area of the mouth of the Congo and the hinterland. The British, dominating commercial activities in the oil rivers, also had their fears. The British Consul in the oil rivers alerted his home government that the French might use their foothold in the Gabon to launch into the Cameroons and Igboland to control the sources of the palm oil trade. It was also at this time that reports began to file in from British traders on the Niger, led by George Tubman Goldie, of French competition and attempts to make treaties on the Niger. The Congo question was fast turning into one of international rivalry, and, as the British were busy deciding what line of action to take, the situation in Egypt was approaching a climax.

Khedive Ismael, the Egyptian ruler, having been dismissed at the request of the French and British governments, was replaced by Tawfiq. Ismael was removed from power because, among other reasons, he refused to carry out the financial reforms which had been initiated in the country by the French and the British. Thus the British were again forced to intervene in Egyptian affairs following the Urabi revolt, ostensibly to restore legality, and the occupation was said to be 'purely temporary'. However, the longer the 'purely temporary' occupation lasted, the more the resentment of the French over the British action grew. The French felt that their country was entitled to a predominant position in Egypt, partly because of their financial investments there, the activities of their officials, and the fact that the whole of the Suez Canal was conceived and executed by de Lesseps, a Frenchman. This predominant position, they felt, had been denied them through the ruthless opportunistic activities of Britain. The feeling of resentment continued to grow, especially among French politicians like Jules Ferry, who realised the need of France for colonial markets and sources of raw materials for industry and felt that France must act quickly in other parts of Africa. This feeling among Frenchmen was a particularly important factor in understanding Anglo-French rivalry during the partition.[17]

The British occupation of Egypt also resulted in German intervention in events in Africa. The rivalry in Egypt was a good opportunity for Bismarck who, after consolidating his Triple Alliance, wanted to keep Britain and France further apart and thus isolate them in international affairs.[18] Besides, by maintaining that their stay in Egypt was temporary, the British had legally allowed the International Debt Commission set up for Egypt between 1876 and 1879 to continue to function. France, in the prevailing circumstances, could not be expected to vote on the British side on the Commission, and Britain had to rely on the vote of Germany. Bismarck naturally expected Britain to compensate Germany for this support and also to realise her dependence on Germany. Britain, however, did not perceive the situation in this way.

In pursuance of Bismarck's intention, for much of 1883 he was sounding British reaction to German claims to Andra Pequena in South West Africa, where Herr Adolf Luderitz, a German merchant, had an ambition to set up a chartered company. All Bismarck wanted was British acquiescence to 'protect' Luderitz and not really to involve Germany in any colonial adventure. British government reaction was initially evasive but eventually it gave the reply that, although Britain had neither claims over Andra Pequena nor the intention of establishing any predominance there, any German claim would infringe British 'legitimate rights'. Britain still intended to continue her policy of commercial and cultural penetration without running an administration that would involve financial costs. In other words, while Britain was opposed to colonial acquisition in the area, she would not tolerate that ambition on the part of other countries. The reply was to cause a change in Bismarck's policy towards colonisation on the part of Germany. Not that he was really interested in colonial acquisition, but his move was essentially diplomatic, directed principally at Britain. In April 1884 Bismarck accepted the treaties concluded by Herr Luderitz. During the same year Bismarck continued Germany's colonial advances by despatching an agent on behalf of the German government who, in anticipation of the British moves in West Africa, concluded treaties which led to the creation of German colonies in Togoland and Cameroon. Most of the new German colonies were designed to border British territories. Bismarck anticipated either of two things eventually to happen: British might realise his intention and become convinced of her dependence on Germany, or an anti-British line on the part of Germany might help in winning over France, now led by Jules Ferry, as Premier.

In June 1884, under the threat of isolation, Britain recognised German protectorate over Andra Pequena. But Bismarck felt the situation had gone beyond that and was bent on pursuing further a Franco-German cooperation. Also in June 1884, Bismarck voted on the International Debt Commission against the proposed British financial reforms in Egypt. This action only served to step up British annoyance, for Britain had been angered by the German annexation of Cameroon, which she had planned to use as the headquarters of the Oil Rivers Protectorate. Besides, in August 1884, the Germans expanded the Andra Pequena Protectorate to include all the coast between Portuguese Angola and the Cape Colony, which was renamed German South West Africa. German efforts finally came to fruition in October 1884, when Germany and France jointly 'invited' Britain to attend a conference in Berlin later in 1884 to discuss the method of establishing international control over the rivers Niger and Congo and also to discuss the means of defining future territorial acquisition in Africa.[19]

The conference was held between November 1884 and February 1885. The Niger question was quickly resolved, as George Goldie had already bought out his competing French rivals. With regard to the Congo, all the powers were aware of their competing claims but were also not prepared for any diplomatic confrontation. The issue was therefore resolved through off-the-conference-table negotiations between the European powers and Leopold's Congo Free State. The result of the various negotiations pertaining to the Congo was that an extensive free trade zone was created, which covered most of East Central Africa and where non-discriminatory taxes were applied only for the purpose of maintaining an administration. Free navigation on sections of the Niger, subject to various controls of the French and the British, was promised with regard to that river. One final thing that emerged at the conference was the definition of 'effective occupation', which regulated the process by which a European power could lay claim to an African territory. And, once again, the Europeans had demonstrated that their problems in Africa could be resolved without dragging themselves to war.

NOTES

[1] Norman R. Bennett, <u>Africa and Europe</u> (New York, Africana, 1975), p.32.
[2] Ibid., p.42.
[3] J.C. Anene, 'Slavery and the Slave Trade', in J.C. Anene and Godfrey Brown, <u>Africa in the</u>

Nineteenth and Twentieth Centuries (Ibadan, University Press, 1966), p.92.

[4] Ibid., p.93.

[5] For an alternative view on the estimate of the number of slaves involved, see Philip D. Curtin, _The Atlantic Slave Trade: A Census_ (Maddison, Wisconsin University Press, 1969) and his 'The Atlantic Slave Trade 1600-1800', in J.F. Ade Ajayi and Michael Crowder (eds.), _History of West Africa_, vol.1 (London, Longman, 1976), 2nd ed., pp.302-30. Curtin is of the view that the figures of those involved given by most authors, especially Africans, are exaggerated. He claims to base his own findings on a combination of 'modern research and statistical methods with ... broad knowledge of the field'. But we thought that, even though other figures may not be too accurate, Curtin's figures consitute a gross underestimation. See also, UNESCO, _The African Slave Trade from the Fifteenth to Nineteenth Century_ (Paris, UNESCO, 1979).

[6] Norman R. Bennett, _Africa and Europe_, op. cit, pp.62-3.

[7] Ibid., p.66ff.

[8] On the British annexation of Lagos, see Robert Smith, _The Lagos Consulate_ (London, Macmillan, 1978) and G.O. Oguntomisin, 'Hostility and Rapport: Kosoko's Changing Relations with the British', _Odu_, no.24, July 1983, pp.78-88.

[9] N.R. Bennett, _Africa and Europe_, pp.74-5.

[10] Ibid.

[11] Ibid.

[12] J.E. Flint, 'Chartered Companies and the Scramble for Africa', in J.C. Anene and G. Brown (eds.), _Africa in the Nineteenth and Twentieth Centuries_, pp.112-14.

[13] Ibid., pp.114-15.

[14] Ibid.

[15] Ibid., and Bennett, _Africa and Europe_, pp.88-9.

[16] Bennett, op. cit., p.89.

[17] J.E. Flint, 'Chartered Companies and the Scramble for Africa', p.118.

[18] On the European alliances of the period see W.L. Langer, _European Alliance and Alignments 1871-1890_ 'New York, Alfred Knoff, 1950), and _The Diplomacy of Imperialism, 1890-1902_, 2 volumes (New York, Alfred Knoff, 1951).

[19] J.E. Flint, 'Chartered Companies and the Scramble for Africa', pp.119-21.

CHAPTER 2

BERLIN AND AFRO-EUROPEAN RELATIONS

Sola Akinrinade and Toyin Falola

By the time the Berlin Conference took off in November 1884, most of the participating countries had already showed interest in acquiring various parts of Africa.[1] The general history of relations between the European powers and the African territories before this time had been one in which the African territories suffered rather than gained. The European countries maintained an informal dominance on these territories via economic and cultural penetration; but by the time the participants at Berlin were through and the provisions of the agreements implemented, the whole of the western coastline of Africa, spanning the Cape of Good Hope to Senegal, with the exception of Liberia, was claimed by the European powers.[2]

The Congo was secured by King Leopold of Belgium through the use of his diplomatic skill. He was able to persuade the United States that his objectives were directed mainly against the slave trade. At the same time he was able to convince important British commercial and humanitarian interests that his regime in the Congo would be far more liberal than either the French or the Portuguese. Leopold went further to convince the French that the proposed colony would fail through insufficient funds, and then negotiated a treaty with France in which the Congo Free State of Leopold would revert to the French in case of bankruptcy. With this agreement firmly secured, France gave its backing to Leopold and the Congo Free State as the administering authority over the Congo.

The situation over the Niger was however different. Tubman Goldie had already united the British traders in 1879 and he fought a bitter commercial war against the French. By the time the conference at Berlin took off, Goldie had already bankrupted the French traders. Moreover, Goldie's agents were concluding treaties with local African chiefs on the Niger, treaties which purportedly gave political and administrative rights to Goldie's trading company. By the time the Congo question was resolved and that of the Niger came up for discussion, the Franco-German friendship was already breaking up, as French politicians were aware that a pro-German policy might enrage French citizens. The result was that the Niger was declared the administrative responsibility of Britain. Rules were then drawn up to guide navigation on the river, but these rules meant nothing, as no international commission was set up to enforce them. Still hesitant about bearing administrative costs, the British government granted a royal charter to the Royal Niger Company, Goldie's company, in 1886 which then proceeded to use this administrative power to establish a complete commercial monopoly in the area.

The British dominant position in East Africa collapsed in 1885, again, through the activities of Germany. Following German intervention in the Cameroons, certain elements in the British cabinet felt it necessary that the government should publicly uphold certain treaties concluded by Harry Johnston, a British naturalist working in East Africa, in order to forestall any German advance into the area. But the British Prime Minister, William Gladstone, did not show much enthusiasm. In November and December 1884, while the Berlin Conference was still on, Karl Peters and some fellow German associates entered Tanganyika and claimed to have concluded treaties inland. Chancellor Bismarck delayed acceptance of the treaties until the conference was over, and on the day following the conclusion of the conference, German protection was granted to Karl Peters and his associates, as well as the right to operate an administration in the area.[3] The German East African Company was then set up in pursuance of this objective.

The situation at that time was bad enough for Britain. The outbreak of the Mahdist revolt in the Sudan[4] and the consequent killing of General Gordon at Khartoum in January 1885 had been unfairly blamed on the government and especially Gladstone; and in March a crisis almost leading to war was brewing between Russia and Britain over Afghanistan. Under such circumstances, Britain could not afford to antagonise Germany. As a result the Germans were allowed a free hand to round off their inland treaties in Tanganyika and establish themselves further up the coast at Witu. The Sultan of Zanzibar was forced to accept the situation, and Gladstone was also forced to acquiesce. Later, the possessions of the Sultan were delimited by a joint British, French and German Commission.[5]

The British attempt to salvage what remained of their position in East Africa again was done with German approval. This, as on the Niger, was through the initiative of private interests. The goal this time was to rule what became known as Kenya by a chartered company headed by Sir William Mackinnon. Mackinnon's association with Kenya, which began with the making of treaties in 1886, could not obtain official approval, as the British government was unwilling to antagonise the Germans and went as far as informing Bismarck in advance of the plans of Mackinnon's association. Bismarck was not interested in exploiting the situation, as he was convinced that the British had learnt their lesson and had realised the need for German support. In fact, Bismarck was becoming alarmed about the colonial situation, for, although he had succeeded in passing the buck of administration to the tables of chartered companies in South West and East Africa, the German merchants in Togo and the Cameroons had rejected that burden and official administrations with the attendant monetary cost. Bismarck sought to bring to a close the East African adventure, and it was agreed between Britain and Germany to divide the mainland along a line from the Umba River to Lake Victoria, with Germany retaining Witu as an enclave within the British sphere of influence. In spite of the agreement, it still took some time before Mackinnon was granted his charter, as the British government was yet to be convinced that serious enough interests were present in East Africa to warrant an official sanction. By way of trade, Kenya had nothing to offer and strategically its value was doubtful.[6]

The strategic usefulness of Kenya was in doubt as long as Britain still nursed plans of withdrawing from Egypt. In actual fact, the Prime Minister, Lord Salisbury, attempted to withdraw in 1887 and reached an agreement whereby Turkey would reoccupy Egypt but allowing for British troops to reoccupy the country and defend the Suez Canal in case of war. The agreement could not be implemented because France, noticing the re-entry clause and with the help of Russia, was able to persuade Turkey to reject it. Lord Salisbury was now aware that withdrawal from Egypt on terms favourable to British interests was not feasible, at least in the near future. Occupation had to continue. The strategic control of Egypt then became a matter of concern for Britain from 1888. The primary interest was the control of the Nile, which was the lifeline of Egypt. The activities of the Mahdists in the Sudan could be ignored in the meantime because, although they possessed the military skill to disrupt things, they lacked the technical skill to pose a threat to the Nile. The immediate danger, therefore, was in Uganda, where the Nile flowed out from Lake Victoria. A European advance from the East African coast was also to be feared. In view of this Mackinnon, who had tried unsuccessfully in 1886 and 1887 to obtain a charter, had one hurriedly placed upon his Imperial British East African Company in 1888. Immediately, a struggle for the sources of the Nile ensued between the British and the German East African Companies. The rivalry was first centred on Equatoria, a province of the old Egyptian Sudan, where Emin Pasha, a German officer, was holding out against the Mahdists. A British relief expedition succeeded in ejecting Emin Pasha from the place before his fellow Germans could reach him. The centre of rivalry then shifted to Uganda. The rival German and British companies both despatched expeditions to Buganda, but the Germans were the first to succeed in concluding a treaty with the Kabaka.

But Lord Salisbury was impatient about the outcome of events in Africa and preferred to negotiate directly with Germany. He offered Germany the British island of Heligoland in the North Sea in return for German recognition of Uganda as a British territory and German withdrawal from Witu in Kenya, and recognition of British protectorate over the island possessions of the Sultan of Zanzibar. Heligoland was of vital strategic importance to Germany, and she joyfully accepted the exchange. The agreement was contained in the Anglo-German (Heligoland) Treaty of 1890.[7]

Italy, established in Eritrea, was the remaining threat to the Nile from the eastern approaches. The Italians had in 1889 concluded a treaty with Emperor Menelik of Ethiopia and had claimed that the treaty gave them protectorate over Ethiopia. A substantiation of this claim would have given Italy control of the Blue Nile. In 1891 Britain decided to recognise the extravagant claims of Italy, but the boundary line of the 'protectorate' was drawn in such a way that it denied Italy direct access to the Nile itself, though she agreed not to alter the flow of the water by building dams on its tributaries.

Local factors, including the rivalries of British and Boer populations, more than anything else, influenced the course of the partition in southern Africa. The British, since the 'Great Trek', had consistently made it a policy to deny the Boers access to the sea, for fear that they might try to secure the support or protectorate of other European powers. The establishment of German South West Africa in 1884 and German East Africa in 1885 further complicated the issue, for there was the fear that the Germans might try to link the two into a single German territory. The problem of the British became complicated when in the same area Portugal made claims to a continuous stretch of territory joining Angola and Mozambique, and the activities of Germany stimulated into action Portuguese ambitions. With this development, it then became necessary for Britain to secure a 'road to the north'. This time, British interests were again pursued through private initiatives; Cecil Rhodes, a wealthy politician was at the head. With his dream of a Cape to Cairo British domination, he began to prospect for minerals north of Transvaal and secured mineral concessions from Lobengula, King of Matabele. A Royal charter was granted to Cecil Rhodes' company in 1889, arming it with powers of administration over the territory. Not long after, the agents of Cecil Rhodes extended their activities to Mashonaland, an area which was a tributary to Lobengula. The company also decided to subsidise the British protectorate of Nyasaland which had recently been established. The 1890s witnessed a bitter rivalry between Rhodes' company and the Portuguese, which was eventually resolved only by the Anglo-Portuguese convention of 1890-1, much to the advantage of Rhodes.

The following three years were to witness the extension of white settlement in Rhodesia, with the extension of the South African railway system into the country and the crushing of African resistance. Rhodes' ambition began to get larger as he now dreamt of a southern Africa fully unified under the British flag. In the plan for the realisation of this dream was the episode that became known as the Jameson Raid. In this scheme, disgruntled 'Uitlanders' were to rise against the Boers in Transvaal, and Dr. Jameson, who was the administrator of the Company in South Africa, would invade Transvaal and come to the aid of the rebels. But the rising did not materialise, and Jameson rode into the waiting hands of the Boers and was captured. The attempt by Germany to use the fiasco to build a European anti-British league failed, as Russia and France refused to cooperate, and in the following years British diplomacy succeeded in isolating the Boers. It was the Boer war of 1899 to 1902 which marked the final act in the partition of southern Africa.[8]

By 1900, the major European powers had taken over political control of most of African lands. There were two important features that accompanied the partition: these were the futility of African resistance and the supremacy of the power and tactics of the European powers. A number of strategies was employed by these powers in acquiring their territories in Africa, the first of which was deception, a tactic which the European powers preferred to refer to as 'peaceful negotiation'. Treaties guaranteeing friendship and protection were signed by the traders from these European countries with African chiefs. Certain clauses were inserted in the treaties by the European merchants which were meant to serve as bait to the Africans, such as promises of compensation, whether monetary or in kind. However, such promises were never fulfilled.

In areas where there were tendencies to go to war with the local chiefs, the European powers resorted to another process of deception, such as inviting the chiefs into their gun boats and deporting them thereafter, thereby removing the impediment to British or French diplomacy. This policy, popularly referred to as gun-boat diplomacy, was used against King Jaja of Opobo between 1886 and 1887.

A second method employed was acquisition through commercial activities. Among clauses inserted in the treaties between the commercial companies and the African chiefs were those that guaranteed free trade on the one hand and a promise of African participation in the commerce on the other. However, the interpretation of these provisions by the European powers was that trade would be carried on only between the parties to the treaties and not with anyone else. Unwittingly, the African chiefs had signed away their commercial independence and replaced it with a most vigorous monopoly, couched in the flamboyant language of free trade. The tactic worked very well in the coastal states, where certain local chiefs expected to benefit personally from the commercial traffic that would ensue. But it was not all the coastal local chiefs who acquiesced in such acts, as exemplified in the case of Kosoko's confrontation with the British at Lagos and the Fante Confederacy, where the leaders refused to be drawn into deceptive negotiations but instead chose to trade with any party that was ready to purchase their commodities.[5]

A third strategy employed involved the use of missionaries. The missionaries without much candour became intruments of colonialism and aided the pacification of certain areas through their well-informed intelligence reports. The activities of the missionaries, for instance, contributed to the imposition of the Pax Britannica in Yorubaland. The returnees (free slaves), who constituted the first core of educated Africans, were close associates of the missionaries, and through them the European powers, especially the British, acted along the coast. This was especially the case in West Africa (see chapter one). Although the missionaries sometimes openly opposed British encroachment, they accepted the British argument that civilisation could come only if British overlordship was imposed on the people.

The final method of pacification involved the military campaign, the most effective of all the strategies. African resistance movements had no chance of success in view of the military and technological gap between them and the European invaders. Moreover, the European merchants and traders along the coast were in the habit of selling obsolete weapons to the African potentates. Such men as Samory Toure, Jaja of Opobo, Nana Olomu of Ebrohimi and Prempeh I of Asante, bought these obsolete weapons and ignorantly thought they had an invincible army and a full arsenal. They went to war only to meet the superior Maxim guns. Apart from the inequality in their arsenals, the military strategy adopted by the Europeans was superior to that of the Africans. The European armies, made up of a handful of men, but well-drilled and disciplined, easily overwhelmed the African multitudes of men whose marksmanship was poor, even when they had the guns. All the states that offered resistance suffered crushing military defeats in the hands of the invading armies of the imperialists.

The response of African peoples and rulers varied from place to place. It ranged from determined but futile resistance; to ready

acceptance, more or less, in places where the advent
of European rule was a deliverance from more
tyrannical rivals and/or neighbours; to a mixture of
the two. The best option open to the African
rulers who were losing their authority to the white
men was to go for the best bargain possible, as the
African states were in most cases too small and
disunited, with poorly armed and ill-disciplined
armed forces, to present any effective resistance,
save in exceptional cases as in Ethiopia, blessed
with an ancient unity, or the Zulu and Asante
nations, which were well-organised. Unfortunately,
the African people did not also possess any sense of
racial unity or racial identity; their states
feared, distrusted and betrayed each other more than
they opposed European control. But more than
anything else, the decisive factor was the military
supremacy of the Europeans, which in the final
resort won the various battles that ensued.

There abound examples of states and rulers that
either accepted, or fiercely (but futilely) opposed,
the invading European army. A good example of a
people that put up a determined but futile
resistance was the Hehe, led by Mkwawa. [10]

The deliberations of the European powers had by
1890 placed the Hehe people within the sphere of
influence of Germany, and the Germans sought to
incorporate them into the new colony of German East
Africa. Located off the principal trade and
communication routes and unaware of what was going
on, i.e. the activities of the Europeans - because
of their isolation - the Hehe were slow to respond
to the overtures of Germany for peaceful
incorporation into their colony. The Germans
preferred a peaceful venture to wars, which were
considered an unnecessary drain on the already tight
colonial budget; but their aspirations for peaceful
co-option of the Hehe failed. Mkwawa and his people
were at the zenith of their expansion and were
unaware of the strength of the European newcomers to
East Africa. An expedition in 1891 was sent by the
Germans to bring the Hehe under control, but with a
crass lack of knowledge of the martial arts of
the Hehe and their confidence in their own
strength, the Germans suffered a crushing defeat as
they were ambushed at Lugalo and lost their
commander, Emil von Zelewski, and most of their
troops. German reaction to this defeat was a
demonstration of the futility of African resistance.
In 1894 a second German expedition was despatched
and it successfully stormed Mkwawa's capital. The

Hehe were effectively defeated, but Mkwawa himself managed to escape, only to commit suicide later, in 1898, as his capture by the Germans was appearing more and more imminent.

There were other outstanding African casualties of the European invasion into the continent, especially in West Africa. King Jaja of Opobo was one of the men who fell victim to the superior tactics of the European conquerors who were acquiring territories in Africa. By 1885, when steps were taken to acquire the Oil Rivers, the acting British Consul, Harry Johnston, resorted to the use of the tactics of character assassination, perfidy and treachery in dealing with Jaja. He was subsequently deported to the West Indies in 1887. However, a lot of presure was put on the British at home for his return. The British were at first slow in giving in but, when they realised that it was only Jaja who could hold the territory together, they finally gave in, and the request for Jaja's return was finally granted in 1891, but he died on the return trip before he could reach home.

Prempeh I of Asanta was another sorry case. Having ascended the throne as Kwaku Dia, he later changed his name to Prempeh I and built up the Asante empire into a formidable position. When the British came, they offered British protection over his territory, which he stoutly refused. For quite some time, Prempeh I held on, but, despite the vigorous opposition he offered, the Asante kingdom became a British protectorate, following his arrest and that of his family. Initially they were detained at the Elmina castle but they were finally exiled to Sierra Leone in 1896. The British went a step further and demanded custody of the coveted Asante golden stool, the symbol of Asante unity. This request was met with vigorous opposition by the Asantes, who preferred shedding their blood to releasing the symbol of their revered ethnic unity. Following the outbreak of open hostility that ensued, Asante was finally annexed to the British Crown in 1900.

Equally, Samony Toure was another man who could have withstood French expansion in West Africa, but the French employed crude tactics in dealing with him, and he was ultimately deported to Gabon, where he died in 1900.[11]

Not every ruler could be like Mkwawa, or all people like his. Those who welcomed the invaders also abounded, and the reasons for their actions are clear. The Nyamwezi of Urambo, for example, had suffered serious decline after the death of their redoubtable chieftain, Mirambo, in 1884. The Urambo had grown increasingly weaker as they were surrounded by aggressive African rivals. It became the task of Mirambo's successor, his brother Mpandashalo, to try and reverse the trend, which he bravely did but met his death in 1890 during an attempt to expel a band of Ngoni raiders. Thus, when the first set of German troops arrived among the Nyamwezi in 1890, the leadership of Urambo was only too ready to welcome them and accepted the protection they offered, which seemed the only available option that could guarantee the continued existence of what remained of their state. For the Urambos, this was a rational and successful decision, although, at that time the long-term implications of their decision to accept foreign rule was not apparent to them.[12]

In areas where resistance was offered to British encroachment, as noted earlier, such movements did not succeed. This was due to a combination of factors. First, was the superior method of European diplomacy which combined deception with promises. African leaders were made to put their states under European protection without actually knowing the full implication of what they were doing. Most of the African rulers were illiterates, and the interpreters employed did not make clear the British or French intentions. This was one of the factors responsible for the subjugation of the African states, for, having initialled the agreements, their leaders would not turn round and deny what they had already acceded to. Secondly, in certain areas the contemporary political situation often contributed to the success of the Europeans. There were cases of internal crises in African kingdoms, and the Europeans seized the opportunity to interfere in the internal political process and supported the more pliant side in each crisis, thereby disintegrating the opposition. This was especially the case in Lagos, where the British supported Akitoye against Kosoko, a rival nationalist who refused to sign any treaty with the British.

The absence of cooperation among the African nationalists was another factor that worked against them. In-fighting among the nationalists enabled the imperialists to employ the tactic of 'divide and rule', as they instigated one group of Africans against the other in order to weaken both of them. Above all, there was total absence of a feeling of racial identity among the Africans which could have generated inter-state alliances against the imperialists. Even in the Sokoto Caliphate, where the Sultan made it a point of duty to defend any and all of his emirates against foreign attack, the duty was impossible to carry out because of the distance between Sokoto and the southern parts of the Caliphate. For example, Ilorin and Bida fell to the British without any significant response from the Sultan.[13]

Among themselves the African states were quite powerful indeed; but were patently weak against the superior European arsenal and strategy. African armies, to be sure, were large armies, but modern war is not a game of numbers, as their soldiers were often ill-equipped, undisciplined and untrained compared with their European counterparts. For example, Samory Toure had 4,000 men, all mounted and with guns; but they were no match for the French army, with only 250 men equipped with repeater rifles and machine guns. In places where they relied on natural frontiers, like large rivers, thick forests and rocky mountains, such natural defences were potent only against fellow African warriors. In fact the big rivers served the Europeans better because they were able to carry more men and weapons in preparation for military encounters than the Africans. Unlike the situation in Ethiopia, African natural defences elsewhere were not impregnable, and African soldiers on the run were easily flushed out of their forest hideouts by the booming sounds of the Maxim guns.

Finally, there was the economic factor. This encompassed the lack of resources to prosecute a long and serious war. The economies of African states were based on farming and trading: there was little manufacturing. But agriculture and commerce are peace-time ventures, which could not be pursued in times of internal crises, like wars. The African states were therefore ill-equipped to support a protracted war. By and large, they depended on the supply of outdated weapons from the coasts. Besides, the need to draft all available hands into the prosecution of the wars had an adverse impact on the agricultural sector as surplus production was soon depleted within a short period. On the other hand, the European invaders, who received their supplies from their home countries, never felt the pinch of hunger. As would be expected, African resistance was short-lived in the circumstances.

Whatever sequence the unfolding events on the

continent followed, almost all African territories were forced to accept European dominance, thanks to the crude military technology and the comparatively small size of the African states. Once completed, the partition of African lands radically altered the course of African history. African rulers lost control of their territories, as such control quickly went to the acquisitive powers: mainly France and Britain. Africa was moved to the stage of world history, as it was divided into artificial units, which in most cases had no bearing to hitherto existing ethnic frontiers. Some kith and kin were divided between rival European powers in such a way that they lost both their co-operative and collaborative approaches to life. For instance, the Ewes, divided between German Togoland and Ghana; the Yorubas, between Dahomey (now Benin Republic) and Nigeria; and the Somalis between Somalia and Ethiopia. The arbitrary demarcation of boundaries is responsible for some of today's irredentist movements in Africa (see also Chapter three). Besides, the states created at Berlin represent the African nations of today. But the Europeans also introduced new ideas, modern communication systems, as well as scientific technology. In addition, there was the adoption of the languages of the colonial masters, principally French, English and to a lesser extent Portuguese, by the Africans to enable them to communicate with each other on the one hand, and with their colonisers on the other.

Social disruption also immediately followed the scramble and partition. Whole villages were wiped out, and men, women and children killed, all in the name of pacification. Besides that, the colonisers also exploited African natural resources. Finally, the partition put Africans in a position of inferiority, whilst their masters assumed the image of demi-gods during the entire period of colonial rule that followed. Such changes had a profound impact on the social and political lives of the Africans. This issue is taken up in the next chapter.

NOTES

[1] On the origins of the scramble see Norman R. Bennett, Africa and Europe (New York, Africana, 1975), Chapter 3, especially pp.84-93; also J. D. Hargreaves, Prelude to the Partition of West Africa, (London, Macmillan, 1966), Chapter 5, p.196ff.

[2] On the West African phase of the partition see J. D. Hargreaves, West Africa Partitioned, Vol.I, The Loaded Pause, 1885-89 (London, Macmillan, 1974).

[3] N. Bennett, Africa and Europe, op. cit., p.96; and J. E. Flint, 'Chartered Companies and the Scramble for Africa', in J. C. Anene and Godfrey Brown (eds.), Africa in the Nineteenth and Twentieth Centuries (Ibadan, University Press, 1966), pp.122-3.

[4] On the Mahdist revolution in the Sudan see P. M. Holt, The Mahdist State in the Sudan, 1881-1898 (Oxford, OUP, 1958); also his A Modern History of the Sudan (London, Wiedenfield and Nicolson, 1967), pp.77-91.

[5] On the European Conquest of East Africa see Kenneth Ingham, A History of East Africa (London, Longman, 1965), Chapters 4 and 5, pp.115-90.

[6] See Kenneth Ingham, A History of East Africa.

[7] On the details of the Heligoland Treaty see A. J. P. Taylor, The Struggle for Mastery in Europe 1848-1918 (London, OUP, 1971), pp.329-30.

[8] For the Southern African phase of the partition see J. E. Flint, 'Chartered Companies and the Scramble for Africa', pp.127-9.

[9] On Kosoko's relations with the British see G. O. Oguntomisin, 'Hostility and Rapport: Kosoko's Changing Relations with the British, 1852-1862', ODU, no.24, July 1983, pp.78-88; and Robert Smith, The Lagos Consulate (London, Macmillan, 1978).

[10] On the Hehe resistance see N. R. Bennett, Africa and Europe, op. cit., pp.111-12.

[11] For various studies on aspects of African resistance to imposition of European rule see articles in Tarikh, vol.4, no.3, and vol.4, no.4., both devoted to the theme of 'European Conquest and African Resistance' (I and II).

[12] Norman R. Bennett, Africa and Europe, op. cit., p.120.

[13] On the military defeat of the various provinces of the Sokoto Caliphate and other parts of Nigeria see Obaro Ikima, The Fall of Nigeria (Ibadan, Heinemann, 1977).

CHAPTER 3

GOODBYE TO BERLIN?
THE PARTITION OF AFRICA RECONSIDERED

Dennis Austin

A.   AFRICA PAST

Towards the end of November 1884 a singular event
took place in Berlin. The big powers of Europe began
to meet in order to divide the African continent
into recognisable pieces. Wolves agreeing on the
spoils. There was nothing unusual in the seizure of
other people's territory as the consequence of war,
but the partition of Africa was on a truly grand
scale, reminiscent of papal pronouncements which
halved the new world between Spain and Portugal. Now
it was another continent and many more partners to
the enterprise, each with a sharpened appetite, each
fearful of losing what might be gained:

> See here, my boys, see what a world of ground
> Lies westward from the midst of Cancer's line,
> Unto the rising of this earthly globe...
> As much more land, which never was descried,
> Wherein are rocks of pearl that shine as bright
> As all the lamps that beautify the sky!
> And shall I die, and this unconquered?

The meeting of these Tamburlaines opened in November
and closed in February 1885, when a General Act was
signed. Fifteen powers attended, and agreement was
reached on a (more or less) peaceful <u>modus vivendi</u>
in respect of the European divison of Africa.[1]
    It was not, however, the case - it could hardly
be - that Africa was undivided before 1884 and
wholly partitioned by 1885. As Scott Keltie
observed: 'In its broad outlines the partition of
Africa was begun and ended in the short space of a
quarter of a century', but there were 'many
finishing touches' to be put to the structure...

The southern frontiers of Morocco and Tripoli
remain undefined, while the mathematical lines
by which spheres of influence of the powers
were separated one from the other are being
variously modified on the do ut des principle
as they come to be surveyed and as the
effective occupation of the continent
progresses.[2]

Like its mirror image, decolonisation, the process
of partition was a drawn out affair. In ancient
times, Mediterranean Africa was overrun by
Phoenicians, Greeks and Romans across the centuries;
then the Arabs subdued the Berbers, and the Turks
followed the Arabs: many more ruins than those of
Ozymandias lie beneath the sands of the Sahara.
Europeans, too, were early arrivals in north Africa,
and the stone-built castles along the west coast,
where slaves were manacled in dungeons - en route to
the Americas - were outposts of European rivalry
from the early 1500s. Even so, Scott Keltie
estimated that as late as 1875 Europe held no more
than a tenth of the continent. The Ottoman Empire
contained much of north Africa; Arab and Indian
dhows still crossed the Arabian Sea and the Indian
Ocean from the Sultanate of Zanzibar; and African
rulers guarded their own domains as chiefs, emirs,
kings and clan leaders, extending or narrowing their
territory as war, migration, drought and famine
dictated.

It was in the last quarter of the nineteenth
century that Europe was all-powerful, when what had
been a constant nibbling and scratching after wealth
gave way to great bites of territory swallowed by
the European powers. They were moved by the best of
motives - the enforced suppression of the slave
trade - and the worst of motives - what Conrad
called the 'vilest scramble for loot that ever
disfigured the history of human conscience.'[3] The
allocation of territory was determined almost as
much by the need to resolve rivalries in Europe as
by the record of discovery in Africa, and the
indifferent neglect of African interests was very
much in keeping with the time.

Yet the remarkable fact is the length of time
these patched up agreements lasted, despite the fact
that changes in ownership continued almost to the
beginning of the end of colonial rule. The Agadir
crisis of 1911, for example, brought an enlargement
of the frontiers of Cameroon as a form of
'compensation to Germany' until 1919, when German

East Africa, South-West Africa, Togoland and Cameroon were re-assigned under League of Nations' mandate to the Allies. Mussolini seized hold of Ethiopia in 1935; the Second World War altered the pattern of occupation in the Horn of Africa. Looking back over the period of partition one can see that the colonial boundaries were never unalterably fixed, either within each empire or between the colonial powers. Uganda yielded whole districts to Kenya and the Sudan; Jubaland was transferred to Somalia from Kenya in 1925; the huge area once known as the colony of Senegal and Niger was re-arranged a number of times into different administrative units. And there was always the moderating influence of what might be called the universality of empire, that sense of belonging to a larger entity - remote but never wholly unperceived - by which the inhabitants of a particular colony were linked to those of a neighbouring or near-neighbouring territory. Common services in East Africa, federal links in L'Afrique Occidentale Francaise and L'Afrique Equatoriale Francaise - even the abortive federation in Central Africa - helped to blur the frontiers of division.

The straight-edged, multi-coloured, neatly-ruled and delineated map of Africa was never as firmly divided as it appeared to be. It was a cartographer's talent, an image of Africa which stood out boldly from the maps but which existed in pure form only in the pages of the atlas. Reality was more muddled. It is worth remembering how long it took to translate into colonially-administered states the 'spheres of influence' carved out by yesterday's heroes on behalf of kings, queens and emperors:

> During the early years of the century the Uganda government had no direct control north of Elgon. The districts were on pieces of a great band of unadministered territory which lay between the administered areas of Uganda, British East Africa, Ethiopia and the Sudan. This band of territory was not only unadministered, it was almost unknown to the colonial officials. Occasionally an expedition would cross a section of it or traders would pass on their news, or there would be rumours of tribal fighting and Ethiopian raids, but that was all.[4]

Does President Mobutu, in all the authenticity of

his African dress, know as much today about the
unadministered areas of Zaire?

B.   AFRICA PRESENT

Having divided the continent, the European powers
governed their new possessions until, exhausted
after the Second World War, they transferred control
to African leaders. How have these ex-colonial
states coped with their freedom? The truth is, they
are mournful... If there is a single image of Africa
today it is surely Durer's picture of Melancholy.
There she sits, surrounded by the discarded
instruments of progress, a dejected putto by her
side, a half starved hound at her feet:

> 'She has lapsed into a state of gloomy inaction
> neglectful of her attire, with dishevelled
> hair; she rests her head on her hand and with
> the other mechanically holds a compass, her
> forearm resting on a closed book. Her eyes are
> raised in a lowering stare.'5

I think that not even today, twenty-five years after
independence, has the shock of that European
conquest been fully understood. A novel of the
quality of Achebe's Things Fall Apart conveys some
of the extraordinary turmoil imposed on African
societies, but the anguish must have been extreme,
and it is still there in the politics of these
sovereign states. In pre-colonial times, even when
afflicted by war or disease or famine, Africans
lived out their lives within an ordered framework of
beliefs and customs, sanctioned by gods and spirits.
Then colonial rule descended, and the initial effect
came close to stupefaction. The disparity of power
was so great, and any attempt at resistance was
crushed by the weight of conquest. In time, of
course, men and societies adjusted, until what had
been alien and wondrous became accepted and prized.
It had happened before:

> 'In place of distaste for the Latin language
> there developed a passion to command it. In the
> same way, our national attire came to be
> favoured, and the toga was everywhere to be
> seen. So the British were gradually persuaded
> to use   amenities which make   vice
> agreeable - arcades, baths and sumptuous
> banquets. They talked of such novelties as
> 'civilisation' when really they were only a

feature of their enslavement.[6]

So it came about that what was once a colonial patchwork is now the foundation of African self-government, and from 1963 the Organisation of African Unity (OAU) made it plain that its members were determined to keep the jigsaw of existing states. Modern Africa had been born in chains and had struggled to be free: it was not a time to risk losing what had been won. There should be no change in the map: it was too dangerous and too difficult, not least because the former colonial boundaries now had the validity of international law. Sovereignty was the basis of a world order of states, and the United Nations gave legal protection to the fact of independence, whether it was Caliban on his island or the leaders of a hinterland republic. When, therefore, the OAU affirmed support for the colonial boundaries, the new association was thought to have been prudently sensible to stick to the map:

'The record of wars in Europe over the territorial definition of Poland or the Balkan states or the Low Countries, or in Latin America over boundary disputes, or over partition in South Asia, was scarcely an attractive precedent for change. African leaders had become committed to an anti-colonialism which had as its aim the capture of the colonial state; but, once the capture was made, the castle keep was quickly defended under a nationalist flag...'[7]

Yet rigidity, too, has had its price. Although African governments are not prepared to alter the rules or recognise the legitimacy of change, a minority has begun to set the rules aside. The cartography is still there, translated into sovereign states, and there are national frontiers on the map; but gradually, almost peevishly, governments have quarrelled with each other and with their own subjects. An island appears in a river and is claimed by two neighbouring states. A frontier runs through one of the great lakes and is disputed. There are claims dating from pre-colonial times, as by Morocco over the Sahara; claims, too, from partition history, as by the Cameroonian and Nigerian governments.[8] And there are secessionists who try to stake out their own particular enclave within an existing state. There is scarcely an African country whose leader is not troubled, or whose fellow citizens are not tormented, by the problem of popular disaffection and inter-state rivalry. By the 1980s one in every two refugees in the world was an African: 5 million out of 10 million. Of the 50 sovereign states, 23 were under military rule, others were governed by soldiers-turned-politicians, none had escaped the threat of an armed coup. The colonial state is creaking and groaning, tugged and pulled this way and that in its structures of control, bullied and divided by rebel leaders, war-lords, <u>banditti</u>, civil war and foreign war. Natural disasters of flood, drought and famine are compounded by human folly, whilst over a large area of southern Africa apartheid constantly threatens not only Africans within the Republic of South Africa, but its neighbouring states. Little wonder, therefore, that Africa is mournful. The level of arms purchases continues to rise, and the war dead now number many hundreds of thousands in Angola, Burundi, Chad, Eritrea, Ethiopia, Mozambique, Nigeria, Rwanda, Somalia, the Sudan, Uganda, Western Sahara, Zaire and Zimbabwe.

In the early years of independence, the newly-sovereign governments clung nervously to the shipwreck of empire. Almost twenty-five years have passed since the heyday of self-government, and the barriers to change are crumbling. The OAU failed to hold all its members to its own principles during the Nigerian civil war; it was uneasily divided over Tanzania's invasion of Uganda, and unable even to meet in 1982 because of the disputed recognition of the Sahrawi Arab Democratic Republic (Western Sahara).[9] There are deep differences today over which side in the civil war in Chad is the 'lawful government'. The continent presents a grim picture of a high dependence on food imports, declining living standards and radical efforts at reform that seem always to fail: the demand of the nationalist movements had been 'freedom', but by 1984 not a single African government had been changed by free elections, not a single state was free from the danger of rebellion.

It is time, therefore, a century after the Berlin Conference, to raise the question whether the frontiers and states created by partition will be able to bear the strain of these African disputes. I sketch below a brief outline of the most serious. The categories run into one another and are not exact, but they offer a convenient frame for discussion.

C. REBEL MINORITIES

There are neo-traditionalists whose case rests on the obvious artificiality of the frontiers-states determined not by national sentiment but chance. If the early adventurers who tracked their way through the mephitic swamps of the Upper Nile and who concluded treaties with as many chiefs as they could waylay, had altered their itinerary, bringing in this area rather than that, or foregoing a particular claim to possession, then both the treaty settlements at Berlin, and the frontiers of modern African states would have been different: villages which became British might instead have come under French or Belgian or Portuguese rule. Accident determined their history. So, the traditionalists argue, the mischance of past events, where fate - for some - took the wrong turning, ought to be remedied. They point to a history distinct from that of the colonial period and assert the need to have states more closely aligned with pre-colonial societies; Ashanti, Yoruba, BaCongo, Matabele, Barotse and Buganda, for example, instead of colonially-fashioned, polyglot states - unstable because ill-founded - such as Ghana, Nigeria, Zaire, Zimbabwe, Zambia and Uganda.

Closely aligned are those - perhaps we should call them proto-nationalists - who have argued, with a gun, that particular regions of existing states - 'Biafra', Katanga, the Southern Sudan, Casamance - constitute defined territories whose inhabitants, linked as much by a common dislike of those who rule them as by any historical unity, ought to form their own state from Nigeria, Zaire, Sudan and Senegal.

A third element (including of course many traditionalists and would-be nationalists) had struggled by armed revolt to wrest control of the state, or part of the state, from its rulers. A particularly brutal example was the civil war in 1972-3 between the Hutu subjects and the Tutsi ruling class in Burundi and Rwanda: the former were successful in Rwanda, the latter in Burundi, both conflicts coming close to genocide. Uprisings in southern Angola led by UNITA, liberation movements in Mozambique, Tigre rebels in Ethiopia, and armed dissidents in Uganda, make nonsense of the 'sovereign state', since the government in the capital controls only what it can while its opponents - and refugees - move in and out of the 'liberated areas' and across frontiers.

D.   IRREDENTISM

A classic derivation from Italian history in the struggle for 'unredeemed lands': bloodily expressed in undeclared wars between Somalia, Ethiopia and Kenya and unresolved since Somalia has no intention of surrendering its claim to redeem the Somali-inhabited areas of Haud and Ogaden in Ethiopia and northern Kenya. On the other side of the continent, the wreckage of a war fought with all the ghastliness of modern weapons litters the Western Sahara, where King Hassan tries to assert his claim to the phosphate-rich, ex-Spanish colony against those who actually live in these inhospitable regions.[10] Colonel Qaddafy is said to have designs on northern Chad through his support in money and weapons for Goukouny Queddie against the southern leader, Hissene Habre. Perhaps to this list we should add Cameroon, which still resents the absorption by Nigeria (following the UN Plebiscites in 1959-60) of the former British Northern Cameroons.

E.   FRUSTRATED NATIONS

Ethiopia has swallowed, though not digested, Eritrea with which it was once federated: prior to 1945 Eritrea was an Italian colony.[11] Until recently it was axiomatic that to be a colony qualified a territory for statehood. Yet neither Namibia, nor the Western Sahara, nor Eritrea has been able to enter that paradise. The explanation of course lies in Pretoria, Rabat and Addis Ababa: meanwhile the claims and the fighting continue. One might add, too, movements based on early colonial history, like the Togoland Congress in Ghana in the 1950s, which once sought to recreate the boundaries of German Togoland.

F.   AGGRESSION

To the Polisario Front, Morocco is indisputably the aggressor, as presumably Colonel Qaddafy is to Hissene Habre in Chad. Amin attacked north-west Tanzania, only to find that he had brought the whole Tanzanian army against him. South Africa maintains a policy of permanent aggression - but South Africa deserves special mention (see below). One may also wonder whether the military in some African states, frustrated at home by ineluctable difficulties which have beset most military governments, will divert attention from domestic problems by using its power at the expense of its neighbours, if only to 'rectify a frontier' or occupy a buffer zone beyond its present boundaries.

G.   SOUTH AFRICA

Maps in Pretoria show a different configuration from those at the OAU headquarters: there is an array of additional pygmy states, granted a form of independence by South Africa.[12] Not dominer pour servir, the former French emblem, but donner pour dominer - an Afrikaner motto? It is a queer notion of self-government, nullified by extreme reliance on South Africa and unrecognised by the rest of the world. Yet it raises an interesting question. If the inevitable actually happens and white rule collapses, a black government would certainly claim all the territory of the present Republic; but perhaps it might claim more, quashing the nominal independence of the Bantustans and stretching its grasp to take in Namibia and the former High Commission Territories of Lesotho, Botswana and Swaziland. On the other hand (and, perhaps, more plausible), if white South Africa were to founder in fragmented disorder, there might very well be residual African states of a kind that produced a different map of the region.

It is proper to add one other factor of disturbance: foreign interference. That, too, is on the increase, and it has brought in the Russians, Cubans and East Germans, as well as the Americans. They are freebooters, operating under the subterfuge of alliances and treaties of friendship, with the consequence that once again international rivalry extends into Africa. The shadow of the Superpowers falls across almost every African conflict. If the CIA is active in Zaire, Soviet agents are hard at work in Benin. Certainly, if it were not for Russian and Cuban help, Lt. Col. Mengistu Haile Maryam in Ethiopia and President Jose Eduardo dos Santos in Angola would find it difficult to maintain even such control as they presently have over their borders. Somalia relies on Arab money and American weapons, but for the arms that oil wealth brings, Col. Qaddafy might be no more than the poor Arab in his tent. Zaire is put together periodically (with American help) by France, Belgium and the IMF. The United States established bases for its Rapid Deployment Force in Morocco, the Sudan and Kenya, (and South Africa) - as if it were an external power located in

Africa - is massively in support of the enemies of
its opponents. How distant now are the early days of
Pan-African hopes and Third World neutrality!

And it is not simply for political influence or
ideological advantage, or for military bases alone
that the Soviet and Western powers are in
competition. The scramble for African resources has
also been renewed. Cobalt and platinum are rare
minerals, along with uranium, diamonds, gold, iron,
copper, phosphates and oil. They are vital to the
industrial world, and it is the combination of rich
mineral deposits and unsteady governments that draws
in the outsider. African states may be able to
change their political spots - transferring from one
patron to another in Ethiopia and Egypt - but not
their economic skin. They remain dependent, the most
developed economically (such as the Ivory Coast)
being the most heavily in debt, and confusion is
added to dependence when, for example, American Gulf
Oil in Cabinda earns dollars for the Marxist
government in Luanda, thus enabling it to pay for
Soviet and Cuban support. The unalterable fact is
that the need for external help enfeebles whatever
government is in office. Look at Upper Volta (now
Burkina Faso), Mali and Niger, where the encroaching
desert makes nonsense of any formal Saharan
boundaries. They are almost too poor to attract
patrons: hence the tenacity with which they cling to
France and the European Community in desperate hope
of relief, relying chiefly on that obsession with
post-colonial links which seemingly bolsters French
prestige. The plight of all the non-oil states -
and some of the oil producers - brings in foreign
experts whose advice for balancing the books and
reducing debts adds to the nervousness of unstable
regimes. In the nineteenth century it was the
intrusion into Africa of explorers, missionaries,
soldiers and administrators that opened the way to
partition. Now there are military advisers,
ideological tutors, financial inquisitors and the
twentieth century equivalent of Victorian
exploration - mass tourism. Where will it end?

H.   THE FUTURE

What is the balance of probability between Africa's
keeping its present form, under its 50 sovereign
states, and some other configuration of the map?
Only Chad approaches the dreadful position of
Lebanon, where zones of occupation are divided
between warring factions and rival armies, spurred

on by powerful neighbours. But is there not a danger that African states may go the same way, as differences of ideology, wealth, power, foreign alliances and national ambition continue to divide the continent? Or will Cabinda be forever part of Angola because the Portuguese decreed it so, and Djibouti, Equitorial Guinea and Benin remain forever sovereign enclaves?

Suppose we examine the problems under three broad categories - annexation, secession and frontier warfare.

I.   ANNEXATION

> Third Fisherman 'Master, I marvel how the fishes live in the sea.'
>
> First Fisherman 'Why, as men do a-land: the great ones eat up the little ones.'

The belief may come close to universal truth, but in fact the international community professes not to approve the practice. It is frowned upon: direct conquest infringes the rules. (Hence the technique of invasion by invitation as in Eastern Europe, Vietnam, Afghanistan and Grenada.) The anger of Morocco in 1982 stemmed from an awareness that, once the OAU gave even provisional recognition to a Polisario government of the Western Sahara, it would be protected by international law. (The OAU has in fact admitted Western Sahara as its 51st member state; November 1984.) Sovereignty is not easily extinguished, and there have been few instances of outright annexation since Russia engulfed the Baltic states. Weak states are dependent, _de facto_, on stronger states, but re-colonisation and annexation would set aside every international convention built up since the end of the war - and contravene the United Nations' charter.

There are additional restraints on African governments. Even if the legality of international status were not enough to safeguard, say, Gabon or Togo, there are external guardians. France in particular watches over its former colonies and may still be prepared to protect them. Moreover, the safety of African states _vis-à-vis_ each other lies not so much in the OAU Charter but in the simple knowledge that to control one's own citizens is troublesome enough without adding other people's problems to the burden. (Tanzania is still suffering the cost of its invasion of Uganda.) If Ethiopia were a strongly centralised, efficient state under confident control, it might (I suppose) seize Djibouti: but the Ethiopian government is beset by troubles, and France keeps a protective eye on its former colony (see Chapter 9). It seems probable, therefore, that, even though there is little of the special relationship between African states which the founders of the OAU had once envisaged - too much blood has been spilt between them - legal, financial military and political difficulties of annexation will prevent any reduction in the actual number of states from its present level.[13]

That leaves out of account the question whether there will be more states, not fewer. Many of the difficulties of the colonial map come from the lassoing together of small traditional states and communities to form much larger territories - Zaire, Nigeria, the Sudan, Chad, Angola, even (relative in size to pre-colonial groups) colonies as small as Sierrra Leone and Uganda. What can be said of the other side of the problem - secession?

J.   SECESSION

I rule out the possibility of peaceful secession, since it is rare for states to yield voluntarily to demands for a separate state. There needs to be a high liberal belief in the popular rights of minorities for a Norway to be able to secede from a Sweden, and African governments are not like that. Enforced secession is a different matter. The Nigerian civil war (1967-70) was a serious affair. Zaire was dismembered in the 1960s, with further outbreaks of violence in the 1970s; and the People's Liberation Front has almost succeeded by force of arms in pushing Ethiopian rule out of Eritrea. About most African states there is an air of uncertainty - nervous governments confronting dissatisfied citizens. When, however, we look at the record of liberation movements and civil wars, the failure of secession has to be explained not only by the balance of military power but by difficulties on the side of the rebels, which go to the heart of the problems.

The first is something of a paradox - the strength of the colonial state. When an army turns out the politicians, the general populace either rejoices or remains indifferent. Allegiance to the political system - any political system - is at a low level, while loyalty to family, clan and

birthplace is intense - scratch a corrupt
nationalist and you usually find a loyal tribalist.
And yet experience of living in the colonial state
runs deep. The indifference is about regimes rather
than the state as such, and it is not difficult to
understand why that should be so. There is now a
settled colonial elite, a colonial language, a
colonial economy, a colonially-trained civil
service and habits engrained over at least two
generations. It is not simply the young and middle-
aged but the elderly who have known only the years
of colonial rule. The post-colonial state stands
guarantor, therefore, of a good many interests built
up over the colonial period.

True, anti-Nigerian sentiment ran high in the
1960s among the Ibo of the Eastern Region, as did
dissatisfaction among the Katangese, with the newly-
independent state of Zaire. But there was then the
daunting problem - a second, fundamental difficulty
to any bid for secession - of finding a clear
identity for the alternative. To be 'Ibo-speaking'
was not enough to engender a wider loyalty to the
region as a basis for a separate Biafran state, for,
if the Ibo distrusted the Hausa and Yoruba, the
peoples of the Delta within the Eastern Region also
took a jaundiced view of the Ibo. It was the
dismantling of the four cumbersome regions of the
Nigerian independence constitution and the promise
of (twelve) new states that did much to win support
for the federal government among the anti-Ibo
ethnic minorities.[14] Similar problems have always
faced the leaders of a would-be Katanga state, and
other bids for statehood in the former Belgian
Congo. The provinces are too divided internally, too
diverse, too incoherent, to sustain a 'state-
within-a-state' as the foundation for a new nation.
The history of caravanserai states, which seem
periodically to disintegrate and from which a
sizeable number of its citizens try from time to
time to escape, is hardly one of stability, but a
non-colonial map of Zaire is even less plausible:
there are no unifying ties strong enough or broad
among its mixed ethnic groups to support any alternative arrangement of the huge territory.
Disintegration in the capital simply leads to
disintegration in the interior.[15]

Third, and perhaps surprisingly, many of those
who have demanded the right to secede are at one end
of a scale of complaints from which they are often
prepared to retreat a little if the opportunity for
change presents itself. Protests against the

colonial boundaries of a state may simply be the extreme expression of discontent with the actual incumbents of the state. The history of the Anya Nya movement in the Southern Sudan is very illustrative. It is one of intermittent guerrilla war and periodic negotiations. A peace treaty was signed in 1972, then fighting flared up again when President Nimeiri curtailed the autonomy of the provinces and introduced Islamic (Sharia) law in the Christian south. It is arguable that even the Eritreans - and they too are divided among themselves - might be reconciled to a reconstituted Ethiopia if there was a change of regime in Addis Ababa from that of Mengistu Haile Maryam. Precisely because African regimes are vulnerable, the guerrilla in the bush may always hope that his time will come, if only to occupy a more congenial place within, rather than outside, the ex-colonial state.

Such hope is likely to be reinforced by a fourth factor, namely knowledge that the secessionist road is very difficult. Like annexation, secession is disapproved of by the international community. Colonies struggling to be free might gain a provisional recognition, but not rebel provinces of a sovereign state. Governments will recognise revolution, or a coup d'état, or treason when it is successful, but not secession. Yet without that approval, rebel leaders are doomed - like the Kurds, Armenians and Basques - to the limbo of perpetual struggle.

One last possibility exists - external help, remembering that it was the Indian army which enabled Bangladesh to secede. Is there a comparable situation in Africa? Probably not. It is frankly difficult to see any non-African forces being dispatched on behalf of secessionist movements. (The only exception might be Chad, because no-one is sure which side is the government.) Even South Africa sees its interests primarily as maximising unrest - keeping the pot stirring - among its neighbours. Foreign money, yes, foreign weapons, certainly, and all the indirect means of intervention that the armoury of the cold war provides, but there is no major interest among external powers in re-partitioning the map of existing states. They wish to control, not to divide, as may be seen in South Africa's willingness to negotiate with Marxist governments in both Mozambique and Angola. That leaves out of account African intervention. There is ample evidence of interference in the affairs of neighbours, from Tanzania's invasion of Uganda, to the sheltering of dissidents from, say, Ghana, in Togo. Will that alter the map? I turn to the last category.

K. FRONTIER CHANGES

It is here, I suspect, that changes will occur, though on a limited scale. The tide of local war already washes back and forth across frontiers that are never clearly demarcated. There are likely to be punitive raids, harrying of border villages, seizure of frontier posts, the de facto occupation of buffer zones and limited fighting of sufficient ferocity to bolster the nationalism of insecure governments. There are grounds enough for dispute and arms to fight them, while the quality of leadership over the past twenty years does not encourage any belief that such conflicts will be settled amicably. Although states will not be annexed, they will be attacked by neighbours; secession may not succeed but guerrilla armies will occupy tracts of territory beyond the control of governments, and it is through such disputes - states buffeted by what they cannot control - that boundaries will become ragged: Libya and Chad, Burkina Faso and Mali, Nigeria and Cameroon, Ethiopia and Somalia, Angola and Zaire, and so forth.

One brief example. Nigeria and Cameroon exemplify the problem since the boundary between them has shifted a number of times and is still contested. The last change was 1961 when the British Cameroons (adminstered as part of Nigeria since 1919) was divided north and south: the northern sectors voted in a UN plebiscite to remain with Nigeria, the south opted to join the Republic of Cameroon. The Cameroon government resents the fact that the vote in the north went against it. Nigeria laments the loss of the southern Cameroons. Ahmadou Ahidjo, then President of Cameroon, once declared that 'le Cameroun septentrional reste et restera ce que l'Alsace-Lorraine a été pour la France à une époque de son histoire'.[16] Well, that may have been the imitative rhetoric of post-colonialism, but, because the boundary remains ill-defined, 'clashes became a constant factor... along the border areas (and) in July 1970 thirty Nigerians were reported killed...' 'A shoot-out between the armed forces of both countries in May 1981... brought the two nations close to the brink of war and reminded everyone that after two decades the border problems had not yet been resolved.[17]

I conclude, therefore, contrary to what at first seemed unlikely, that the African map will not change substantially. Forever Djibouti, Rwanda and Benin, forever Cabinda, forever Zaire: sovereign mice and sovereign elephants. Were the ghosts of the Berlin conference to reassemble this centenary year, they would surely be astonished by the eclipse of European power, but they might be equally surprised to note how closely the map of independent African states resembles the partitioned map. Lord Salisbury observed:

> 'We have been engaged in drawing lines on maps where no white man's foot ever trod; we have been giving away mountains and rivers and lakes to each other, only hindered by the small impediments that we never knew exactly where the mountains, rivers and lakes were.'[18]

Yet the lines became engraved on the map and then settled into sovereignty. It is part of the strange phenomenon of our age that sovereign mouse and sovereign elephant pretend an equality of status, though grossly unequal in stature. The effect is plain. New disparities of power have brought about new spheres of influence, not as the prelude to re-partition or re-colonisation but as part of the shifting world of international relations. The difference between 1884 and 1984 is the lack of concert among the big powers: do ut des has yet to be re-incorporated as a principle of give and take.[19] Instead, there is mistrust - mistrust between the powers and between the strong and the weak. No dominant state can be quite sure of its avowed clients, no dependant fully trust his supposed benefactor. Looking at the map in 1985, it would not be difficult to mark out spheres of influence - Soviet, American, French, South African, Nigerian, Egyptian, Libyan - although each would be inexact and unstable. There are other maps one could draw, not of sovereignty and political control but of market forces, labour migration, religious beliefs (including an Islamic-Christian frontier) and ideological persuasion. They too would be uncertain guides to present problems, for conflicting forces are at work among indeterminate states, and the African continent is in as sad a plight today as it was a hundred years ago. Yet in relation to the question raised at the beginning - whether the territories shaped by colonial rule will outlast their current troubles – the answer is almost certainly, yes, if only because no alternative appears possible. And since states mature by custom over time, the absolute need to continue in existence may bring a weary endorsement of the map.

NOTES

[1] Britain, France, Belgium, Spain, Italy, Germany, Portugal, Austria-Hungary, Denmark, Holland, Russia, Sweden, Norway, Turkey and the United States. The General Act dealt with six specific subjects, including freedom of trade in the Congo Basin, suppression of the slave trade and 'rules for the future occupation' of the continent.

[2] J. Scott Keltie, Encyclopedia Britannica 1911, 'Partition of Africa'.

[3] Quoted from Norman Sherry, Conrad and His World (London, Thames & Hudson, 1972).

[4] James Barber, Imperial Frontiers (Nairobi, East African Publishing House, 1968), p.8.

[5] Erwin Panofsky, Albrecht Durer (London, 1948), p.11, commentary on Durer's 'Melancolia'.

[6] Tacitus Agricola. It would be easy to substitute 'English' for Latin, the 'dark suit' for toga and 'Africans' for the British.

[7] Dennis Austin, Politics in Africa (Manchester, University of Manchester Press, 1978), p.27.

[8] e.g. 'a politician from the former French colony of Niger invoked the Berlin Conference of 1884-5 to defend his country's claim against Dahomey to the island of Lete in the Niger river, asserting that "since 1885 the island had always belonged to Niger". The politician forgot that the administrative entity of Niger was not yet in existence at that time.' (S. Touval, 'Africa's Frontiers', International Affairs, October 1966.) In this respect history is what can be made from different pasts; one must make up one's nationality as one goes along.

[9] In 1966 four African states recognised 'Biafra' (Tanzania, Zambia, the Ivory Coast and Gabon). Nyerere's invasion of Uganda violated all the OAU rules concerning 'non-interference'. When 26 of the 50 OAU members recognised the Polisario Front as the government of Western Sahara, the Secretary-General of the OAU admitted it to membership, whereupon Morocco and its allies boycotted the organisation.

[10] The Polisario guerrillas are supported by

Algeria, the Moroccans are armed by the Americans.
Moroccan claims also derive from Spanish rule, which
was abandoned in 1975 in favour (after some
hesitation) of a division of the territory between
Morocco and Mauritania until 1978, when a coup
d'état ended Mauritania's involvement in the war.
[11] Eritrea was incorporated into Ethiopia by a
decision of the United Nations which also proposed a
federal basis of unity that was never implemented.
[12] See Hegel, G.W.F., 'As a result of war,
nations are strengthened, but peoples involved in
civil strife also acquire peace at home through
making wars abroad', in Philsophy of Right,
translated by T. M. Knox (Oxford, OUP, 1965), p.292.
The states created or proposed by South Africa so
far are: Transkei, Ciskei, Kwazulu, Lebowa, Venda,
Gazankulu and Bophuthatswana.
[13] The likelihood of voluntary amalgamation on
the lines of Zanzibar and Tanzania in 1964 seems
unlikely in present conditions. The stress is on
sovereignty. The most one can hope for is
'functional cooperation' and that too is marred by
disputes between neighbouring states, as in the
expulsion from Nigeria of some 2,000,000 migrants
early in 1983, and some 700,000 in 1985.
[14] Dislike of Ibo domination was also a
principal factor in the (British) Southern Cameroons
plebiscite in 1961, when a majority voted to
transfer from Nigeria to the Cameroon Republic.
[15] Where there does exist a coherent,
centralised, traditional structure that might become
the basis of a new state, it is usually part of a
larger, colonial territory - Buganda in Uganda,
Ashanti in Ghana, the Fulani and Hausa emirates in
Nigeria, Barotseland in Zambia. The little kingdom
of Swaziland - a pre-colonial, post-colonial state -
is a good example of what might have been, had
partition followed traditional boundaries, but what
kind of patchwork quilt of African micro-states
would that have produced?
[16] Quoted in Ndifontah Hyamndi, International
Politics and British Cameroons (London, Macmillan,
1984).
[17] Ibid., p.265.
[18] Quoted in J. C. Anene, The International
Boundaries of Nigeria, 1885-1960 (London, Longmans,
1970), p.3.
[19] It is faintly present in current arguments
between the United States, South Africa and Angola-
plus-Namibia.

CHAPTER 4

BRITAIN AND ANGLOPHONE AFRICA*

James Mayall

Governments, it is widely held, have an obligation
to defend the national interest, whatever that
elusive aggregate is deemed to be. The governments
of great powers often see themselves, in addition,
as shouldering an extra obligation, namely to
contribute to the balance of power and in other ways
to underwrite the values and institutions of
international society in the interest of stability.
Of course, these values and institutions must
operate to the advantage of the great power, but,
since they are regarded as public goods the benefits
of which cannot be monopolised, it is only fair, or
at least inevitable, that he who pays the piper
shall call the tune.

Such, very roughly, was the attitude of British
governments in their relations with the rest of the
world during the period of British pre-eminence,
say from the defeat of Napoleon to the end of the
Second World War. Throughout this period the latent
tensions between a narrowly defined conception of
national interest, the maintenance of the British
Empire on which British pre-eminence partly rested
and the general practices and conventions of
international society may have been recognised by
some of the more far-sighted politicians,[1] but they
were never publicly acknowledged. The proposition
that what was good for Britain was good for the
Empire and good for the world was as firmly held
(and with considerably less public embarrassment) as
the notorious view of the American politician who
held that what was good for General Motors was good
for the United States. It provided the broad
framework of a self-confident foreign policy.
British pre-eminence, never in any case as secure
as it can be made to look in the after-flow of
nostalgia, has long departed the international

scene, and with it has gone the self-confidence and the framework of foreign policy. It was not a Marxist but the late Ian MacLeod, one of the most percipient of post-war Convervatives, who once noted that the attitudes and policies of British pre-eminence had never been self-sustaining: they rested on three material advantages; on the fact that the British had pioneered industrial capitalism; on the existence of the British Empire, which had provided a large, open market for British manufactures and had significantly augmented the country's diplomatic and military strength, and on the British navy.[2]

Overtaken by her industrial competitors, stripped, albeit with a minimum of actual as opposed to rhetorical fuss, of her Empire by an alliance between nationalism abroad and liberalism at home, and with no permanent naval presence East of Suez since the late 1960s, the contemporary problem for British governments in their relations with the non-European world can be fairly accurately, if somewhat negatively, described as damage limitation. In this regard, Britain is arguably not so different from the other industrial democracies: they all wish to cooperate with Third World countries in ways which will do as little as possible to undermine the existing distribution of power and influence within international society. For British governments, however, this general problem poses a sharper utilitarian dilemma, namely how in an uncomfortably competitive world to transform the legacies of pre-eminence and Empire from liabilities into assets.

In no part of the world has this general problem presented British governments with greater difficulties than in their relations with Africa. The broad strategy for effecting the transformation - decolonisation within the Commonwealth - was announced to the world with the granting of independence to Ghana in 1957. But what exactly were the British up to? 'If we want things to stay as they are', Giuseppe di Lampedusa makes one of his characters say in The Leopard, that marvellous novel about the confrontation between the old Sicilian order and Italian nationalism,'things will have to change'. Was this what Harold Macmillan meant when in February 1960 he warned the South African parliament to adapt to the wind of change that was blowing across the African continent? Nkrumah, the first legatee of the old order south of the Sahara, certainly feared so: neo-colonialism, he warned, was the worst kind of imperialism because, unlike the real thing, it constituted the exercise of power without responsibility.

But if that was their main purpose - to keep the old imperial show on the road - at the time most British ministers and officials, untrained then as now in dialectical historicism, would probably have denied it; they were reacting, as always, pragmatically and as they saw it honourably, to the challenge of the moment. Thus, for some time they resisted the argument of General Assembly Resolution 1514, which held that lack of preparation for self-government should not be used to delay independence, but not so much out of opposition to the principle (principles have seldom been debated in Britain in the abstract), as because the presence of settler communities with entrenched political privileges, as in Central Africa, created practical obstacles to disengagement, or because the concept of an independent state, dependent from its birth on budgetary assistance, was anathema to those trained in the principles of sound administration and Treasury control.

By the middle 1960s, however, it was clear that any such doubts had been brushed aside; the British government (first under the Conservatives and then Labour) had decided to seek the country's fortune in Europe as and when the French would permit them to do so; the Commonwealth sentimentalists on the Left and far Right had been brushed aside, and what remained of the Empire was to be scuttled as decently, but also as quickly, as possible. The Central African Federation was broken up in deference to the wishes of the United Independence Party of Northern Rhodesia and the Nyasaland Congress Party. Grants in aid were accepted as a reasonable price for disengagement in Malawi, Sierra Leone, the former High Commission Territories in Southern Africa, and even Gambia was finally allowed to acquire independence with no more than a theatrical nod in the direction of an economically viable Senegambian Federation. Only the anomolous constitutional status of Rhodesia frustrated the strategy and constantly interfered with attempts to create a network of low key, but still special, relationships between Britian and her former colonies. Fourteen years after Ian Smith's unilateral declaration of independence in 1965, the military, economic and political constraints under which the three major parties involved in the conflict were operating, i.e. the Zimbabwe Nationalist, Rhodesian whites and the governments

of the Front Line States, unexpectedly provided a
new Conservative administration with the diplomatic
opportunity to secure the settlement that had
eluded its predecessors. With the implementation of
the Lancaster House Agreement, British sovereignty
was finally removed from the African continent.
Whatever the future problems of British-African
relations, there are no residual imperial
commitments, such as those that exist in the
Falkland Islands, which seem likely to lead to the
projection into Africa of British military power.

In the contemporary international order, with
its emphasis on territorial integrity and anti-
colonial self-determination, liquidation of imperial
commitments is certainly a necessary but not a
sufficient step in the transformation of liabilities
into assets. Once the major assumption of imperial
pre-eminence - that British and African interests
were the same - had been abandoned, the
establishment of a framework for post-colonial
relations required, in addition, the identification
of mutual interests between Britain and the
successor states. In this chapter I shall concentrate
on three broad areas within which this search for
mutuality has been conducted. These are respectively
the organisation and management of the international
economy; bilateral relations, primarily economic in
character which occur within this framework, and the
overall political organisation of international
society. In all three areas, particularly the last,
which is overshadowed by the unresolved conflicts of
southern Africa, the legacies of British global pre-
eminence and imperial involvement have created both
problems and opportunities, which distinguish
Britain's African policies from those of the other
industrial powers: the record of achievement, in
other words is mixed.

A.   THE ORGANISATION OF THE INTERNATIONAL ECONOMY

The contrast between Britain and the other former
imperial powers is nowhere more evident than in the
field of international economic organisation. The
obvious comparison is with France and Germany.
During the colonial period, all three countries
hoped (sometimes in vain) that their overseas
possessions would contribute to their overall
economic and political strength, but the economic
philosophies on which they based their policies led
them to pursue this common aim in different ways. As
the first industrial nation, Britain was the first

country to champion the doctrines of economic liberalism as not only being in her own interests but also in the interests of the international community generally and of world peace.[3] Trade and investment, of course, still followed or rather accompanied the flag, but so long as she remained the workshop of the world, Britain was for the most part able to rely on indirect methods for preserving imperial markets and sources of supply.

Had the Third World then existed - at the time of the scramble for Africa the concept had not been dreamt of - it would have begun on the Rhine: Germany under Bismarck was the first country to insist on the sovereign right of protection as an instrument of development and as a means of closing the 'gap' with industrial Britain. It was not at this point the liberal economy that Germany challenged so much as the proposition that it knew no frontiers. In France, the mercantalist tradition of economic state-craft and the government's willingness to protect the economy for political and cultural ends, had never been broken. France, like Germany, also acquired her African empire from a subordinate position in international society, circumstances conducive at the best of times to protection rather than open markets. In any event, the economies of France's African colonies were notoriously bound to the metropole with hoops of iron: colonial agricultural products were subsidised and provided with a guaranteed market; France in turn monopolised the colonial markets and guaranteed, i.e. controlled, the CFA franc, a service which she still performs. When France signed the Treaty of Rome it was on condition that her partners shared the cost of supporting francophone Africa in return for the partial and largely theoretical opening up of their markets, i.e. to the other five members of the EEC only. Nigeria, supported by Britain and the other Commonwealth African states challenged the legitimacy of Part IV of the Treaty within the GATT on the grounds that the Agreement permitted the creation of Customs' Unions but not the creation of new preferences. Here, then, at the outset of the post-colonial period was a significant convergence of African and British interests: both stood to lose from the creation of a privileged trading relationship between francophone Africa and the Six.

On this issue, however, the Afro-British alliance was defeated. The Nigerian challenge to the association concept in the GATT failed, and first

the East African countries and then Nigeria itself
negotiated their own agreements with the EEC to
protect their own interests.[4] Nevertheless, it is
probably fair to claim that, in their general
approach to the role of the developing countries in
the institutional structure of the world economy,
Britain and Commonwealth Africa remained in
agreement. Both sides were initially in favour of a
global regime to cover the relationship between the
industrial and developing worlds.[5] Only after its
bid to join the European Community was successful
did the British position on this issue finally
change, and even then, typically, the conversion was
not to the principle of special trading
relationships. On the contrary, left to itself, no
British government would have chosen to assert that
the Euro-African Community of interest in which it
was now involved was intrinsically different from
and stronger than the mutual interest shared with
other parts of the new Commonwealth, in particular,
the countries of south Asia. British support for the
Lome Convention was for practical reasons: it
provided a solution to the problem of the residual
Commonwealth preferences which, in the absence of a
Convention, would have lapsed following British
accession. On the other side, Nigeria, whose
representatives played a leading part in the
negotiations, viewed them in a similarly pragmatic
light; they provided an opportunity for concerting
West African economic policies in parallel with the
ECOWAS project and more generally for exercising
continental leadership (see also Chapter ten).
But if on one level - that of dealing with
consequences of the creation of the EEC and
Britain's subsequent accession to it - there has
been a broad convergence of British and African
interests, on another - that of dealing with African
and Third World demands for structural reform and a
New International Economic Order - there has been a
significant divergence. So long as it was a case of
tinkering with the liberal market system there was
no real problem. Indeed, to begin with, Britain
tinkered with it herself as a way of dealing with
the costs which arose when she yielded her position
of pre-eminence to the United States. From the
signing of the Atlantic Charter onwards, the
Americans had sought the abolition of the
Commonwealth preference system and the sterling
area. The demands were resisted; preferences were
frozen but not abolished and for a time the sterling
area was actually strengthened, as the British

attempted to deal pragmatically with the post-war
dollar shortage. But these policies were tactical,
essentially a means of playing for time, rather than
a credible attempt to influence the long-run
structure of the international economy; and in time
they fell apart and were abandoned in response to
pressures from within Africa itself and from
outside.[6] Thus, for example, the British not only
developed sectors of the East African economies to
meet British needs but developed also the system of
common services on which the East African Community
was subsequently based. British investors,
particularly those in Kenya, stood to gain from the
regional integration of the economy; another
example, it might be argued, of a smooth transition
from an imperial identity to a post-colonial, some
would say a neo-colonial, mutuality of interests.
But as Eliowany Kisanga has shown, when new and
often more powerful multinational investors began to
compete with the British they often found it
advantageous to deal with the national governments
rather than with community institutions, thus
reinforcing the already impressive centrifugal
forces within the region.

The close monetary relations between Britain
and Commonwealth Africa similarly suffered with the
demise of the sterling area. Unlike France, Britain
had, in any case, never attempted to extend the
control of the Bank of England over Commonwealth
African economies. With the approach of
independence, one after the other Britain's African
colonies secured an independent central bank as one
of the essential supports of sovereign
statehood.[7] And even before the final liquidation
of the sterling area, most of independent Africa had
prudently diversified their reserve holdings away
from a total dependence on sterling. Such relatively
gradual shifts in economic power and diplomatic
orientation - towards Europe in the British case,
away from Britain in the African - were in a sense
only to be expected within the open market order.
The British might regret the weakening of their
privileged position in Africa, vis-à-vis their
competitors, but they had no grounds on which to
complain about it. The Africans on the other hand
said vociferously that they, after all, had never
been consulted about the desirability of an open
market trading system. Following the lead given by
Algeria to the Group of 77 in 1974, they
increasingly pressed for a radical restructuring of
the international economy to give them a greater

say in its management, to transfer resources from rich to poor according to a criterion of need, and to enhance the prices of raw materials, on which most of them depended, through indexing, compensatory finance and the creation of a financially independent and politically powerful Common Fund for commodities. As the least developed group of countries within the Group of 77, the Africans were the most insistent on the creation of an institution which would not merely stabilise commodity prices (a move which the British were more willing than some to concede) but increase the flow of resources to themselves.[8] In advancing these demands, Third World governments were proposing a system of positive income redistribution, analogous to that carried out by some Western governments within their own societies since 1945. Indeed, President Nyerere has suggested that the creation of such a global Keynesian system is essentially a matter of will and that there is no essential difference in this regard between the domestic and the international context. There is, it should be noted, a body of opinion in Britain as in the other industrial countries, which endorses the re-distributive thesis of the NIEO campaign - it forms, for example, the broad orientation of the original Brandt Commission report - but it is <u>not</u> a view which is shared by the Thatcher administration <u>or</u> any of its predecessors. On the contrary, British governments have repeatedly made it clear, in their actions if not in ministerial speeches, that they believe the analogy between the Welfare State and the international community to be false.

In official British thinking on international economic affairs, there is a crucial distinction between fair trading rules and aid - the former are based on the typically negative liberal principle of non-discrimination. This principle, it is held, can be stretched to embrace the notion of preferential access for developing countries, but not to include a collective mechanism for automatic income redistribution. The reason is that aid is viewed as a discretionary matter and, therefore, as an expression of a political relationship. Although the London-based Commonwealth Secretariat has established for itself a useful role in mediating between the two sides on North-South issues, the British government itself does not stand out from the other members of OECD as more accommodating to African interests. In terms of the broad framework of the international economy, Britain remains a <u>status</u>

quo power, despite the decline of its political and economic influence on the continent, while the African Commonwealth countries are revisionists, despite the fact that many of them are ruled by a political class which personally benefits from its association with foreign capital and despite the growing economic disparities between the Commonwealth African countries themselves.

B.   BILATERAL RELATIONS

In their approach to bilateral relations with African countries as much on the general issue of multilaterialism, the style of British and French post-colonial policies stands in sharp contrast towards one another. The special relationship between Paris and the francophone African countries, although subject to some dilution, continues to be guaranteed by a series of bilateral political and military, as well as economic, treaties. Since the abrogation of the British-Nigerian Defence Pact in 1962 and of the Simonstown basis of agreement with South Africa two years later, there has been no British equivalent. The Commonwealth represents an English language, post-imperial association but, although from its creation in 1966 Britain has remained the largest contributor to the Secretariat, the emphasis has been deliberately placed on the multilateral character of the Organisation; and so far as Africa and Asia are concerned, it has been most active, and arguably effective, as an informal lobby on general North-South issues, rather than as a channel through which Britain can maintain a privileged position in its former colonies. In the past there has even on occasions been talk of Britain's withdrawal or expulsion from the Commonwealth. The Thatcher government, however, clearly values the Organisation and has reason to be grateful to Commonwealth countries for their support in the Zimbabwe negotiations and at the time of the Falklands War in April 1982; but even so, its commitments towards the Commonwealth are both less precise and almost certainly ultimately more dispensable than its commitments towards either the EEC or the Atlantic Alliance.

There is a further difference between Britain and France which throws light on the British problem of translating imperial liabilities into post-colonial assets. France remains the centre of a powerful (even if in a global sense a minority) culture area based on the French language. It is not merely a question of shared intellectual habits and life-style, although both of these are important. It also provides France with a comparative advantage in the securing of contracts, as any analysis of the European Development Fund will quickly demonstrate. By contrast, Britain not only surrendered its global pre-eminence but surrendered it to another English-speaking nation whose traditional anti-colonialism was perfectly compatible with economic and cultural competition with Britain for influence in Commonwealth Africa. Since at independence all former British colonies set about diversifying their external relations, and since the United States had greater resources at its disposal, it quickly established in educational as well as economic and political matters a rival, and in some cases a stronger, magnetic field of attraction to the former metropolitan power.

Too much should not be made of Britain's decline vis-à-vis the United States. In the overall conception of the Pax Americana, Africa had low priority. Once the rigidities of the Cold War had been established, the rulers of the Imperial Republic were generally content to leave the 'policing' of peripheral areas to their allies who were familar with the terrain. In the early years of American globalism, Africa presented Americans with no equivalent to Dien Bien Phu, and as time went on they became positively anxious to share the burden wherever they could with the former colonial powers.[9] Nevertheless, except in matters which came before the Security Council, which I will discuss in the final section of the chapter, in its bilateral relations with African countries, Britain increasingly returned to its original role as a nation of shopkeepers. Its primary concerns, in other words, were the protection of trade and investment and the provision of aid both as an inducement to African governments to stay within the liberal market order and as a more direct buttress to British exports.

Let us take first the question of aid. In broad terms the British aid record fairly accurately reflects the country's economic standing amongst other members of the OECD. Britain is the fifth largest donor overall, after the United States, France, West Germany and Japan, although when expressed as a percentage of GNP (0.35 per cent in 1980) the British performance is better than that of the United States (0.27 per cent) and Japan (0.32 per cent) but considerably worse than that of France

(0.64 per cent) and Germany (0.44 per cent).[10] About a third of Britain's bilateral financial disbursements (£1,326 million in 1980) have traditionally gone to Africa, although when technical assistance is included the continent accounts for about half the total aid effort.[11] In addition, about 30 per cent of British aid (£526 million in 1980) is channelled through multilateral agencies, a significant proportion of which, of course, ultimately goes to Africa.

What criteria govern the British aid programme in Africa? Apart from saying that it is intended to maintain, and on occasions enhance, the area of inter-dependence and mutuality of interests, in other words to lubricate Anglo-African relations, it would be misleading to interpret its growth and pattern according to a deliberately pre-conceived economic or political strategy. On the contrary, as a glance at the pattern of disbursements will indicate, the programme continues to bear the imprint of particular problems which arose in the context of decolonisation - in 1975, for example, 82 per cent of British aid still went to Commonwealth Africa, a proportion of which has since been whittled away as a result of Britain's accession to the EEC and as a result of a deliberate government policy of diversification, but only marginally.

Within Commonwealth Africa, southern and east African countries have obtained the lion's share of British aid transfers: in 1977 southern African countries took £38.5 million, East Africa £23.4 million and West Africa £13.5 million. These figures reflect (or perhaps conceal) special circumstances. Kenya dominates the East African scene: between 1963-1979, Kenya was the second largest British aid recipient after India, receiving £180 million, much of it to finance the Land Transfer Programme for buying out British owned farms in the country. In southern Africa, the smaller countries, Malawi, Botswana and Lesotho, are not only major consumers of British technical assistance but also to begin with (although no longer) recipients of grants in aid, while Zambia, also a major recipient of technical assistance (a consequence of the wildly uneven development of skilled manpower under the Central African Federation) became a major recipient of financial aid after 1975 as a result of the collapse of copper prices and the Rhodesian crisis.[12] Since the independence of Zimbabwe, the pattern of concentration on southern Africa has been reinforced as a result of reconstruction aid to that country and Britain's qualified support for SADCC. The relatively low aid figures for West Africa reflect on the one hand the fact that those countries which have been highly dependent on British assistance, for example the Gambia and Sierra Leone, had very small budgets, and on the other the fact that Nigeria, the African country which is most important to Britain, decided after the quadrupling of oil prices in 1974 against seeking capital aid from the UK and other major donors.[13] Of the African countries outside the Commonwealth which have attracted significant amounts of British aid - aid to non-Commonwealth Africa as a whole represents about 10 per cent of the total - the principal recipients have been the Sudan and Egypt which were once administered by Britain although outside the formal machinery of the Empire, and Ethiopia, the one African country which escaped the European scramble.

Within Britain itself, official opinion, and in the end policy, has generally followed some way behind changes of view and fashion within the professional community of Western aid experts. Thus, for example, under the Labour administration which held office between 1974-1979 there was a conversion to the philosophy of basic needs which echoed a similar change of orientation by the World Bank at the same time,[14] while the present Tory government, which has been in the vanguard of the Western monetarist revolt, has not only reduced aid overall, in line with the general cutback of government expenditures but has also increased the Aid Trade Provision (ATP) i.e. that proportion of the Aid budget which is earmarked to meet specific requests for export assistance by British industry which might otherwise fall foul of GATT and OECD rules on export subsidies.[15] Such changes of direction, however, are more a question of degree than of kind: although the British aid programme has never given rise to the degree of controversy within Parliament as has customarily greeted the American programme with Congress, its supporters have always had to argue that it is not merely right to provide concessionary finance but that there are also material returns to Britain from doing so. It was the Labour government which accompanied its basic needs strategy with the introduction of the ATP, which its Conservative successors, egged on by the CBI, have sought to strengthen.

In 1977 the overall proportion of aid which was tied to the procurement of British goods and

services was estimated at 65.8 per cent.[16] In a
ministerial paper written the following year, the
then Minister of Overseas Development, Mrs. Judith
Hart, defended the programme in terms which make
clear the reasons for the bi-partisan support which
it has generally enjoyed despite the influential
voices which have from time to time been raised
against it:

> There are two basic ways in which the aid
> programme helps British industry. By helping
> foster income creation and widely distributed
> income growth in the developing countries, it
> increases the overseas markets for British
> goods. In the process it also provides
> opportunities for aid financed exports both
> under bilateral and multilateral aid
> arrangements.[17]

On the first count, moreover, even the British
contribution to multilateral agencies, justified in
the last analysis as support for the system of
liberal multilateralism, also yields a more direct
return. Of all World Bank loans to developing
countries in 1980, the UK share of procurement was
just over 6 per cent, but in East Africa it was 16.4
per cent and in West Africa 9 per cent. The British
share was even higher in soft loan credits (IDA) to
East Africa, 17.5 per cent compared with an overall
share of procurement in developing countries
generally of 12 per cent.[18] These figures suggest
that Britain's comparative advantage in Commonwealth
Africa has not been completely eroded. In dealing
with a nation of shopkeepers, it seems, there may be
some circumstances in which the familiar corner shop
still has the edge over the more powerful but
anonymous supermarket.

We should not be deceived, however, by such
homely analogies. It is the activities of the major
industrial corporations such as Lonrho, ICI and the
oil companies, together with British banks and
financial institutions which dictate the pattern of
trade and investment. As with aid, this pattern is a
product of Britain's colonial involvement in Africa -
thus despite a rapid growth in the immediate post-
colonial period, in the mid-1970s about 70 per cent
of private investment and about 60 per cent of
British trade with independent Africa was still
within the Commonwealth.[19] In this case, however,
the legacy of the past has revealed an uncomfortable
paradox: while government to government aid

relations have given rise to relatively few political problems,[20] the steady expansion of private sector links over which the government has only the most indirect control (through Commonwealth and now EEC preferential arrangements, among others) has increasingly exposed them to criticism from their African trading partners.

The reason is well known. Both aid and private investment are heavily concentrated in two countries, the Federation of Nigeria and the Republic of South Africa. With its emergence as a major oil exporter, and hence as a major importer of capital and manufactured goods, Nigeria jumped to being Britain's twelfth largest market in the world and its fifth outside Europe.[21] Simultaneously, it became a more important market than South Africa, which had traditionally enjoyed pride of place in Britain's economic relations with Africa and thereby assured itself of British protection at the United Nations whenever, for example, the African countries demanded the imposition of economic sanctions in an effort to force the Republic to abandon its policy of separate development. When Britain's stake in the rest of the continent is added to its stake in Nigeria, it is possible to argue that there has been a massive shift in the balance of British interests and that as a consequence the African countries, acting under the leadership of the Nigerian government, are now in a position to face Britain with the necessity of an historic choice between white and black Africa.

That Britain has so far been able to avoid this choice is also well known. The explanation must be sought in Africa, as well as in Britain itself. Not only is it as difficult in Africa as anywhere else to persuade countries to engage in collective economic sanctions when they would have to bear the cost of imposing them themselves, but the African countries generally need the industrial world more than they are needed. For a time, Nigeria's oil wealth seemed to exclude that country from this general rule and indeed gave a certain credibility to the idea of counter-sanctions; but the world-wide recession and the development by Britain of North Sea Oil, which is in direct competition with the Nigerian product, suggests that its exemption is more apparent than real. In any event, while there have been token expropriations of British interests - Barclays Bank and British Petroleum - which have been defended as warnings to Britain over its southern African policies, these have been isolated incidents (for which there are also more parochial explanations) and have made no serious impact on Britain's £500m. investment in the Nigerian economy.

Within Britain there are well-organised pressure groups, such as the Anti-Apartheid Movement and the United Nations Association, which regularly campaign for an embargo on British trade with South Africa and for disinvestment, and which are supported at least in principle by influential sections of the Labour and Liberal Parties and by the Trades Unions. No British government can afford to ignore such opinion completely, particularly now that it is possible to argue that Britain's historical entanglement with South Africa is putting at risk other, potentially more important, British interests. As a result of such pressure, indeed, the Government was persuaded in the mid-1970s to strengthen its alternative strategy of 'positive engagement' by devising a code of conduct for British investors, the fore-runner of the EEC code of conduct and the set of principles which the Reverend Sullivan successfully persuaded a majority of US corporations with South African interests to adopt.

Pressure on successive governments for disengagement from South Africa has predictably engendered a counter-pressure in the form of the well-organised, and well-financed activities of the United Kingdom South Africa Trade Association (UKSATA). This Association, which claims to have the backing of most of the 'British companies with significant investment and trading interests in or commercial dealings with the Republic of South Africa and many of the medium and smaller British companies'[22] and is supported by a small but vocal group of Members of Parliament, regularly disseminates information on such matters as the value of British trade and investment (in 1982 £348m. and £11,000m. respectively); the impact on British employment from a policy of disengagement (an estimated addition of 250,000 to the unemployment figures), and the fact that 'access to South African metals and minerals (platinum, chrome, vernadium and manganese) is as necessary to the industrial west as access to Middle East oil'. No British government can afford to ignore this pressure either, and indeed, while Labour administrations have been generally more eager to dissociate themselves from South Africa politically and in sporting and cultural affairs[23] - for example it was not until 1964 when Harold Wilson first became

Prime Minister that Britain joined the United States in imposing a unilateral arms embargo - they have been as adamant as their Conservative opponents in resisting both domestic and international pressure for the imposition of sanctions.

Since the economic as well as diplomatic isolation of South Africa is official OAU policy, it is inevitable, therefore, that South Africa should continue to cast a shadow over Britain's relations with the rest of the continent. Were it not for its South African entanglement, it is at least conceivable that, with the surrender of all its sovereign claims, the continent would have been made safe for the descendants of the Manchester school of economists who had been opposed to colonial expansion from the beginning. As it is, however, it is largely because South Africa constitutes a general problem for the international order in the outcome of which Britain has an historic interest (other considerations apart, among the 40 per cent of South African whites who are of British descent, a substantial although undisclosed proportion still holds British passports) as well as the purely material interest sketched above, that Britain remains politically embroiled in African affairs. It is to this final problem of Afro-British relations that I now turn.

C.   SOUTH AFRICA AND INTERNATIONAL ORDER

In the period between 1945-50, the political map of the post-war international system was drawn; it was not to be altered in any fundamental way until the early 1970s and much of it, indeed, survives to the present day.[24] Among the governments of the Western powers, two versions of this map circulated freely and some of the most intractable contemporary international problems - including the problem of South Africa - partly arose from the inconsistencies between them.

The first map, that of the United Nations, established, so to say, the new constitutional order for international society. As with the new economic order its form mirrored the values of its most powerful members, the liberal democracies and particularly those of the United States. The major concession to realism in the shape of the Security Council and the power of veto which was granted to its five permanent members, ensured that the interests of the old imperial powers could not be lightly brushed aside; but at the same time the commitment in the Charter to the right of national self-determination and fundamental human rights, when combined with the anti-colonialism of the two emergent great powers (they had not yet fulfilled de Tocqueville's prophecy by being dubbed super-powers), was sufficient to guarantee that the parliamentary procedures of the world body would be used to maintain relentless pressure on the imperial powers to dismantle their colonial systems and on their right to invoke Article 2 (7), which insulates domestic jurisdiction from outside interference, as a defence against such pressure.

Within this first constitutional map South Africa suffered from guilt by association. Only two kinds of state were envisaged, those which were already independent and whose domestic arrangements were constantly immune from scrutiny, and those which were to be created by de-colonisation, the withdrawal of the Europeans back across the colour line to their own homelands. South Africa, an independent state since 1910, was not immune, however: its traditional policy of racial segregation, even before the National Party reinforced it by the introduction of full-scale apartheid after 1948, was too blatantly at variance with the majoritarian principles under which first Asian and then African nationalists successfully demanded independence. As a result, from 1946, when the Indian government first raised the question of South African discrimination against the Asian community in Natal at the United Nations, South Africa's racial policies have been the subject of annual debate and censure. The simultaneous refusal by the South Africans to place the mandated territory of South West Africa (Namibia) under the UN Trusteeship Council created another issue of contention: not only was South Africa an anomalous state in the eyes of the new Afro-Asian bloc, it had committed the cardinal sin against the new constitutional order by refusing to prepare for independence those whose destiny had been placed in its care by the mandate 'as a sacred trust'.

In the early post-war period, the British Labour government repeatedly refused to associate itself with this international campaign against South Africa, arguing that its racial policies were not a proper subject for UN debate and even questioning, on the advice of Foreign Office lawyers, the opinion of the International Court of Justice in 1950 that South Africa needed the permission of the UN before it could modify the status of South West

Africa. The reasons for their attitude were complex, partly determined by their desire to have neither the principle nor the pace of de-colonisation dictated from outside (except to a limited extent with the respect of the Trusteeship territories) but partly also by considerations of a more immediate strategic and political character.

The second map of the post-war world, that of the Cold War, determined the major international alignments from the late 1940s to the present day. But, as we have already noted, initially the common Western stand against what was perceived as an imminent threat of Communist expansion, concealed a more friendly rivalry between the United States and the residual force of British imperialism. This placed the British Government in a difficult position: inasmuch as they feared Soviet designs against their global interests, they needed to enlist American support beyond Europe as well as in the North Atlantic area, but insofar as this would require the Americans to lend formal support to British imperial arrangements, proposals for an extension of the Western Alliance, i.e. into the South Atlantic, stood no chance of gaining Congressional support. As Ritchie Ovendale has been able to show in a recent article, based on material from the British archives which has become available under the thirty year rule, it was in this context that the Labour government formulated the basic policy towards South Africa which, with relatively minor fluctuations, has been followed ever since.[25]

The basic problem which they feared had three aspects. The first was strategic. So long as the Americans were unprepared to commit themselves to the defence of British and Western interests in the Middle East, the British would need all the support they could muster within the Commonwealth. As a professed anti-Communist power, South Africa stood ready and willing to help (despite their hostility to the UN the South Africans had sent an air force unit to Korea). The fact that after 1948 the South African government contained men who were deeply hostile to Britain persuaded the Atlee government of the importance of doing nothing which would jeopardise the strategic relationship between the two countries. The second aspect was economic. Besides being the source of many of Britain's strategic raw materials, in the immediate post-war period, South Africa was one of the few countries with which Britain had a favourable balance of trade, a consideration which gave it access to South African gold production to provide much needed backing for sterling area reserves. Finally, the third aspect was political. It was deeply embarrassing for the government, which had both initiated Britain's imperial withdrawal from India and introduced the Welfare State at home, to find itself bound by interest rather than sentiment to a government, most of whose policies it deeply abhorred.

The solution which the Labour party devised and which all British governments have adhered to ever since was to make the best of a bad job. On the one hand, there was no alternative to cooperation; on the other, any latent South African expansionism should be checked, in the first instance by refusing to incorporate the High Commission territories in the Union, as had originally been envisaged in 1910, and then by constructing a bloc of pro-British territories to the North. In presenting the paper which outlined this policy to the Cabinet the Commonwealth Secretary, Patrick Gordon-Walker, explained it in the following way:

> 'Britain should be ready to develop those relations with the Union that bind her to us and make her unwilling to risk a break with us ... these relations are also in our direct interest. Chief amongst them comes cooperation in defence and in economic matters. Also important is to give the Union what help and guidance it decently can at the United Nations. Those who argue that, because we dislike the Union's native policy, we should ostracise her and have nothing to do with her completely fail to understand the realities of the situation. Such a policy would not only gravely harm us in the defence and economic fields; it would also weaken our power to deter South Africa from foolhardy acts from fear of breaking with us. It would immediately and directly reduce our chances of holding the Territories, which form a vital part in any policy of containing and confining the Union's influence and territorial expansion in Southern Africa.[26]

It may seem far-fetched to claim that this policy has survived the events of the past thirty years, including withdrawal of South Africa from the Commonwealth, the collapse of the Central African Confederation, fourteen years of rebel government in

Rhodesia and the disintegration of the sterling area. Reflection, however, seems to support its essential validity. The changes that have occurred in Southern Africa have been despite British policy rather than because of it. At the United Nations, British governments have fought a long rearguard action against the African campaign to turn South Africa into a pariah state, only to join the majority in criticising apartheid in the General Assembly once the British Empire itself had been effectively liquidated and, even then, drawing a sharp distinction between criticism and action. Whenever there is a demand for sanctions under Chapter 7 of the Charter, the British government, along with the other Western powers, can be relied on to veto it, using whatever arguments are ready at hand to justify their action. It can be plausibly argued, of course, that it is the threat of sanctions, rather than their imposition, which is what matters and that it is their ultimate uncertainty about continued Western support which has persuaded the South African government to undertake even such cautious and half-hearted reforms as it has embarked upon. Maybe. On the other hand, the current stalemate in the Namibian negotiations suggests very strongly that, whatever the situation in the past, the South Africans now know that they have successfully called the West's bluff. It is true that Britain has now ceded to the United States leadership in designing the containment policy, but, whatever differences there may be between the two governments over the line to be pursued within the Contact Group, it seems unlikely that they are fundamental.

Meanwhile, as in the past, the British government tries to have it both ways, i.e. to cooperate and contain simultaneously. Formal defence cooperation, it is true, has been abandoned (it is very doubtful whether this has been extended to the contact between the intelligence services), but economic cooperation remains as strong as ever, and the British government continues to foster relations at all levels of South African society, for example, by sponsoring visits of Verlichte members of parliament to Britian and in other ways seeking to encourage domestic reform. It would be a brave man, however, who claimed that these efforts were accompanied by much hope. The collapse of the Central African Federation was the biggest blow to the early containment policy, but, with the independence of Zimbabwe and the establishment of

SADCC, it has arguably been revived. Whether, in the face of African opposition to South Africa from within the country, even more than from outside, Britain can continue to have it both ways is uncertain. Probably in the long run it cannot. But for so long as the two maps of the international system cannot be reconciled, British governments are likely to conclude, as in the past, that the only option open to them is to make the best of a bad job. Their policy has never been popular in independent Africa, but there are few signs of radical change.

* An earlier version of this chapter was presented at a Conference on Africa and the Great Powers, University of Ife, Ile-Ife, Nigeria, in June 1983.

NOTES

[1] For example, Disraeli, speaking in 1852 about Britain's remaining colonial presence in North America. 'These wretched colonies will all be independent in a few years and are a millstone round our neck.'

[2] Ian Macleod, 'Reports of Britain's Death', Foreign Affairs, October 1966, pp.89-97.

[3] Peter Cain, 'Capitalism, War and Internationalism in the Thoughts of Richard Cobden', British Journal of International Studies, Vol.5, No.3, October 1979, pp.229-47.

[4] The Nigerian agreement was a victim of the Civil War and was never implemented, largely it has been claimed because the French deliberately delayed ratification.

[5] For example, the British supported the Commonwealth argument about non-reciprocity as the appropriate basis for North-South relations as opposed to the contrary position adopted under the first two Yaunde Agreements.

[6] See Arthur Kilgore and James Mayall, 'The Residual Legatee: Economic Relations in the Contemporary Commonwealth', in John Groom and Paul Taylor (eds.), The Contemporary Commonwealth (London, Macmillan, 1984).

[7] Y. Bangura, Britain and Commonwealth Africa: The Politics of Economic Relations 1951-1975 (Manchester, Manchester University Press, 1983).

[8] See Geoffrey Goodwin and James Mayall (eds.), A New International Commodity Regime (London, Croom Helm, 1979).

[9] For a fuller discussion of this point, see

James Mayall, <u>Africa, The Cold War and After</u> (London, Elek, 1971).

[10] <u>Development Cooperation</u>, 1982 Review (Paris, OECD 1982, pp.204-5).

[11] Guy Arnold, <u>Aid in Africa</u> (London, Kogan Page, 1979), p.39.

[12] <u>Ibid.</u>, pp.40-43.

[13] Olajide Aluko, <u>Essays in Nigerian Foreign Policy</u> (London, Allen and Unwin, 1981), p.62.

[14] The new British policy was set out in a White Paper published in 1975 under the title <u>More Help for the Poorest</u>. For a critical discussion of this policy see Arnold, <u>op. cit.</u>, pp.45-50.

[15] Daniel Nelson, 'Pounds of Flesh', <u>Far Eastern Economic Review</u>, 19-25 November 1982.

[16] Arnold, <u>Aid in Africa</u>, p.45.

[17] <u>Ibid.</u>, p.47.

[18] Vince Cable, 'British Interests and Third World Development', in Robert Cassen, Richard Jolly, John Sewell and Robert Wood (eds.), <u>Rich Country Interests and Third World Development</u> (London, Croom Helm, 1983, p.194).

[19] British Information Services, Central Office of Information, <u>Britain and the Developing Countries, Africa</u> (London, January 1977), p.7.

[20] Two exceptions were the disputes between the British and Tanzanian governments in the mid-1960s over the latter's refusal to pay colonial Civil Service pensions, and with Idi Amin's regime in Uganda over the mass expulsion of Asians and abuse of fundamental human rights. Both disputes led to a suspension of British aid.

[21] <u>See</u> Alec Parrett, 'Trade Patterns, the Two-Way Pull', <u>Africa</u>, no.73, September 1977, pp.97-8.

[22] UKSATA, <u>British Trade with South Africa: A Question of National Interest</u> (London, UKSATA, August 1982).

[23] The Annual Report of the MCC contains the following interesting report of the discussion which took place after the Test and County Cricket Board had agreed to make ineligible for selection for England a group of players who had undertaken a private tour of South Africa in 1981: 'A member expressed concern as to whether the decision by the MCC Committee to support the ban was truly representative of the views of Members. He also mentioned that the cricketers involved might still take legal action. He informed the meeting that, of the ten resolutions passed by sporting bodies in favour of breaking sporting links with South Africa,

eight had been proposed by the Soviet Union.'

[24] For a fuller discussion of this process see the Introduction to James Mayall and Cornelia Navari (eds.), <u>The End of the Post-War Era: Documents on Great Power Relations, 1968-75</u> (Cambridge, Cambridge University Press, 1981).

[25] Ritchie Ovendale, 'The South African Policy of the British Labour Government, 1947-51', <u>International Affairs</u>, Vol.59, no.1, Winter 1982/83, pp.41-58.

[26] Quoted in <u>Ibid</u>., p.57.

CHAPTER 5

FRANCE'S INVOLVEMENT IN SUB-SAHARAN AFRICA: A
NECESSARY CONDITION TO MIDDLE POWER STATUS IN THE
INTERNATIONAL SYSTEM

Daniel Bach

Twenty-five years after the independence of most
African countries, French influence and involvement
in the affairs of the continent remain far more
significant than those of other former colonial
powers. Since 1960, successive French presidents
have all considered of particular importance the
preservation of close relations with Africa, and
beyond differences in policy implementation, a
remarkable continuity may be observed in this
respect. French interests in Africa are diverse and
complex and, insofar as state policies are
concerned, they cannot be merely interpreted in
economic terms. In particular, external trade and
investment on the continent are far less significant
than in other parts of the world, where French state
policies retain a much lower profile. More
importantly, perhaps, Africa remains the only area
of the world where France retains sufficient
influence as to guarantee its claims to middle power
status in the international system.

A.   DE GAULLE'S POLICY: PRESERVING THE STATUS QUO

Maintaining the stability and the continuity of
Franco-African relations was a decisive feature of
General de Gaulle's policy as first President of the
Fifth Republic (1958-1969). With a few exceptions
(Guinea and Mali), the independence of francophone
African countries did not provoke any radical
changes in their relations with France. Relations
established during the colonial period were
continued through the implementation of the policy of
'cooperation' defined in 1960-1961. As it then
appeared, the preservation of the Communauté
established by the 1958 constitution would have
proved very costly, while refusing demands for

independence might have threatened the future of France's relations with its former colonies.[1] De Gaulle's view of relations with Africa was, in several respects, then, the expression of a tradition initiated by the theoreticians of colonial expansion under the Third Republic. Political and strategic considerations, far more than economic or financial motives, underlined the French President's African interventions. The franc zone contributed in no small way to the achievement of de Gaulle's fundamental aim: restoring France's status as a middle power. Economically, Africa represented but a small percentage of France's external trade, but the cooperation agreements often provided French companies with situations of quasi-monopoly. Within international organisations, francophone votes comforted French policies and increased their significance. Gaullist policy moves tended to the establishment of close, strongly personalised relationships, which accounted for the preservation of the existing strong networks of influence.

In Africa, those francophone countries which had signed cooperation agreements with France maintained with each other privileged links within sub-regional groupings, such as the Union Africaine et Malgache (UAM) or the Organisation Commune Africaine et Malgache (OCAM).[2] These institutions provided a framework for the definition of common positions and policies in liaison with France. Important guarantees were in return offered to those heads of states close to France: economic and financial aid but also military support, if necessary. In February 1964, French troops intervened in Gabon, after President Leon Mba was overthrown by what looked like a pro-American coup. Four years later, General de Gaulle agreed to commit French troops in Chad, where the revolt of Frolinat threatened the stability of François Tombalbaye's regime. At times French policy involved semi-official interventions designed at de-stabilising such regimes as that of Sekou Toure - whose demand for independence in 1958 was resented as an ideological challenge to continuing French presence in Africa.[3]

Another well-known policy move concerned Nigeria during its civil war (1967-1970). De Gaulle's policy of support for Biafra in 1968-1969 was largely motivated by geo-political considerations and was meant to dismantle the Nigerian state, considered as a pole of attraction and a potential threat to the preservation of French

influence in neighbouring francophone West African
states.[4] In Nigeria, as in the case of Guinea, de
Gaulle's policy largely ignored economic considerations: Guinea was viewed as one of the richest
francophone West African states in 1958, and French
businessmen tried without any success to prevent a
total break, which Sekou Toure did not wish either.[5]
In the case of Nigeria, most French companies
operating in the country did not support secession
but could do little to oppose de Gaulle's support
for Biafra. Far more effective were the pressures
applied by francophone leaders like Diori Hamani of
Niger or Ahmadu Ahidjo of Cameroon. Despite pressure
from Felix Houphouet-Boigny and Jacques Foccart -
the Elysée adviser on African affairs - General de
Gaulle started reconsidering his position early in
1969.[6] By then, it was becoming apparent that
Biafra's secession might dramatically affect the
unity and stability of the neighbouring states.

B.   GEORGES POMPIDOU: REORDERING PRIORITIES

After the election of Georges Pompidou in June 1969,
French policy in sub-saharan Africa entered a
transitional period. In order to transform France
into a competitive commercial and industrial power,
Pompidou sought to facilitate the expansion of the
activities of the private sector abroad. In
addition, a system of financial guarantee against
political risks within the franc zone was instituted
in 1971. The French president also encouraged
industrialists to organise trade and business
missions on the continent and considered that 'the
stage of aid' was 'outdated' and that countries like
Ivory Coast or Cameroon primarily needed private
investment in order to complete their
industrialisation.[7] Simultaneously, an aid policy
aimed at reducing the cost of cooperation links for
France's public finances was adopted. To this
effect, aid was expected to acquire a more technical
character while contributing to the growth of the
productive sector in the African states concerned.
The closer links between public aid and private
flows of capital went along with a net decline in
French overseas development aid and appeared
unacceptable to a majority of francophone African
countries. A crisis followed which affected OCAM
(abandoned by Zaire, Congo, Cameroon, Chad,
Madagascar and Gabon) as well as bilateral links
with France: demands for renegotiating the
cooperation agreements were strongly expressed in

the early 1970s. French President Georges Pompidou vainly attempted to ignore them.

Throughout his term of office Pompidou sought to reduce the weight of France's costly economic, political and military commitments in Africa. French troops were withdrawn from Chad. Relations with new partners such as Nigeria were developed. In 1975, Nigeria became France's biggest trading partner in sub-saharan Africa - President Senghor of Senegal complained the year before that 'France is more dynamic in Nigeria than in francophone black African countries'.[8] Despite the reluctance of the 18 francophone countries associated with the EEC, Georges Pompidou encouraged the opening of global negotiations towards an agreement between the African Caribbean and Pacific (ACP) countries and the EEC. This attitude was in accordance with the Heath-Pompidou agreement of 1972, but it also reflected France's interest in gaining access to larger markets other than those of the francophone African countries. In that respect French policy departed sharply from that of General de Gaulle. In West Africa, however, Georges Pompidou publicly supported francophone initiatives towards the establishment of the Communauté économique de l'Afrique de l'ouest (CEAO), which took place in Abidjan in 1973 in order to counterbalance Nigeria's mounting influence in the sub-region.[9]

C.   VALERY GISCARD D'ESTAING'S NEW ECONOMISM

The African policy of Valery Giscard d'Estaing did not dramatically depart from previous French policy in Africa. The search for new markets, still a major preoccupation, acquired renewed acuity along with the concern over preserving France's access to strategic minerals from the African continent.[10] The specificity of France's policy showed through a polarisation of politico-economic relations around a few francophone (Gabon, Cameroon, Zaire) and non-francophone (Nigeria, South Africa) states. This policy at times challenged old solidarities - relations between France and the Ivory Coast were subsequently in disarray between 1979 and 1981. The international context was dominated by the opening of the African continent to influences other than those of the former European colonial powers, which were in any case in decline. As a result, Giscard d'Estaing's African diplomacy renewed the interventionist policies of de Gaulle. French troops intervened in Chad from 1977 onwards, in Zaire (first indirectly in 1977, then directly a year later), in Mauritania during 1978, and in Central Africa in 1980. Besides these overt military commitments, which took place without any parliamentary control, other military actions were undertaken secretaly. In 1974-75, covert support was provided to the UNITA and the FLCE (Front de libération de l'enclave de Cabinda). French complicity was also strongly alleged when a group of mercenaries attempted to invade Benin in 1977 and in the mercenary-led overthrow of the regime of the Comoro Islands a year later.[11]

The multiplicity of French interventions in Africa reflected the persistence of a strong French interest in the affairs of the continent - the increasing number of participants to the annual Franco-African summits also confirmed the positive response met by some of the Giscardian diplomatic initiatives. Under Giscard d'Estaing French policy in Africa now went along with a global vision of the evolution of the continent, which did not seek to challenge that of the other western powers. In sub-saharan Africa, in particular, French policy lost its specificity which under de Gaulle led to the opposing of United States' policy in the Congo and in Gabon, as well as confronting US, Soviet and British support to the Federal Government of Nigeria during the civil war.

Economic and financial considerations permeated France's African policy, as clearly illustrated in the Abelin report of 1975 and the evolution of aid flows. A closer association of private investment and public aid was advocated so that both could maximise the expansion of French exports and investment in the continent.[12]

Besides francophone Africa, Nigeria and South Africa became France's main trading partners. For example, French exports to Nigeria doubled between 1975 and 1978. And by 1980, Nigeria had become France's thirteenth biggest customer in the world. Nigeria was also France's third oil supplier in 1981. In southern Africa, despite mounting protests, economic relations between France and South Africa also developed significantly during this period. South Africa's share of France's trade with the continent increased from 7.8 per cent to 11.1 per cent between 1975 and 1980. In 1976 a major contract was signed for the construction of two nuclear plants by French companies at Koeberg in South Africa.

D.   FRANCOIS   MITTERRAND: EXPECTATIONS   VERSUS
     CAPABILITIES

While Francois Mitterrand's election in May 1981
aroused considerable expectations in France, in
Africa the socialist president's accession to power
was viewed with mixed feelings. Governments closely
associated with Giscardian policies (Gabon, Zaire,
Central African Republic) were concerned over the
policy changes announced by the socialist party's
Africa programme; whilst the socialist regimes (in
Benin, Congo, Angola, Mozambique and Ethiopia)
welcomed the prospects of improving their relations
with France.
        France's African policy did not undergo the
radical changes which some African countries had
feared, or hoped. The African policy of Mitterrand
should be analysed against the background of the
initial policy pledges of his government. Policies
implemented should also be seen within the context
of (i) the political evolution of the continent and
(ii) the activities of other extra-African powers
towards the continent's problems and conflicts.
        The security of the continent, the
socialist programme insisted in 1981, should be
dealt with by the Africans themselves and
'discussions for collective security guarantees
ought to be favoured' along with 'inter-African
defence agreements' and, more generally, 'OAU
interventions'. Circumstances however forced the
socialist government to overlook this principle on
several occasions during the following years. Yet,
Mitterrand's overall approach to conflicts on the
continent consistently insisted on the need to
promote a peaceful negotiation of conflicts and
avoid the risks of East-West confrontation in
Africa.
        Not surprisingly, the French policy line in
southern Africa and in Chad was significantly
different from that of the Reagan Administration. In
southern Africa France always argued that the
departure of the 15,000 to 20,000 Cuban troops and
Soviet advisers based in Angola should not be linked
to the independence of Namibia. Until France decided
to withdraw from the five-nation contact group on
Namibia, its support for the views of the Front Line
States looked sometimes ambiguous, but it retained
its importance as the United States stuck to its
policy of 'constructive engagement' towards South
Africa. In July 1985 France announced a freeze on
future economic relations with South Africa and

initiated a United Nations Security Council resolution condemning the apartheid regime and advocating the adoption of voluntary economic sanctions against Pretoria.[14]

In Chad, French policy initially supported the view that, since the Libyan troops' intervention of December 1980 was requested by Chad's legal government, the legitimacy of the military presence should not be challenged. A policy of détente was accordingly adopted by France at a time when the United States, Egypt and the Sudan were all getting increasingly committed to supporting Hissene Habre's military resistance to the government forces in that country. In October 1981, several tons of light arms were flown from France to Chad in order to consolidate the positions of its central government and break its imposed tête-à-tête with Colonel Khadaffi. France also actively supported the formation of the inter-African force which was sent to Chad in accordance with the resolutions of the OAU Nairobi summit of 1981 after the withdrawal of Libyan troops in November that year.[15] The inability of the African peace force to restore law and order in Chad was equally a failure for France's policy in that country. The government of Hissene Habre, who came to power in late May 1982, was none the less recognised by Paris. Moreover, in August 1983, at the request of the new Chadian President and under pressure from several francophone African states, Mitterrand reluctantly agreed to send French troops to Chad in order to stop the movement of Libyan troops in the south of the country. Neither the OAU nor Chad's neighbours were able to ensure a peaceful settlement of the conflict, nor, indeed, guarantee the country's stability and territorial integrity. At the same time, France did not want direct confrontation with Libya in Chad. Thus, in September 1984, a bilateral agreement was signed between Tripoli and Paris, providing for the withdrawal of Libyan and French troops in Chad amidst a storm of cricitism in France, Chad and francophone Africa.

As shown in the case of Chad, Mitterrand's active pursuit of a policy of 'positive' commitment to the affairs of the continent could not ignore the African states' demands for security and stability. This in turn considerably reduced France's capacity to apply pressure for the respect of human rights - a major policy guideline in the socialist government's Africa programme. Thus, the long-standing commitment of the 'Eritrean national reality' and its 'people's right to self-determination' were overlooked in the joint communiqué which was adopted during the visit of France's Foreign Minister, Claude Cheysson, to Ethiopia in January 1982.[16] Furthermore, the regignation of Jean-Pierre Cot, France's Minister for Cooperation and Development, in December 1982, publicly confirmed that relations between France and francophone Africa would not involve any radical reorientation.

After the formation of the first Mauroy government, in June 1981, a few shortlived attempts at changing relations between France and francophone Africa occurred. This was of grave concern to such leaders as David Dacko (Central African Republic), Omar Bongo (Gabon) and Mobutu Sese Seko (Zaire). Early in July 1981, François Mitterrand and his Prime Minister refused to receive the Central African Prime Minister, who had travelled to Paris in order to discuss the future of relations between the two countries. The First Secretary to the French socialist party, Lionel Jospin, also refused in the same period to receive the Gabonese President, who was on a visit to Paris, and instead met opponents of his regime. This particularly irritated President Bongo at a time when the French press was querying the dubious relations which he had had with the Giscardian regime.

Not long after the episode, France was forced to abandon its 'new' African policy. At a time when the United States appeared ready to provide alternative assistance to those francophone countries adversely affected by France's policy, criticisms of their anti-democratic nature were progressively toned down in Paris. As early as August 1981, during the Cameroon-Nigeria border conflict, the then Cameroonian President, Ahmadou Ahidjo, secured French arms without any difficulty. Truly, in Zaire, instructions to the French officer cops in charge of training the Zairean army were modified so as not to get them involved in the internal affairs of the host country. In spite of unrelenting human rights' violations by the Mobutu regime, in September 1981 the French presidential adviser on African affairs, Guy Penne, announced during his visit to Kinshasa a consolidation of bilateral cooperation between the two countries. In November that year, the Paris Franco-African summit definitely and publicly confirmed the willingness of France's new leadership to consider state to state relations independent of the logic of human rights: Zaire, it was now agreed, would organise the next conference.

The May 1982 visit of Mitterrand to Niger, Ivory Coast and Senegal was primarily aimed at reassuring traditional partners in francophone Africa that the new President did not seek to 'depart from previous policies'.[17] The President also emphasised, however, that 'we do not want France's military presence to be confused with intervention in the internal affairs' of the African states concerned. In Niger, where President Kountche feared Libya's growing influence in the region, Francois Mitterrand went further and warned that, 'France will not only stick to its commitments to the security but it will also ensure that the conditions of this security should be even better protected if this is necessary'.[18] By 1984, defence agreements were still in force between France, Ivory Coast, Djibouti, Gabon, the Central African Republic, Senegal and Togo. French troops were also stationed in these countries at their own request (see also Chapters 7 and 9).

Reorganising aid structures and modes of intervention initially constituted a priority for the new French government, which had envisaged the creation of a vast ministry of Third World affairs so as to 'break with old and perverse neo-colonial habits' and bring to an end a 'cooperation policy (which) was conducted so far in a paternalistic manner'.[19] In effect, the reform which was implemented in late 1982 involved a much more modest extension of the activities of the Ministry of Cooperation and Development, now in charge of overseas aid to francophone and non-francophone Third World countries. Simultaneously, great concern was shown at convincing francophone countries in Africa that aid commitments to them would not be scaled down as a result of the reforms. Pledges to an overall increase in overseas aid from 0.36 per cent of France's GDP in 1980 to 0.7 per cent by 1988 were reiterated. During the Least Developed Countries' Paris conference, later at Cancun, or during the Versailles summit of June 1982, François Mitterrand also advocated an increase in international aid and the stabilisation of commodity prices. These appeals found some receptive ears within the EEC but none from the United States. In France, where Jean-Pierre Cot once wrote that 'generosity towards the Third World identifies itself with France's enlightened interest', the increasing financial and social difficulties faced by successive governments imposed a reconsideration of some of the earlier policy moves. These could not be pursued in isolation from other western and socialist industrialised countries. France had advocated the stabilisation of Third World revenues within the context of co-development agreements likely to promote the harmonisation of North-South interests. In 1982, France accordingly accepted to purchase uranium from Niger and gas from Algeria at prices higher than those of the international market. Both contracts, however, had to be renegotiated as they imposed an increasingly heavy burden on French public finances at a time of sharp decline in world prices and increasing competition between industrialised countries. To a large extent, the evolution of Mitterrand's African policy has been shaped by such extra-national considerations at a time of increasing internal financial and social difficulties. In this respect, one might wonder whether France still has the means of fulfilling its ambitions insofar as its African policy is concerned.

NOTES

[1] P. Quantin, Les méandres d'un discours fleuve (Bordeaux, Centre d'étude d'Afrique noire, 1978).

[2] D. Bach, 'L'insertion de la Côte d'Ivoire dans les rapports internationaux', in J. F. Médard and Y. A. Faure (eds.), Etat et bourgeoisie en Côte d'Ivoire (Paris, Karthala, 1980), pp.252-67.

[3] G. Chaffard, Les carnets secrets de la décolonisation (Paris, Calmann-Levy, 1967), tome 2, pp.165-268, and J. Baulin, La politique africaine d'Houphouët-Boigny (Paris, Eurafor-Press, 1980), pp.47-85.

[4] D. Bach, 'Le général de Gaulle et la guerre civile au Nigéria', in Centre d'étude d'Afrique noire et Institut Charles de Gaulle, La politique africaine du général de Gaulle, 1958-1969 (Paris, Pedone, 1981), pp.331-45.

[5] D. Bach, 'L'insertion de la Côte d'Ivoire', op. cit.

[6] Ibid.

[7] Le Monde (Paris), 10 and 12 February 1971.

[8] In Afrique contemporaine, (73), 1974, p.43.

[9] D. Bach, 'The politics of West African economic co-operation: CEAO amd ECOWAS', Journal of Modern African Studies, XXI, 4 (1983), pp.605-23.

[10] For a detailed analysis cf. D. Bach, 'La France en Afrique sub-saharienne: contraintes

historiques et nouveaux espaces économiques', in S. Cohen and M.-Cl. Smouts (eds.), <u>La politique étrangère de Valery Giscard d'Estaing</u> (Paris, Presses de la Fondation Nationale des Sciences Politiques, 1985), pp.284-310.

[11] <u>Ibid</u>.

[12] République française, <u>Rapport sur la politique de coopération présenté par Pierre Abelin, Ministre de la Coopération</u> (Paris, la Documentation française, 1975), pp.52-7.

[13] 'Le parti socialiste et l'Afrique sub-saharienne' (Paris), mimeo, 1981.

[14] <u>Le Monde</u>, 28 and 29 July 1985.

[15] D. Bach, 'La politique francaise en Afrique depuis le 10 mai 1981', in Centre d'étude d'Afrique noire, <u>Année africaine 1981</u> (Paris, Pedone, 1983), pp.236-53; J.-F. Bayart, <u>La politique africaine de Francois Mitterrand</u> (Paris, Karthala, 1985).

[16] <u>Ibid</u>.

[17] <u>Interview</u>, Radio France Internationale, 17 May 1982.

[18] Statement in Niamey, mimeo.

[19] Agence France-Presse, <u>Bulletin quotidien d'Afrique</u>, 30 May 1981.

[20] <u>Le Monde</u>, 8 July 1981.

CHAPTER 6

PORTUGAL, MOZAMBIQUE AND ANGOLA: TRENDS TOWARD FUTURE
RELATIONSHIPS

Fola Soremekun

When Mozambique became independent on 25 June 1975
and Angola followed suit on 11 November of the same
year, together they had closed a major chapter in
the history of a European colonising power in
Africa.[1] De-colonisation efforts for both countries
had been difficult, but the one for Angola had been
particularly so.[2] There was some order when the
Portuguese handed power to Samora Machel, leader of
the FRELIMO. As for the Angolan situation, power
was handed to no one in particular but only to the
phantom entity - 'The Angolan People' - as the
Portuguese High Commissioner, Cardoso, withdrew
into Luanda Bay early in the afternoon of 10
November.
        Angola was on the brink of Civil War as the
MPLA's authority was being disputed by the other two
rival political parties, FNLA and UNITA. The latter
party remains to this day to haunt the MPLA
government. In Mozambique, the major dissident group
disputing FRELIMO's supremacy was finally to
coalesce in the form of MNR (Mozambique National
Resistance).[3] Clearly, in their de-colonisation
efforts, the Portuguese had been inept and had left
behind them a legacy of confusion and anger. Thus,
as 1975 moved to a close, the trend of any future
relationship between Portugal and her former
colonies looked bleak. The aim of this chapter,
then, is to examine what has happened between the
two sides since 1975.

A.   THE BURDEN OF THE COLONIAL PAST

In order to get our subject in proper focus, we have
to project against the background of the past, the
recent and the remote. For Angola and Mozambique,
the wounds inflicted by the colonial situation were

still fresh at independence. To arrive at independence they had to fight bloody guerrilla wars for more than a decade. Both sides suffered grievously in terms of human lives lost, not to quantify the ill-feeling and hate that wars generally generate. Wars tend to excite the pristine instincts of men and sharpen their awareness for their past. Winning the war for independence was for the Africans in Angola and Mozambique the culmination of a fifty year period of a particularly harsh colonialism. While they might have talked about '500 years of Portuguese colonialism', in reality the previous 450 years had witnessed intermittent small wars against Africans, shifting tribal alliances with or against the Portuguese, resulting in captives in slave trading, which made Angola 'The Black Mother' - source of millions of slaves to the New World.[4] Today, the under-population of Angola and Mozambique bears witness to the barrenness and destructiveness of those years.[5]

Until the 1980s there was no questioning the fact that the Africans in the two colonies were the 'sons of the soil', engaged with the Portuguese in a 'love-hate', inconsistent relationship, full of contradictions. As the pressures of the 'New Imperialism'[6] impinged upon the Portuguese, they, in their own turn, squeezed the Africans and subjugated them by force.[7] The Portuguese were not unlike other colonising Europeans who mouthed the shibboleth of having a 'civilising mission' that they were destined to impart to the Africans. Portuguese conquistadores of this period, like Artur de Paive and Mousinho de Albuquerqueas, were not unlike Lugard and Harry Johnston of British colonial Africa.

To govern their newly-conquered areas was not going to be effective, however, until after World War I. Between the 1890s and then, and in order to soothe world opinion, they substituted 'contract labour' for slave labour. They promulgated laws of 'trabalho obrigatorio' (obligation to work). In Mozambique, African migrant labour to the South African mines was established by treaty with the South Africans. The period of the Portuguese occupation and attempts to rule Angola and Mozambique was a period singularly marked by unprecedented psychological and physical attacks by the colonialists on the Africans. African ways of life, culture and their very existence were attacked. The very humanity of Africans was questioned. Portuguese hatred for the Africans was

unabashed; they were called 'savages' and
'indigenes'. Administration was sketchy. The stage
was being set, however, for the most repressive
colonial period, starting in the late 1920s when
Portugal herself was close to economic collapse.

The paladin who came to the rescue was the
economist, Professor Antonio de Oliveira Salazar. He
was to stay to rule the country until 1968, when
Macelo Caetano, another Professor of Law, took over
until the military overthrew him on 25 April 1974.
The Salazar/Caetano period, which spanned at least
forty years, was a time of perpetual tension for the
Africans.[8] The fascist regime appealed to the
pristine instincts of its countrymen, basing its
spirit on that of 'nacao una' - one nation. The
regime demanded and exploited African labour to
achieve many of its economic goals.[9] It imported
Portuguese people into the colonies to compete with
Africans. It also accentuated a pseudo-philosophy
of development, based on the supposed special
qualities of the Portuguese, which made them
amenable to the tropics, using Gilberto Freyre's
Lusotropicalism.[10]

The regime believed that Angola, Mozambique and
Portugal were one: and so Portugal had no colonies,
only 'Overseas Provinces'. Hence, there was no need
for Africans to seek to be independent. To enforce
its wishes, the regime used a very efficient secret
police - the PIDE. All those who dared to show
traces of opposition were ruthlessly dealt with;
they were jailed, tortured, killed or driven to
exile. To buy off world-wide criticisms of its
corporative economic practices, which excluded
foreign investments, the regime by the late 1950s
started to invite western multinational corporations
to invest in the colonies. The purpose of this
action was to tie them and powerful countries like
the United States, Britain and West Germany to a
posture of defending their interests, should African
nationalism threaten to uproot Portuguese
pretensions.

In the wake of the national consciousness
sweeping Africa after World War II, Angolans and
Mozambicans could hardly stand aside and continue to
accept colonial humiliation. The Africans were
forced to start a war to liberate themselves in
February/March of 1961. The war was to drag on for
thirteen years in Angola and for ten years in
Mozambique. The long war strained the relationship
between the Portuguese and the Africans. PIDE
activities were widened and further tightened. The

whites in Angola and in Mozambique were very often so frightened that they would form quasi-legal vigilante groups to fight the guerrillas. One such group was the OPVDCA of Angola.[11] Despite divisive efforts by the regime, African political parties in exile with the shared aims of obtaining freedom for the colonies functioned within an informal organisation called the CONCP (Conference of the Nationalist Organisations of Portuguese Colonies).

The three parties which were involved in this organisation - the MPLA, FRELIMO and PAIGC (African Party for the Independence of Guinea and Cape Verde) - were of 'leftist' orientation and coordinated all their activities. Apart from that, the Africans started an international campaign to inform the world about the nature of Portuguese colonialism and solicited aid in toppling it. They however avoided recourse to racism as a philosophy of their struggle because it would deter them from achieving their carefully calculated political aims. For, in spite of the hypocrisy involved in the Portuguese claims that they were not racists, they were truly far better than other colonial powers in this respect. Angolan and Mozambican guerrillas were very disciplined, well-trained and possessed clear-cut political objectives. A Mozambican nationalist guerrilla had this to say:

> '... In our units and on our missions we have often come across unarmed Portuguese civilians. We didn't harm them. We asked them where they were coming from, we explained our struggle to them, our sufferings; we received them kindly. We do this because our struggle, our war, is not against the Portuguese people; we are struggling against the Portuguese government ... which is also exploiting the Portuguese people themselves.'[12]

The burden of the colonial wars - as they were affecting the Portuguese people at home, both economically and socially - was what in part propelled General Antonio Spinola in early 1974 to publish his Portugal and the Future, searching for a new order in the empire. He was not making radical proposals - but even his conservative idea of giving some autonomy to the overseas provinces was too progressive for Caetano. Unknown to Caetano, however, were several young army officers, who were no less disillusioned with the colonial wars and who decided to stage a coup d'état on 25 April 1974. One of

their cardinal aims was to de-colonise quickly[13]
Between that time and late 1975, which witnessed the
transition to independence in Angola and Mozambique,
there was a lot of racial tension, violence, death,
venality, strange political manoeuvres and sheer
political ineptitude on the part of the Portuguese
authorities to be the proper referees. The injuries
of the past, the haste of the present and the
haziness of the future had combined to confuse the
governing authorities and their wards alike. Many
whites, who feared black majority-ruled governments
in the two colonies, started fleeing back to
Portugal, while others went to South Africa. Some
siphoned away foreign exchange, others sabotaged
machines and disrupted transportation facilities,
whilst some of the rich among them financed white
conservative secret armies to create trouble. This
was more rampant in Angola because of its rich
natural resources and its great economic potential
for development.

In a speech at the investiture of the
Transitional Government in Mozambique on 20
September, 1974, and at the 24th Session of the
Organisation of African Unity Liberation Committee
on 8 January, 1975, Samora Machel gave a graphic
description of not only the Mozambican colonial
heritage but also that of Angola. He was soon to
preside over a country of more than 98 per cent
illiteracy, while Neto would be able to claim 'only'
90 per cent illiteracy for Angola.

> 'Colonial plunder combined with the colonial
> war, left us with economic bankruptcy.
> Colonialism contracted debts running into
> hundreds of millions of dollars. Industry is on
> the verge of coming to a halt, and commerce is
> suffering from a shortage of goods. The people
> are hungry and ill-clad. The social situation
> inherited is equally chaotic. After five
> centuries of colonial domination, practically
> no Mozambican doctors, economists, engineers,
> jurists, etc., have been trained. The colonial
> war has left us a sombre heritage: one and a
> half million people interned in concentration
> camps, who have to be reintegrated into
> society; thousands of bomb and massacre
> victims, widows, orphans, cripples, etc. ... In
> urban zones and concentration camps the enemy
> spread the most degrading vices: alcoholism,
> drug addiction and prostitution.'[14]

At the independence ceremony in Angola, Neto, taking power for MPLA, could only hope that his government would right the types of wrongs so common to Portuguese colonial Africa. He attacked the Portuguese government for its handling of the de-colonisation process, noting that it 'tacitly legitimised through its silence and passivity the ... fascist international brigade' which had lined up against the Angolan people. The Angolan people, he said further, had no quarrel with the Portuguese people. He continued to say, however, that by

> 'putting a final end to colonialism and decisively barring the way to new colonialism, the MPLA ... affirms its ... intention radically to change the present structure ... the objective of economic reconstruction will be to satisfy the people's need ... never voracious imperialism.'[15]

What lay ahead after independence in the relationship between the erstwhile colonial master and the Angolans and Mozambicans is what we turn to next.

B.   FROM INDEPENDENCE TO THE FUTURE

For those who could read between the lines, Neto's statement that Angola would radically change its political and economic structure should have been a clear indication that the Western structures in that country must go. This was to be extended to Mozambique also. We have aleady pointed out that both countries, being members of CONCP, were wont to follow parallel leftist policies. After independence, both came out clearly and openly to embrace Marxist-Socialist policies.[16] From January 1976, when Angola was about to win its 'Second War for National Liberation', it started its policy of nationalisation of virtually all Portuguese-owned enterprises. This was greeted with howls of execration in Portugal, particularly among the right-wing elements, with the most pressure coming from the 'retornados' (the Portuguese who had recently fled from the colonies). In Mozambique, the government's nationalisation of private homes alone led to the mass exodus of whites, reducing their number by the end of 1976 to less than half of the 100,000 who were in the country in pre-independence days.

The nationalisation policies of the MPLA

government adversely affected Portuguese economic interests in the country. None the less, there was always a latent feeling in the metropole that somehow relations with the fledgling African states had to be improved. Some revenge or the righting of wrongs was usually expected from the newly-independent states. Relations between Portugal and Angola started to improve by late February 1976. This was just three and a half months after independence! There had been a lively, if not acrimonious, debate in the Portuguese Parliament about this issue. It would seem that to delay recognition any longer might well lead to further alienation of the country. Furthermore, there was also the feeling that Portugal might still salvage its honour by leaving the door open for future cooperation and offer the hand of friendship.

The official recognition of the Peoples' Republic of Angola by Portugal came on 22 February 1976. The two countries started to negotiate over matters pertaining to Angolan debts in Portugal and the capital and property claims of Portuguese citizens in Angola. Other matters negotiated included Portuguese aid to Angola and diplomatic arrangements. But it was still going to be close to a year before the Portuguese opened their embassy in Luanda! There were still other sensitive issues, such as the question of nationality or citizenship for the Portuguese in Angola. The Angolan Nationality law passed in 1977 gave Angolan citizenship to those who had lived in the country for ten or more years. On their part the Angolans asked Portugal to give them technical aid. How much was this to be? How and when were all outstanding issues to be resolved and accomplished? The increasing presence of Eastern Bloc personnel and aid in Luanda at that time became a matter for internal political discussion in Portugal, as there were many - especially those influenced by the 'retornados' - who did not want to aid a country whose ideology was hostile to that of the West - the philosophy in which the majority of the Portuguese believed. Portugal wanted to enter the European Economic Community. It also wanted to get an IMF loan. If it were to cuddle too much with Marxist Angola and Mozambique, would it not face reprisals from the European countries and the United States? These were some of the dilemmas facing a small, poor country like Portugal.

Fortunately for Portugal's relationships with her former colonies, the position of the presidency in the Portuguese constitution gave some leeway to any determined man who occupied the position to carry on parallel diplomacy. In late 1976, Ramalho Eanes became both President of the country and Chairman of the Portuguese Armed Forces Chief of Staff. Eanes had risen through the military ranks, had served in Angola and Mozambique and had an understanding of the problems created by colonialism. Although he was not actively perceived as one of the plotters of the 1974 coup, he had enough prestige among many Portuguese officers, which was sufficient for him to emerge into his position. Eanes had a balanced view of Portuguese needs and concerns toward Europe as well as to the erstwhile colonies. He believed that European stability would depend increasingly on the stability, security and economic development of Africa.[17]

He started to act on this belief by sending feelers out to his fellow presidents in Lusophone Africa. As a result of his diplomatic initiatives, in January 1978 Luis Cabral of Guinea Bissau visited Lisbon. The visit of Cabral paved the way for better relations with the other former colonies. Indeed, Cabral was to act on many occasions as a go-between to better Portuguese-African relations. He was instrumental in bringing Eanes and Neto together in his country in June 1978. Although not much that was concrete came from this meeting, the 'Spirit of Bissau' was significant for the latent potentials of such a meeting for the future. No special or privileged position for Portugal was accepted by Neto, nor were the Portuguese to send their 'cooperantes' - technical help - quickly enough.

It is pertinent to ask why Neto agreed to meet Eanes at that time. By 1978, much steam had gone out of the enthusiasm of pre and immediate post-independence activities in his country. Furthermore, the MPLA was in trouble at home. The party, constantly riddled with factions, was almost falling apart. Race and ethnicism, studiously eschewed in the past, were rapidly being embraced by some of the prominent members of the party, like the erstwhile Minister of the Interior, Nito Alves. These 'Fractionalists' as they were called, also believed in giving way to the extreme left of the party ideology, so much so that they staged an abortive coup[18] in May 1977. And, furthermore, although UNITA was temporarily supine, it was already beginning to regroup. The Eastern Bloc help which Angola was receiving was not enough. The chief of the bloc, Russia, was over-fishing in Angolan waters and re-exporting Angolan coffee on the world market at substantial profit to itself.

Neto and his party needed help from the West in the form of investments and technical know how. In September 1977, Neto, full of disappointment, was to call for a new Angolan Revolution.[19] The Portuguese, for their part, had been watching developments in the country carefully in the light of allegations that some Portuguese elements had influenced Alves. None the less, the aid promised by Portugal was slow in coming. Then, in September 1979, Agostinho Neto died suddenly and just as his political acumen and personality were beginning to have a positive impact in attempts at normalising his country's relations with Portugal. At about the same time, there was a swing to the right in Portuguese politics as Sa Carneiro, of the PSD, and Freitas do Amaral, of the CDS, joined forces with some centre parties and monarchists (PPM), thereby giving them a majority in parliament.

The conservative coalition was bent on reversing the gains made in both Portugal and its former overseas colonies between 1974 and 1975. As would be expected, their policy brought the right wing Prime Minister, Carneiro, into direct conflict with President Eanes and the Council of the Revolution. Carneiro wanted to curb the powers of the President by seeking a referendum which would give him (Carneiro) the power to strike out the socialist clauses in the Constitution. As for Freitas do Amaral, the Foreign Minister, he was not only anti-Eanes, but also anti-Angola and Mozambique. According to the new Foreign Minister, Portugal's

'... external policy ... will be a policy that is clearly pro-European and pro-western ... there will be no trace of 'Third Worldism', non-alignment or any distant reserve in our Atlantic solidarity (sic).'[20]

Although he admitted later that there would inevitably still have to be some relations with the former colonies, none the less he was opposed to his country's earlier policy of seeking close links with them. According to Amaral, the policy was full of uncertainties and fluctuations. The Foreign Minister was even said to have been a secret supporter of one of Mozambique's dissident parties which had called for an outright break in diplomatic relations with

Mozambique after a Portuguese citizen, who had been found guilty of sabotage, was executed by the MPLA. A motion of censure was subsequently passed against the government in Luanda. However, a Portuguese delegation later visited Maputo for discussions with Mozambican officials. The trip was a success, as most Portuguese citizens in detention in Maputo awaiting execution for treason and sabotage had their sentences commuted to jail terms. The crisis was none the less the most serious between the two countries since Mozambique became independent in 1975.

The tension engendered by the crisis had its roots in the attempt by Maputo to halt the activities of dissidents operating from Ian Smith's Rhodesia. The rebels were aided and abetted by the Ian Smith regime to make sorties into Mozambique and sabotage its strategic installations and transport system. This opposition to Mozambique coalesced and later became known as Mozambique National Resistance, led for a while by the late Orlando Cristina. Today the group is still active and is headed by Evo Fernandes, its General Secretary*. The MNR had always had the support of some Portuguese businessmen like Jorge Jardim and Manuel Bulhosa, whose businesses were nationalised after independence. Other former settler elements also supported it. Most of the dissidents, both from Angola and Mozambique, now numbering up to 800,000, live mainly in South Africa. Portugal had to balance the needs of making her people secure in South Africa against those of maintaining good relations with Mozambique.

None the less, the death of Sa Carneiro and his Defence Minister, Amaro da Costa, in an air crash during the heat of the Presidential election campaign in December 1980, led to the appearance of Francisco Pinto Balsemao as Prime Minister. Balsemao, fortunately, was not as totally opposed to Eanes' (who had been re-elected) policies as his predecessor. Within two years, however, this Democratic Alliance was to fall apart, due to factors outside the scope of this chapter. Eanes however continued to pursue his policy of rapprochement with Portugal's former African colonies. Thus, by November 1981, relations with Mozambique had more or

---

* We should point out, though, that the MNR ceased operating from Rhodesia after it became independent in 1980.

less been normalised to such an extent that
President Eanes visited Maputo (and later went on to
Dar es Salaam and Lusaka).

In April 1982, he paid an official visit to
Angola. He took time off to visit the war zone, as a
gesture of solidarity with the Angolans and to
empathise with their problems - for which his hosts
praised him. It was also a direct slap in the face
for UNITA and its South African allies. In June of
the same year, Pinto Balsameo also made a state
visit to Mozambique and to Zimbabwe, bringing in tow
a galaxy of Portuguese businessmen. In the
communiqués issued after the state visits, apartheid
was roundly condemned. And at the international
trade fair then taking place in Maputo, Portugal
secured $40 million worth of orders from Mozambique.
Lisbon also won the prize for featuring the best
pavilion.[21] It was within this atmosphere of elation
and cordial relations that Portugal and Mozambique
signed the agreement whereby Mozambican army
officers would be trained in Portugal. Arms would
also be supplied to Mozambique under the treaty.
This was clearly an important agreement, because it
somewhat diversified Mozambique's sources of arms'
supplies, which had hitherto been exclusively from
the Eastern Bloc countries. The treaty was also
meant to deal a heavy blow to the MNR menace. This
menace had been very serious and had consistently
diverted Mozambican resources away from the urgent
goal of internal economic development. For a country
often prone to floods and droughts, heavy
involvement in military campaigns could indeed be
very devastating.

By 1983, however, relations between the two
countries started to grow sour. The same was true
for Portuguese-Angolan relations. What was
responsible for this development? The reasons could
be found in the tangled situation in southern
Africa. Angola is dedicated to the support of SWAPO
and at the same time she is determined to fight
against the dissident South African-backed UNITA.
Behind South Africa stood the United States, which
under Reagan has not hidden its determination to
oppose the Marxist-Leninist states in southern
Africa. On the other hand, Mozambique is dedicated
to the support of the ANC of South Africa. But how
did Portugal fit into all this tangle?

South Africa had continued, since Reagan's
assumption of office in 1980, to bomb economic
targets in both Angola and Mozambique in retaliation
for their nationalism. More than this, however, she

also accelerated her support for MNR and she continued to occupy a large portion of the southern part of Angola, saying it was trying to prevent the Cubans and SWAPO forces from disrupting her own interests in Namibia. Portugal's interest on the other hand was to look after the welfare of its citizens in South Africa, to maintain and improve upon its commercial interests in Angola and Mozambique and to be able to enter the European Common Market. By 1983, Mozambique and Angola were under so much military and economic strain that they wanted some solutions to, or at least some abatement of, their plight. It was at this juncture that Mario Suares became Portuguese Prime Minister in June 1983. Thereafter, Portugal became involved in virtually all negotiations involving Mozambique and Angola on the one hand and South Africa and the United States on the other over the southern Africa situation. It should be noted that up to February 1982 the UNITA office in Lisbon was headed by the controversial Norberto de Castro, a Portuguese retornado from Angola. He was replaced by Fernando Wilson dos Santos, who had been active for UNITA as the Secretary for Information in London and the United States. He carried special papers in Lisbon, where UNITA had high level contacts with media organisations through which it distributed war communiqués.[22]

In Luanda and Maputo there was the strong suspicion that Portugal had been given the role of intermediary for economic projects of a neo-colonial nature in southern Africa.[23] Lisbon was seen to be fostering not only its own interests in the region but also those of the United States and South Africa. It was noted in Luanda and Maputo that, since Soares became Prime Minister, contacts between Lisbon, Washington and Pretoria had increased substantially. Matters came to a head between June and August 1984, when the leaders of Angola and Mozambique respectively charged that the United States and South Africa with the help of Portugal were trying to force them to negotiate with their dissident elements in their countries. They blamed the 'free circulation and presence of the representatives of counter-revolutionary groups' in Lisbon on Portugal, which they also accused of helping to train some of them as top administrators.

In retaliation for Lisbon's pro-South African and pro-American postures in southern Africa, Angola decided not to invite Portugal to the Luanda International Trade Fair held in late 1984. This was in spite of the fact that in the one held the previous year 90 Portuguese companies had attended and won substantial contracts. Angola also ordered its oil company, Sonangol, to exclude the Portuguese State Oil Company, Petrogal, from block 4 oil exploration on the Angolan continental shelf. Before then Petrogal had been negotiating for a 10 per cent share in the offshore oil at Ambrizette. Angola then started to angle for economic support from Spain - Portugal's ancient enemy and rival. There was also talk of Angola moving its embassy from Lisbon to Madrid. But in an interview in December 1984, the Portuguese Foreign Minister, Jaime Cama, denied Portuguese support of the MNR. He averred, moreover, that many countries (which he did not name) were trying to spoil the cordial relations between Portugal and her former colonies. Portugal, he said, refused to be anybody's scapegoat. It was only a small nation trying to live in peace in the world.[24]

As for Mozambique's charges, it would seem that, since Machel himself had signed the Nkomati Accords (March 1984) with South Africa, he believed in part that the MNR would shortly be eliminated as the Accords called for the withdrawal of help from South Africa for that group, while Mozambique would not permit the ANC to use its territory to launch attacks against South Africa. There were indeed some MNR supporters still in Portugal, but it had not been clear whether or not the Portuguese government was moving quickly enough to silence them in the interest of cordial relations with Maputo. Mozambique's complaints came in the wake of continued attacks from the MNR five months after the Nkomati Accords. The question, however, was this: if Portugal was really not supporting the MNR and South Africa had stopped supporting it, was MNR able to continue to function? Mozambican newspapers accused some members of the Portuguese government of having questionable connections with the MNR. They named the Minister of State, Antonio Almeida Santos (a long-time resident of Mozambique before independence) and Carlos Mota Pinto - who was both the Deputy Prime Minister and Defence Minister - as the men who urged the MNR to be intransigent. Mozambique's complaint against Portugal forced the South African government to declare on 3 October 1984 that it was doing all it could to help in dismantling the MNR. Curiously, the Portuguese were apparently nonchalant about the lives of some of their citizens in Mozambique, 30 of whom had been killed as a result of MNR attacks. The situation was temporarily brought under control when Samora Machel met Mario Soares on 3 November 1984 in India during the funeral of Indira Ghandi. Machel was reported to have told Soares that only his personal friendship for him and for President Eanes had prevented him (Michel) from publicly embarrassing Lisbon by naming those Portuguese who were still actively supporting the MNR.[25]

The rumblings over this issue continued into 1985. At a meeting in Sao Tome in mid-February 1985, the Lusophone African Presidents issued a communiqué stating their concern over Portuguese support for the dissidents. The Portuguese Prime Minister, Mario Soares, in response held a meeting with the ambassadors from Lusophone African states and pledged that his government would 'not allow Portuguese territory to be used as a base for operations against the legitimate governments of Angola and Mozambique'. His government, he said, would 'prevent the actions of complicity of Portuguese citizens in the de-stabilisation of these countries. We all have an interest in the rapid return of peace to Mozambique and Angola ... without counting the fact that there are many Portuguese citizens among the victims of these situations'.[26] It remains to be seen what the Portuguese Prime Minister will do in a concrete way to mollify the Africans.

In late March 1985, Portugal was informed that it would be formally admitted into the European Economic Community in 1986. This move could augur well at least for Mozambique and her battered economy, as Portugal could help to secure free entry into the EEC for her primary products. The Soviet Union and the Eastern Bloc do not seem to be in a position to provide markets and other assistance necessary for Mozambique's long-term economic development. So far there has been no indication that she is even being encouraged to be an associate member of their Council for Mutual Economic Assistance (COMECON). At Portuguese nudging and, no doubt with the possibility of substantial gains in the future, Mozambique had recognised West Germany's position in West Berlin in 1982. The move removed the last barrier to increased aid to Mozambique by the EEC. However, what the other implications of Portugal's entry into the EEC will be for its future relations with Lusophone Africa as a whole remain to be seen.

C.   CONCLUSION

The future lasts a long time and is full of
unforeseen events and circumstances. If we are to go
on projecting into the future, by the trend of the
relations between Portugal and her former African
colonies, continued conflict would seem to be in
store. It has been a sad fact that the history of
the Portuguese in Angola and Mozambique has been one
of continued conflicts over the centuries.[27] The
African peoples have always resisted injustice. Even
now that they are politically free, they are still
enmeshed in the problems of the past. In freedom
they want to keep something of the inherited
Portuguese structures in order to avoid economic
collapse, while trying out something new - Marxist-
Leninism. The past, of course, will not die and
continues to reassert itself - perhaps in the form
of Portuguese Conservatives wanting at least a
modified past in these countries. The past also
reasserts itself in the persistence of Portuguese
culture - language and other usages which are still
being accepted by the newly-independent countries
in spite of the incessant conflicts on the political
and economic fronts. In order for us to get a
picture of what the real future may be in the
relations between Portugal and these African
countries in the long run, we may get some pointers
by looking at what now obtains between other past
colonial powers and their former colonies - like
France and Britain - world-wide. For the immediate
future, the unfinished political and economic
business in southern Africa will be the major
determining factors.

NOTES

   [1] Lourenco Marques, <u>Noticias,</u> 25 June 1975.
<u>Angola: 11 de Novembro de 1975 Documentos da
Independencia</u> (Luanda, Ministerio da Informao,
1976).
   [2] Fola Soremekun, <u>Angola: The Road to
Independence</u> (Ife, University of Ife Press, 1983),
pp.1-10. Also see index listing the many political
parties seeking power. Franz Wilhem Heimer,
'Decolonization Conflict in Angola: An Essay in
Political Sociology' (Geneva, IUHEI, 1979), Passim.
   [3] Here is a list of some of the Mozambican
'parties':
   MNR Mozambique National Resistance was formed
   after independence but its roots went to the

transitional government period between September 1974 and June 1975. Jorge Jardim, a white Mozambican industrialist, and a few others like him have been connnected with this organisation.
Other parties which were rivals to FRELIMO were:
COREMO Mozambique Revolutionary Committee. Was formed about 1965, led by Adelino Gwambe, who was ousted about a year later, and came to be led by Paulo Gumane. It had its headquarters in Lusaka before Mozambique's independence.
GUMO United Group of Mozambique formed before the military coup of 25 April 1974. It was essentially a lobby group of people of many races who wanted strong ties with Portugal after independence. FRECOMO Mozambique Common Front, led by Joana Simiao, also formed in 1974.

[4] Basil Davidson, The African Slave Trade: Precolonial History 1450-1850 (Boston, Little, Brown), pp.80-1. Lawrence W. Henderson, Angola: Five Centuries of Conflict (Ithaca, Cornell University Press, 1979), p.94. Philip D. Curtin, The Atlantic Slave Trade: A Census (Madison, University of Wisconsin Press, 1969), pp.3-13.

[5] Henderson, op. cit. pp.94-8, and Thomas H. Henriksen, Mozambique: A History (London, Rex Collings, 1978), pp.75-7.

[6] Eric Axelson, Portugal and the Scramble for Africa (Johannesburg, Witwatersrand University Press, 1967), gives details of this subject.

[7] Examples abound about the subjection of African kingdoms. The Portuguese were able to occupy Bié plateau, a strategic area in southern Angola, by crushing Ndunduma, 'The Thunder'. For reactions later, see Fola Soremekun, 'The Bailundu Revolt, 1902'. African Social Research, 16 December 1973, pp.447-73. A typical Mozambican example was that of the crushing of Gungunyana of Gaza. See Douglas L. Wheeler, 'Gungunyana', in Norman R. Bennett (ed.), Leadership in Eastern Africa: Political Biographies (Boston, Boston University Press, 1968), pp.167-220.

[8] James Duffy, 'Portuguese Africa, 1930-1960', in Peter Duignan and L. H. Gann (eds.), Colonialism in Africa, 1870-1960, Vol.2 (Cambridge, Cambridge University Press, 1970).

[9] Rene Pellisier, 'Angola: Economic dynamism and the policy of deliberate change', Optima, Vol.23, No.3, September 1973, pp.115-135. Antonio

Figueirdeo, Portugal: Fifty Years of Dictatorship (Middlesex, Penguin Books, 1975), p.216.

[10] Gilberto Freyre, O Mondo que Portugues Criou (Rio de Janeiro: Livraria Jose Olympie, 1940). This book should be read in its entirety to get the gist of Lusotropicalism. For criticisms, see Roger Bastide, who once described it as a 'sentimental ideology of underdevelopment', 'Lusotropicology, Race and Nationalism and Class Protest and Development in Brazil and Portuguese Africa' in Protest and Resistance in Angola and Brazil (Los Angeles: University of California Press, 1972), pp.225-40. Allen F. Isaacman, The Tradition of Resistance in Mozambique (Los Angeles: University of California Press, 1976), pp.186-9.

[11] Organizacao Provincial de Voluntarios e Defesa Civil de Angola (Provincial Organisation of Volunteers for Angola's Civil Defence).

[12] Joaquim Maquival, quoted in Eduardo Mondlane, The Struggle for Mozambique (Baltimore, Penguin Books, 1969), p.160.

[13] Lisbon, Expresso, 26 April 1974. The entire edition of this newspaper is significant for the first steps of the historic change-over. The young army officers formed a Junta of National Salvation. See Luis Ataide Banazol, A Origem do Movimento das Forcas Armadas (Lisbon, Prelo Editora, 1974), pp.33-5.

[14] Samora Machel, 'Message to the 24th Session of the Liberation Committee of the OAU', Dar es Salaam, 8 January 1975, in The Tasks Ahead: Selected Speeches of Samora Machel (New York, Afro-American Information Service, 1975), p.101.

[15] Angola: 11 de Novembro de 1975 Documentos da Independencia (Luanda, Ministerio da Informacao, 1976), text of speech, pp.119-25.

[16] Angola: Socialism at Birth (London, MAGIC, 1980), passim. For a list and level of state participation in other foreign-owned enterprises see Angola: Reconstrucao Nacional, nd. np. Documentos: Terceira Reuniao Plenario do Comite Central do MPLA. Luanda 23-29 Outobro 1976 (Luanda, Edicao do Secretaria do Bureau Politico do MPLA) nd. See also 'Resolucao sobre os principios directores das relacoes exteriores', pp.51-5.

[17] Shirley Washington, 'Toward a New Relationship', Africa Report, March-April 1980, p.18.

[18] 'Report of the Political Bureau ... on the attempted coup d'etat of 27 May 1977' (Luanda, MPLA Information Bulletin No.4, July 1977). Fola

Soremekun, 'The MPLA Dissidents', _African Perspectives_, no.1, September/October 1977, pp.9-10 and 32.

[19] Agostinho Neto, Discurso, 'Precisamos de fazer uma nova revolucao', (Luanda) _Jornal de Angola_, 16 September 1978.

[20] Quoted in Washington, _op. cit_, p.21.

[21] Shirley Washington, 'Mozambique: Portugal's New Initiative', _Africa Report_, November-December 1982, p.12.

[22] For full details of the allegation see 'Conspirators in Lisbon provoke Crisis', _Africa Now_, October 1984, pp.82-3.

[23] _Africa Now_ (London), October 1984, pp.82-3.

[24] See interview with Portuguese Foreign Minister, Jaime Gama, _Africa Now_, December 1984, pp.50-1.

[25] _Africa Now_, December 1984, p.52.

[26] _Sunday Sketch_ (Ibadan), 17 February 1985.

[27] One of the most recent interpretations of Angolan and Mozambican history showed this clearly. Three of the most recent books in English in this vein are: Lawrence W. Henderson, _Angola: Five Centuries of Conflict_ (Ithaca, Cornell University Press, 1979); M.D.D. Newitt, _Portuguese Settlement on the Mambezi_ (London, Longman, 1973); and Allen F. Isaacman with Barbara Isaacman, _The Tradition of Resistance in Mozambique_ (Los Angeles, University of California Press, 1976).

CHAPTER 7

THE SOVIET UNION, ANGOLA AND THE HORN OF AFRICA: NEW
PATTERNS IN AFRO-EUROPEAN RELATIONS

James Mulira

The 1917 socialist revolution in Russia laid a solid
foundation for Afro-Soviet relations. Since then,
the USSR has emerged as an influential power on the
continent of Africa. The Soviet presence has
affected the course of Africa's political, economic
and social development. In one of his first major
policy statements, V. I. Lenin, the leader of the
Bolshevik government, pledged his country's support
to colonial Africa. In pursuit of this objective,
subsequent Soviet leaders have rendered invaluable
diplomatic and material support to anti-colonial
movements in Africa in their quest for national
independence. The same support has been, and is
still being, rendered to independent African states
in their struggle against neo-colonialism.
      The Western powers, most of which had been
colonisers, have strived to counteract the growing
influence of the USSR on the continent, which they
still regard as their sphere of influence. The
competition between the West and the USSR for
influence on the continent has led, in recent years,
to a dangerous rivalry that has been detrimental to
Africa's interests. The pro-Soviet African states
have received massive economic and military aid,
which they have utilised in de-colonisation and
national development. In return for this aid, they
have made available to the USSR their economic
resources, strategic air and sea ports' facilities
for the pursuit of Soviet national and international
objectives. Soviet impact on Africa's development
has been remarkable, despite the fact that effective
contacts between the two began only in the early
1960s. This chapter intends to review, analyse and
determine the extent to which Soviet and Western
powers' policies towards Africa since independence
have affected the course of developments on the

continent. Angola and the Horn of Africa have been used as case studies because they have in recent times attracted the most intensive superpower rivalry on the continent. Today, they are the most important priority areas for both the USSR and the other superpower, the USA.

In the political field, the Russian ideologists claim that the Soviet Union is internationally duty-bound to assist all anti-colonial and anti-imperial movements anywhere in the world.[1] This therefore qualifies anti- colonial movements in Africa for Soviet support. The Leninist thesis that 'imperialism is the highest stage of capitalism'[2] was invoked to find solutions to colonial problems. The anti-colonial movements in Africa were supposed, according to the Soviet strategists, to complement the Commintern in internationalising the revolution and were consequently actively supported by Moscow.[3] The Commintern and its affiliates, such as the International Trade Union Committee of Negro Workers (ITUCNW) collaborated with the Pan-Africanists and early African nationalists, such as George Padmore, Jome Kenyatta and Kwame Nkrumah, and laid a firm base for future Afro-Soviet relations.[4]

Soviet efforts towards the de-colonisation of Africa were crowned in its successful UN resolution of 1960, which called upon all colonial powers to grant independence to their colonies without further delay.[5] This act endeared the USSR to many colonial subjects who, from then on, viewed the USSR as a champion of Africa's independence. Africa's leaders viewed Soviet anti-colonial policies favourably, and most of them established diplomatic relations with Moscow immediately after achieving independence. Since the early 1960s Soviet influence has been felt in almost all facets of Africa's development to the extent that in some countries it has replaced Western influence. African countries whose independence was achieved through violent military means - Angola, Mozambique and Zimbabwe, plus the nationalist guerrillas of ANC and SWAPO - received and are still receiving massive Soviet military aid in their struggle for independence. Even some of those which achieved independence through non-violent means received both Soviet diplomatic and financial support, which was useful after the final victory.

The amount and the nature of Soviet aid to a particular African state is always determined by its political, economic and strategic importance to the

USSR. Somalia, under socialist Siad Barre, was one of the biggest recipients of Soviet economic and military aid in Africa, because it satisfied the above conditions.[6] Somalia adopted a socialist rhetoric and programme because Barre deemed both as the only option that could unite the then divided Somalia. He also calculated, and rightly so, that by identifying with socialism he would attract Soviet economic and, particularly, military aid which he so badly desired in his irredentist ambitions against Ethiopia. In reality, however, Barre was not a socialist, nor was he for socialism. He merely used it as a means to an end. None the less, his limited commitment to the socialist ideology came to the open when he admitted in 1977 that, 'I am a nationalist first, a Moslem second and a Marxist third',[7] which led to the deterioration in his relations with the Soviet Union. However, the limited ideological influence which the Soviet Union temporarily exercised in Somalia posed some challenge to the western democratic institutions which Mogadishu had inherited at independence. This is because in foreign affairs socialist Somalia supported Soviet policy and denounced the West over a number of international issues, such as the Vietnam war, the Middle East conflict and southern Africa. Until 1977, Somalia was one of the most trusted allies of the USSR in Black Africa, and the Kremlin exercised far more influence on the government in Mogadishu than the Western powers.

Ethiopia, on the other hand, was a staunchly pro-Western state before 1974. Although Ethiopia had never been formally colonised by Western powers, she nevertheless adopted Western political, economic and social institutions up until the end of the imperial regime in 1974. Ethiopia, apart from Liberia, was the most trusted African ally of the USA in Africa. Washington used Ethiopia as her major base to protect her economic and strategic interests, both on the continent and in the Middle East. But, after the overthrow of the Emperor in 1974, Marxist-Leninist ideology became the official ideology of Ethiopia under Colonel Mengistu in 1976. It was taught in schools and in the universities; socialist rhetoric and symbols were also adopted. The Provisional Military Administrative Council (PMAC) - the Derg - adopted the socialism in its drive to solve the prevailing problems of class division, tribalism and economic inequalities, etc., which had not been solved by the previous regime under Western 'democracy'.[8] The Derg was essentially socialist in

name but not in action, because its leaders
persecuted the Marxists and refused to form a
communist party to guide the nation towards the
achievement of socialist goals, for fear of losing
the revolution to militant Marxist intellectuals.
The Derg under socialist guise has carried out
important social reforms, such as the most sweeping
land nationalisation scheme in Africa, under which
24,000 peasant organisations were formed. The Derg
has successfully carried out reforms in the urban
areas under the neighbourhood association system,
known as Kabeles.[9] These socialist reforms have
given a large number of Ethiopians a new sense of
participation and freedom which they never enjoyed
under the monarchy.[10] The USSR has reluctantly
accepted to cooperate with the national democractic
regime of the PMAC in spite of its refusal to form a
communist party. Moscow acquiesced in this state of
affairs in order to protect its vital strategic
interests in the country. Besides, Moscow also hopes
that one day nationalism in Ethiopia will give way
to international communism.

Angola's independence, unlike that of Somalia,
was achieved through a protracted and bloody armed
struggle. The three major liberation movements in
the country drew their respective support from the
two rival superpowers: the USSR and the USA. Angola
thus represents a unique case in the history of
Africa's liberation struggles, because it is only in
Angola that independence was won in the midst of
ideological rivalries between the two superpowers.
The MPLA - Popular Movement for the Liberation of
Angola - led by the late Augustinho Neto was, and is
still being supported by the USSR. Frente
Nacional de Libert cao de Angola - the National
Front for the Liberation of Angola (FNLA) - led by
Holden Roberto, was supported by the USA and her
allies; and the splinter group from FNLA, Uniao
Nacional pro Independence Total de Angola (UNITA),
led by Joanis Savimbi was supported and is still
being supported, though indirectly, by the USA and
its allies. The Soviet Union has exercised the
greatest political influence in Angola among the
superpowers. Neto, the MPLA leader, who had been
connected with the communists since 1959 and who had
visited Moscow in 1964 for military support, was the
major linchpin in Soviet-Angolan relations.[11] He
drew a lot of influence from Moscow and Havana, and
Castro was one of his best friends.[12] It is likely
that Castro also influenced his political outlook,
and the Cuban troops that came to assist him in 1975

could be traced to these early contacts.

The Soviet decision to assist Marxist MPLA was both ideologically logical and politically pragmatic; because a socialist government in Angola would be expected to serve Soviet interests. With Soviet assistance the Marxist MPLA ousted the Western-backed FNLA and UNITA from the capital on 9 July 1975 and controlled 12 out of 15 provinces.[13] Since then, Soviet presence and influence have been assured. The USSR justified its support to the MPLA and its continued stay in Angola on the grounds that it was invited to assist a truly nationalist party against Western puppet rival parties - the FNLA and UNITA.[14] This accusation was backed by the revelation that the FNLA leadership had established strong contacts with the CIA since 1959, and that it was being backed by Washington in its efforts to oust the MPLA government.[15] The USA began to offer direct aid to the rival movements of the MPLA when the Civil War intensified. For example, President Ford authorised $14 million for the CIA's overt actions in Angola.[16] This was followed by arms shipments to the FNLA and the UNITA forces. All these measures were taken by the US to protect its huge economic investments in the region especially those in Zaire and South Africa.

US actions in Angola alarmed the USSR and led her to increase her assistance to the MPLA. The extent of Soviet commitment to Marxist MPLA's victory can be demonstrated by the fact that at independence in 1976 it had committed $90 million to Angola, its largest military aid in Black Africa; it also had one of the largest number of Soviet military advisers on the continent in that country. Besides, the 16,000 Cuban troops in Angola, the largest contingent in Africa, were air-lifted by the USSR to back up the MPLA troops.[17] Soviet military aid to Angola has been increased astronomically in view of the increased guerrilla activities of UNITA, backed by South Africa and the Western powers. For example, by 1981 there were 20,000 Cuban troops in Angola, 5,000 East Europeans and several thousand Soviet military advisers. These figures made Angola the leading recipient of Soviet bloc military aid on the African continent. This has been complemented by a 20 year friendship and cooperation treaty between USSR and Angola, worth $2 billion in 1982, the largest Soviet financial commitment to Black Africa.[18] By the end of 1983, the USSR was exercising the strongest influence in Angola, surpassing that of the US and its allies, including Portugal, the erstwhile colonial power. Soviet influence in Angola and in the Horn has enabled Moscow to establish strong economic and trade ties with states whose economies were traditionally dominated by Western multinational corporations. Soviet economic aid, according to earlier Soviet views, was not profit-motivated, unlike that of the Western donors, and was intended to protect the newly-independent states against capitalist exploitation.[19]

A more realistic analysis of Soviet economic aid policy emerged under the Brezhnev era. Since then, Soviet economists have regarded Soviet aid as mutually beneficial to both the recipient and the donor.[20] Again, they have recently stressed the importance of economic interdependence and argued that the theory of the 'two world economies' has been substituted with a 'single world economy' theory under which socialism and capitalism are mere sub-systems.[21] The Soviet Union thus ensures that it invests its aid in a 'secure' country. As one Soviet economist argues, 'a socialist country engaged in economic assistance to a developing country should be guaranteed not only a recovery of its actual expenditure but also a definite return on the resources invested'.[22] Furthermore, the Soviet Union has lately denounced the concepts of self-reliance and regional cooperation adopted by some African states, because, according to Moscow, such developments would deprive the industrialised nations of vital raw materials and markets.[23] The above views by Soviet economists tend to conform to similar ones held by the Western powers.

Soviet aid programmes, however, differ from those of the West in some ways. For example, Western aid is dispensed bilaterally or multilaterally under international agencies. But Soviet assistance programmes are always bilateral and carry a lower interest rate of 2½ to 3 per cent per annum; with a one year grace period and an average of a 12 year repayment period. Western aid programmes, on the other hand, carry higher interest rates but with longer grace and repayment periods. Most Soviet aid has been in the form of repayable credits. For example, out of the $1.8 billion offered to Africa from 1954 to 1977, only $50m. was offered in grants. In contrast, about 40 per cent of Western aid is always offered as grants.[24] The choice and amount of Soviet aid are determined by a number of factors: the actual or potential strategic importance of the recipient to Soviet security interests; the potential by the USSR to reduce American and Chinese influence in the recipient country or region; the ideological stand of the recipient, and finally the importance of the recipient to Soviet markets.[25] The above principles upon which USSR aid is offered are underscored by a Soviet official thus, 'The provision of credits by our country is not based on any political, military and other economic conditions that are unacceptable to a developing country. However, it would be unjustifiable to reach the conclusion that the Soviet Union is indifferent concerning to whom, and on what conditions, to grant credits. This would ignore the demands of reality.'[26]

Somalia up to 1976, Ethiopia and Angola since 1977, have received the largest share of Soviet economic and technical aid in Black Africa, because they satisfied most of the above conditions under which Soviet aid is offered. Although Somalia had been a British Colony and had established strong economic links with that country, she none the less became increasingly dependent on USSR economic aid and markets following her adoption of a socialist path of development. Soviet interests in the strategic port of Barbera were the single most important factor that prompted it to offer Somalia the second largest Soviet economic aid package in Black Africa.[27] The aid was important for Somalia in several ways: (i) the availability of Soviet economic assistance increased the number of donors for Somalia and also decreased her dependency on former colonial powers, which most independent African leaders would wish to do, (ii) the aid was utilised for some key developmental projects in Somalia, such as dam construction, communications and agriculture,[28] (iii) in the technical field, Soviet experts contributed much to Somalia's development, and by 1977 Somalia had attracted the largest number of Soviet experts in Black Africa,[29] and finally (iv) several hundred Somalis have benefited from the generous Soviet education aid programme, and Somalia at one time had one of the largest contingents of African students in the USSR.[30] Trade relations between Somalia and the USSR were also good, although the former continued to depend overwhelmingly on Western markets.

Although Ethiopia before the revolution received less Soviet aid than Somalia, Addis Ababa was nevertheless amongst the largest recipients of Soviet aid in Black Africa. One plausible explanation of this situation is that the Soviet

Union wanted to gain a foothold in the pro-Western country because of its strategic points around the Indian Ocean. However, Soviet aid was virtually unutilised under the Emperor, possibly for fear of offending the USA. Russian economic aid to Ethiopia was increased after the revolution, and the Marxist regime in Addis Ababa has fully utilised it for some of the most important development projects in the country, such as the construction of the first major oil refinery at Assab.[31] But in spite of its excellent relations with the USSR, Ethiopia has continued to depend more and more on the Western donors, notably the European Economic Community (EEC), which has offered a credit facility of up to $200 million for the 1980-85 period. Besides, out of the $120 million loan listed in the 1979/80 budget, three-quarters of it came from the World Bank, the EEC and China. Western economic aid to Ethiopia has increased since Mengistu's regime began paying compensation to the owners of the nationalised companies, particularly American owners.[32] The Soviet Embassy in Addis Ababa claims that the USSR and Ethiopia have signed agreements for 60 major development projects.[33] These projects, plus the twenty year friendship and cooperation treaty between the two countries, are probably going to reduce Ethiopia's dependence on the Western aid donors and will give the Soviets more economic influence in the country in the long run.[34] The Kremlin already claims that the volume of trade between the two countries has increased 15 times since the revolution. The future trend therefore points to growing Soviet economic influence in Ethiopia, but it is unlikely that it will lead to the complete severance of the country's trade links with the West, which are still very strong. In that regard, it is interesting to note that the West responded 'positively' to the appeal by Mengistu for assistance to end the famine in some parts of Ethiopia in 1984 and 1985.

In the technical field, as well as in the sphere of education in particular, Soviet assistance has been substantial. The number of Ethiopian students in the USSR at the time of the revolution in 1974 stood at 500. But in the 1979/80 academic year Ethiopian students numbered over 1,600, the largest contingent of African students in the country.[35] It is hoped in Moscow that Soviet-trained Ethiopian students will eventually go home and assume positions of responsibility, which would enable them to influence policy in favour of the

Soviet Union.

Marxist Angola, unlike Ethiopia and Somalia in the Horn of Africa, received far less Soviet economic aid for the period up to 1977.[36] Most Soviet aid to Angola was in the form of military assistance, which was more urgently needed by the MPLA to fight the civil war. However, under the economic cooperation agreement between the two countries, a number of important projects have been undertaken in Angola, such as the construction of dams and oil refineries.[37] Whilst Soviet economic links with Angola have not eliminated Western economic ties with the Luanda regime, they have certainly reduced Angola's dependence on the West, particularly her former colonial master, Portugal. If and when the cooperation agreement is fully implemented, it will make the Soviet Union Angola's most important economic partner in the world. In the meantime, however, Angola's fisheries, diamonds, bauxite, coffee and gold are being exported to the Soviet Union in exchange for Soviet chemicals, heavy machinery and so forth. For her part, the USSR has acknowledged Angola's importance as a source of raw materials.[38] Despite the increasing importance of the USSR as an economic and trading partner of Angola, Western countries have continued to play an important role in the country's economic development, particularly in the oil industry, where American oil companies are playing a major role.[39] Angola's decision to allow both the East and the West to participate in its economic development is intended, among other things, to diversify its economy to avoid overdependence on one power bloc.

The Horn of Africa and Angola are today among some of the most important strategic areas on the continent, in the superpowers' evaluation. They have therefore led to the most intensive rivalry between the USSR and the USA for influence and control. The massive Soviet economic and, more importantly, military assistance to these states has been prompted mostly by strategic considerations. Angola's strategic importance includes, among other things, her long coast line and excellent harbours on the Atlantic Ocean, as well as her communication links with Zambia, Zaire, Zimbabwe and South Africa. Whoever commands influence in Angola would have substantial naval, military and economic influence in Zaire, in the south Atlantic and in South Africa. Bruce Handler summarised such a prospect and the West's reaction thus:

'Soviet planners were attracted to Angola's harbour at Luanda and Lobito if not for any other reason than the fact that Western analysts showed alarm at the prospect of Soviet warships in Africa's deep water ports. Soviet berths in Angola and the Peoples' Republic of the Congo are viewed as a threat to the oil route from the Persian Gulf. Even without the presence of Soviet bases, the denial of the Angolan coast to any future south Atlantic defense pact, comprising the USA and Western Europe would be viewed as a serious omission by them.'[140]

The USSR quickly utilised the strategic ports of Lobito and Luanda for its South Atlantic naval force and has posed a threat to the NATO presence in the Atlantic Ocean. Moscow has also freely used the same ports for its import and export trade with Angola and the neighbouring African states. Soviet presence in strategically located Angola has moreover enabled the Kremlin to exercise some influence in the neighbouring states and to challenge the presence of the Western powers in those states. For example, from Luanda, Moscow gave effective aid to Zimbabwean guerrillas, which scared Britain and her allies into granting independence to Southern Rhodesia to abort the possibility of installing a Marxist regime there similar to the one in Luanda. Again, the USSR has offered military assistance to both ANC and SWAPO guerrillas, using Angola as a base. The recent decision by South Africa to withdraw its troops conditionally from southern Angola as well as the new moderate policy adopted towards Namibia's independence could be attributed to the mounting pressure on South Africa by the Soviet-backed SWAPO guerrillas based in Angola. Although President Reagan's mild condemnation of Pretoria's apartheid policy could be attributed to US-based as well as other international pressure groups, it could also be connected directly with attempts by Washington to neutralise or reduce Soviet influence in southern Africa, in the wake of the failure of America's policy of 'constructive engagement' with the pariah regime of President Botha.

The superpowers have rendered massive military aid to Angola and the Horn of Africa to sustain in power regimes which allow them the use of strategic bases in those states. African leaders have been very receptive to superpower military aid, which they use

to quell internal opposition, to appease the
national armies and for the irredentist ambitions of
some. In the 1970s and the early 1980s, the Soviet
Union readily gave military aid to strategically
important African countries but especially those in
the Horn and Angola, to: (i) undermine or reduce
Western and Chinese economic political and military
influence in those states; (ii) assist client states
to enhance their internal security and stability;
(iii) asssist national liberation movements either
directly or by proxy, and finally (iv) extend the
Soviet defence perimeter in support of its global
interests.[41] Since the 1970s Soviet military aid to
Africa has consistently surpassed economic aid, in
spite of the continent's urgent need for more of the
latter. For example, Soviet arms transfer to Africa
(excluding Egypt) was over $2 billion for the period
1972 to 1977. Sub-Saharan Africa alone accounted
for £1.4 billion[42] in the same period. Yet economic
aid to the continent (excluding Egypt) for the
period from 1954 to 1977 was a mere $1.84 billion.[43]
Marxist MPLA readily received Soviet military
assistance during the civil war against Western-
backed FNLA and UNITA. It was postulated by Moscow
strategists that a victorious MPLA would protect
Soviet interests in Angola and allow it to use the
country as a base to further its influence on the
continent. The importance of Angola to the USSR is
illustrated by the fact that Luanda attracted the
larget Soviet military aid in Black Africa, which by
1976 was already worth $190 million.[44] Apart from
that, 400 Soviet military advisers and up to 19,000
Soviet-backed Cuban troops assisted the MPLA forces
in their final victory against its Western-backed
rivals.

In order to counter the perennial South
African invasions of, and the guerrilla activities
of UNITA in, Angola, the USSR has had to increase
its military aid to MPLA government forces
tremendously. Moscow trained the 35,000 strong
regular army of the MPLA and equipped it with T34s,
T55s and the most recent T62 tanks. These are
complemented by heavy artillery 122mm, 130mm and
152mm guns, self-propelled SU100 heavy anti-tank
weapons, BM21 rocket launchers, etc., and by the
20,000 Cuban troops. In the new air defence system,
the SA surface-to-air missiles are complementing
the SA3 and SA6 systems, and the MIG.24 assault
helicopter gunships. Angola has allegedly shot down
several South African Mirage and Impala bombers and
also claimed to have knocked out several South

African tanks by December 1983, using Russian-supplied weapons.[45] Meanwhile, the Soviet Union has acquired the strategic air and sea ports of Luanda and Lobito for her TU-95 Bear and ASW patrols.[46]

In pursuit of strategic objectives in the Horn of Africa as in Angola, Moscow extended massive military aid to Somalia, which amounted to $181 million by 1977; making it the second largest Soviet military assistance package in Black Africa.[47] In the same year, there were 5,000 Soviet military advisers in that country, the highest number in Black Africa.[48] At the time, Somalia also had the largest number of African military personnel undergoing training in the USSR.[49] The strategic importance of Ethiopia has since 1977 attracted the largest Soviet military aid in Black Africa, unprecedented both in terms of the amount involved and the sophistication of weapons supplied. For example, at the peak of the Ogaden war between Somalia and Ethiopia in 1977, the USSR committed to Ethiopia arms worth $1 billion, 20,000 Soviet-backed Cuban troops, 1,500 Soviet military advisers, twenty Soviet warships in the Red Sea, 400 Soviet made tanks and 50 MIG fighter bombers, among other military equipment.[50] Soviet military aid commitment to Ethiopia amounted to $2 billion in 1979, one of the largest Soviet military aid commitments to developing countries and comparing favourably with Soviet military assistance to Egypt in the early 1970s.[51] With this size of military assistance, the Ethiopian army became one of the best-equipped armies in sub-Saharan Africa. As Soviet influence increased in Ethiopia, the USSR also became the most dominant military power in the Horn of Africa.

The Ogaden war was not only the first major war involving two independent African states but was also the first in which two rival superpowers directly supported the belligerents on the African continent. The Horn of Africa is today a high priority area for the USSR on the continent, and it has jealously kept its recent achievements there, such as the strategic Dahlak Islands in the Red Sea, 30 miles off Massawa, which has increased Soviet naval advantage in the Indian Ocean. A US navy commentator lamented the new Soviet strategic achievements thus, 'the strategic consequences of this is (sic) to tighten further the Soviet grip on the mouth of the Red Sea ... in crisis the USSR forces would be in a position to intercept traffic moving from the Mediterranean through the Suez Canal and south along the Red Sea.'[52]

The wider implications of Soviet military involvement in the Horn of Africa are: (i) the region has been so militarised that most of its developmental resources have been diverted to purchasing expensive Soviet and Western arms and to maintaining large national armies, foreign troops and advisers. For example, since 1977 the largest single area of government spending in Ethiopia has been on defence; arms deals with the USSR between 1977-80 totalled $2,000 million. The repayment arrangement has to be both in hard currency and in barter form, involving Ethiopian exports. However, the barter system had to be discontinued after some time because it created an acute shortage of badly-needed foreign exchange for Addis Ababa.[53] (ii) Soviet military presence in Ethiopia has also increased USA-USSR rivalry in the region and has turned it into a new centre of international competition and tension, which is dangerous to the interests of Africa. Seen from the perspective of Ethiopian national interests, however, Soviet military aid has enabled the country to maintain her independence and territorial integrity against the irredentist ambitions of one of her neighbours, Somalia. While the West has remained critical of massive Soviet presence in the region, the Kremlin, in turn, has accused Washington of not only initiating the militarisation of the region but also of trying to use its new bases in Somalia and Mombasa for furthering its expansion and aggression into the continent.[54]

CONCLUSION

Ideologically, the USSR tended to identify with socialist-oriented states in Africa, such as socialist Angola and Somalia before 1977, and Ethiopia after 1977, because they accepted Soviet advances as well as being somewhat anti-Western and anti-imperialist. The leaders of socialist Somalia and Ethiopia have none the less behaved more often as African nationalists than scientific socialists, as confessed by Siad Barre and as shown by the refusal of Colonel Mengistu to form a communist party. Again, the real commitment of the MPLA to develop Angola along the scientific socialist lines of Marxist-Leninism is yet to be proved. The socialist rhetoric has been selectively and effectively used by leaders of all three states for the purposes of achieving national unity and support for their regimes at home. In Angola, the socialist ideology was used to achieve a measure of unity in a country which was, and is still, beset by tribal and ethnic cleavages. The success of this ideology in Angola is however limited, as tribal and ethnic divisions are still rampant and are reflected in the three major political parties: MPLA, FNLA and UNITA. In Ethiopia, however, the socialist ideology has been fairly successfully utilised for the purposes of winning support for the Derg from workers and peasants against pro-imperial groups in the country. The creation of workers' communes and the land nationalisation policies under Mengistu have been fairly successful. Somalia successfully used the socialist ideology under Siad Barre to achieve national unity and to obtain support initially from the USSR, which he used against Ethiopia. Socialism however ceased to be an important ideology for Somalia when the Soviet Union switched its support to Ethiopia during the Ogaden war.

In the economic field Soviet aid has benefited the recipients in several ways. For example, Soviet aid to countries in the Horn and Angola has lessened their hitherto overwhelming dependence on the former colonisers' markets, thereby boosting their sense of independence. The availability of USSR economic aid has also diversified and increased the choice of markets and range of goods to choose from by these states and has accordingly increased their opportunities to bargain for more favourable terms from donors. This was difficult when the Western multinational corporations had the sole monopoly over the markets of these countries. Some of the Soviet economic and technical aid has been utilised on some key development sectors in Angola and in the Horn; mining, agriculture, refineries, etc. It must be noted, however, that the Soviet aid programme has had some unfavourable aspects, too, such as the short grace and repayment periods. In some states, such as Ethiopia, foreign exchange earning exports have been bartered for non-revenue generating projects, such as the purchase of arms. The USSR as a donor country has ensured that the capital it invested in the three countries was not only recovered but that it yielded for her favourable economic and political dividends.

Militarily, and viewed from the perspective of the interests and objectives of the regimes in power in the three African countries concerned, Soviet military aid has been of enormous benefit to Angola and Ethiopia in particular. Without USSR and Cuban military assistance, the MPLA would not have been able to achieve a military victory over its rivals in the country. Somalia's Siad Barre would also have found it much more difficult to sustain himself in power without Soviet military aid, which he used to quell internal resistance to his rule and to rally support from the army and the civilians for the war against Ethiopia in 1977. In the case of Ethiopia, the victory against Somalia would have been long and difficult, were it not for the massive Soviet and Cuban military assistance. Russian military and technical aid has helped all the three states in training and building some of the most modern and most effective armies in Black Africa.

Soviet military assistance is not without its drawbacks. For instance, it led to the militarisation of the recipients and encouraged civil wars in Angola and the Horn, resulting in heavy human casualties. Secondly, the wars have diverted a lot of scarce economic resources to the purchase of arms instead of using them on more pressing economic development schemes such as the control of drought in Ethiopia as well as the promotion of agricultural development. Finally, the air and ocean port facilities which have been provided by these states to the USSR and USA navies and air forces have increased international rivalry among the superpowers, which have used these bases as new centres of international competition, a situation which is very dangerous for the survival of the African continent. All in all, the Soviet presence in Angola and the Horn of Africa has made a tremendous impact on the political and economic development of these states, with far-reaching implications for the continent and international relations generally. For instance, the USSR now has far more influence in Angola and Ethiopia than the Western powers, which still reluctantly regard these areas as their traditional spheres of influence. Moscow has for its part used its fairly strong presence in the Horn and Angola to increase its influence elsewhere on the continent at the expense of the Western powers.

The Western powers, especially the USA, need to review their policies in the Horn of Africa and Angola if they are to minimise the growing influence of the USSR. Several steps can be taken to achieve this objective: it is necessary for there to be a change of US policy towards South Africa which until recently stressed 'constructive engagement' with the apartheid regime. 'Constructive engagement' has been widely condemned, both in Africa and by anti-apartheid groups throughout the world. The anti-apartheid demonstrations by American groups at the South African Embassy in Washington, plus the increasing criticism of Pretoria's racist policies among leading US Republicans and Democrats, are believed to have persuaded President Reagan to denounce the apartheid system and to call instead for positive changes in southern Africa. African reaction to the new American moves has, however, been cautious. It is hoped that America will put pressure - both political and economic - on the Pretoria regime to grant independence to Namibia, offer political concessions to black South Africans and thereby reduce tension in southern Africa. If US policy in southern Africa is seen in Africa to be pro-black majority rights in South Africa, it will win friends and influence in Black Africa for Washington and will consequently reduce Soviet influence in the continent, particularly in pro-Soviet states such as Angola. Similarly, US policy in the Horn of Africa needs some readjustments to make it more accommodating of the Marxist regime in Ethiopia, increase its economic aid to that famine-ravaged country and finally decrease its open support for her opponent in the region, Somalia. Such a policy posture is likely to lead to an increase in US influence - both economic and political - in the region. It must be stressed here, however, that such a significant change of US policy is unlikely to take place under the hawkish and extremely conservative Ronald Reagan. Thus, Soviet influence in the Horn and in Angola will continue for the foreseeable future; a new pattern in Afro-European relations which have hitherto been dominated by the capitalist Western countries.

TABLE 7.1: SOVIET ECONOMIC ASSISTANCE COMMITMENTS TO ALL DEVELOPING COUNTRIES, AND TO AFRICAN COUNTRIES, 1954-77 (Millions of US Dollars)

Country	1954-1958	1959-1964	1965-1969	1970	1971	1972	1973	1974	1975	1976	1977	Total 1954-77
All developing countries	988	3,047	2,556	194	870	598	622	563	1,264	945	392	12,932
Africa	-	757	251	51	197	17	10	10	73	369	21	1,840
Algeria	-	227	1	1	189	-	-	-	-	290	-	716
Angola	-	-	-	-	-	-	-	-	-	10	-	11
Benin	-	-	-	-	-	-	-	5	-	-	-	5
Cameroon	-	8	-	-	-	-	-	-	-	-	-	8
Central African Empire	-	-	-	-	2	-	-	-	-	-	-	2
Chad	-	-	-	-	-	-	-	1	1	-	-	2
Congo	-	10	-	-	-	-	4	1	-	-	-	14
Equatorial Guinea	-	-	-	-	1	-	-	-	-	-	-	1
Ethiopia	-	102	-	-	-	-	-	1	2	-	-	105
Ghana	-	87	-	-	-	-	-	-	-	-	1	94
Guinea	-	73	95	-	-	-	-	2	-	-	1	201
Guinea Bissau	-	-	-	-	-	-	-	-	1	11	-	11
Kenya	-	48	-	-	-	-	-	-	-	-	-	48
Malagasy	-	-	-	-	-	-	-	-	-	-	-	13
Mali	-	55	11	-	-	12	-	-	-	-	-	80
Mauritania	-	-	4	-	-	-	1	-	-	-	-	5
Morocco	-	-	44	-	-	-	-	-	-	-	-	98
Mozambique	-	-	-	-	-	-	-	-	-	3	-	3

Niger	—	—	—	—	1	1	—	2
Nigeria	—	—	7	—	—	—	—	7
Rwanda	—	—	—	—	1	—	—	1
Senegal	7	—	—	—	1	1	—	8
Sierra Leone	—	28	—	—	—	—	—	28
Somalia	57	9	24	—	—	—	63	154
Sudan	22	42	—	—	—	—	—	64
Tanzania	—	20	—	—	—	—	19	40
Tunisia	28	1	—	—	—	—	55	82
Uganda	16	—	—	—	—	—	—	16
Upper Volta	—	—	—	1	—	—	—	6
Zambia	—	6	—	—	—	—	—	6

Sources: Central Intelligence Agency, National Foreign Assessment Center, Communist Aid to the Less Developed Countries of the Free World, 1977, ER-78U (Washington, DC, November 1978), p.5; supplemented by the 1975 and 1976 editions of the same publication.

121

TABLE 7.2: SOVIET, EAST EUROPEAN AND CUBAN ECONOMIC
TECHNICIANS IN AFRICA, 1976, 1977

Country	Soviet and East European Technicians		Cuban Technicians	
	1976	1977	1976	1977
Total, all developing countries	45,345	58,755	4,385	6,575
Africa	27,320	34,290	4,105	5,900
Algeria	6,625	6,200	10	15
Angola	525	700	3,000	4,000
Ethiopia	150	250	0	400
Ghana	50	105	0	0
Guinea	550	710	0	–
Kenya	25	–	0	0
Liberia	–	15	–	–
Libya	10,000	15,000	0	0
Mali	300	375	0	0
Mauritania	50	60	0	0
Mozambique	–	500	–	400
Nigeria	200	–	0	0
Somalia	1,500	1,050	0	30
Sudan	50	125	0	0
Tanzania	150	165	200	200
Tunisia	400	650	0	0
Uganda	75	30	0	0
Zambia	225	125	0	0
Other	6,445	8,230	895	855

Sources: Central Intelligence Agency, National
Foreign Assessment Center, Communist Aid
to the Less Developed Countries of the
Free World, 1977, ER-78-10478U
(Washington, DC, November 1978), p.9, and
CIA Communist Aid to the Less Developed
Countries of the Free World, 1976,
ER-77-19296 (Washington, DC, Central
Intelligence Agency).

TABLE 7.3 SOVIET ARMS TRANSFERS TO AFRICA, 1967-76
       (Million current dollars)

Country	Value of Transfers
Algeria	315
Angola	190
Benin	1
Central African Empire	1
Chad	5
Congo	10
Egypt	2,365
Equatorial Guinea	5
Guinea	50
Guinea Bissau	5
Libya	1,005
Madagascar	1
Mali	25
Morocco	10
Mozambique	15
Nigeria	70
Somalia	181
Sudan	65
Tanzania	30
Uganda	65
Zambia	10
Total	4,424

Source: US Arms Control and Disarmament Agency,
           World Military Expenditures and Arms
           Transfers 1967-76, Publication 98
           (Washington, DC, ACDA, July 1978) table
           VII, pp.158-9.

TABLE 7.4:   SOVIET MILITARY ADVISERS IN AFRICA

Country	1976	1977		1976-77
Algeria		600	600	600
Angola	500	500	500	170- 200
Congo				400
Equatorial Guinea	25	23	50	200
Ethiopia		500	500	
Guinea	75	130	125	110
Guinea Bissau	50	65	50	
Libya	800	1,000	1,000	300
Mali			175	30- 40
Mozambique	50	200	200	200- 250
Nigeria				50
Somalia	1,000	1,500		2,500-5,000
Sudan	90			80- 90
Uganda	300	300		300
Other	1,010	847	2,515	
Total	3,900	5,715	5,715	4,940-7,540

Source: US Central Intelligence Agency, Communist Aid to the Less Developed Countries of the Free World, 1976, ER-77-10296, (Washington, DC, August 1977), table 3, p.4; CIA estimates published in US Congress, Joint Economic Committee, Allocation of Resources in the Soviet Union and China - 1978, Hearings, 95th Congress 2nd Session, 26 June and 14 July 1978, p.90; CIA, Communist Aid to Less Developed Countries of the Free World, 1977, ER-78-10478U (Washington, DC, November 1978), table 2, p.3; US Library of Congress Congressional Research Service, 'The Soviet Union and the Third World', Issue Brief, no.IB77101 (Washington, DC, 12 December 1977), table III, p.11.

TABLE 7.5: AFRICAN MILITARY PERSONNEL TRAINED IN
THE SOVIET UNION, 1955-76

Country	Number of Personnel
Algeria	2,025
Benin	25
Burundi	75
Chad	75
Congo	350
Egypt	5,675
Equatorial Guinea	200
Ghana	175
Guinea	850
Guinea Bissau	1,100
Libya	1,250
Mali	350
Morocco	75
Mozambique	300
Nigeria	550
Somalia	2,400
Sudan	325
Tanzania	1,425
Uganda	700
Zambia	75
Other	650
Total	17,650

Source: US Central Intelligence Agency, Communist
Aid to the Less Developed Countries of the
Free World, 1976, ER-77-10296 (Washington,
DC, August 1977), table 4, p.6; CIA,
Communist Aid to Less Developed Countries
of the Free World, 1977, .ER-78-10478U
(Washington, DC, November 1978), table 3,
p.4.

NOTES

[1] Roger Kanet, The Soviet Union and the Developing Countries (Baltimore, John Hopkins University Press, 1975), p.3.

[2] V.I. Lenin, Imperialism: The Highest Stage of Capitalism (Moscow, Progress Publishers) no date.

[3] Roger Kanet, The Soviet Union and the Developing Countries, p.3.

[4] Joukoff Edmond and R. North, Soviet Russia and the East 1920-27 (New Jersey, Stanford University Press, 1957), pp.53-65; and George Padmore, The Life and the Struggle of the Negro Toiler (Maddison, Red International of Labour Union, 1931); and J. Kenyatta, 'An African Looks at British Imperialism', Negro Worker III, no.1, January 1933, p.21.

[5] Jan Triska and D. Finley, Soviet Foreign Policy (London, Macmillan, 1967).

[6] J. Bowyer Bell, 'Strategic Implications of Soviet Presence in Somalia', Orbis vol.19, no.2, (Philadelphia, Summer 1975), pp.402-11.

[7] David Lamb, 'Russia in the Somalia They Helped to Develop', Los Angeles Times (Los Angeles), 2 October 1977.

[8] Ethiopian Ministry of Information, Ethiopia Tik The Origin and the Future Direction of the Movement (in English), mimeographed 20 December 1974.

[9] Marina Ottaway, 'The Theory and Practice of Marxism-Leninism in Mozambique and Ethiopia', in D.E. Albright (ed.), Africa and International Communism (London, Macmillan, 1980), chapter V.

[10] Paule Heinze, 'Communism and Ethiopia', Problems of Communism (Washington, May-June 1981,) p.55.

[11] John A. Marcum, The Angolan Revolution, vol.1 (Cambridge, Mass., MIT Press, 1969), p.28.

[12] Michael T. Kouffman, 'The Three Men who Control Angola's Warring Factions', The New York Times (28 December 1975), and Daily Telegraph (London, June 1975).

[13] William E. Shanfele (Jr.), US Assistant Secretary of State for African Affairs, The African Dimension of the Angolan Conflict (Washington, DC, State Department, Bureau of Public Affairs, 6 February 1976), p.2.

[14] 'Angola's National Forces', International Affairs no.3, (Moscow, March 1963), pp.116-17.

[15] Jivi Valenta, 'Soviet Decision-Making on the Intervention in Angola', in D. Albright (ed.),

Africa and International Communism, chapter IV, pp.95-6.

[16] See J. Stockwell, *In Search of Enemies: CIA Story* (New York, Norton, 1978), p.161.

[17] Joseph P. Smaldonein, 'Soviet and Chinese Military Aid and Arms Transfer to Africa: A Contextual Analysis', in W. Weinstein and T.H. Henricksen (eds.), *Soviet and Chinese Aid to Africa* (New York, Praeger, 1980), pp.85 and 100. See also *The Soviet Union and the Third World: A Watershed in Great Power Policy*, Report to the Committee of International Relations, House of Representatives (Washington, Library of Congress, 8 May 1977), p.107.

[18] *Africa Research Bulletin* (henceforth ARB) (Economic and Technical Series) 15 January – 14 February 1982, p.6324.

[19] V.L. Yamalov, 'Soviet Assistance to the Under-developed Countries', in *International Affairs*, no.9 (September 1959).

[20] A.A. Gromyko, 'Soviet Foreign Policy in Africa', *International Affairs* (September 1967).

[21] Elizabeth Krial Valkenier, 'The USSR, The Third World and the Global Economy', *Problems of Communism* (July – August 1977).

[22] I. Shamarai, 'Problems of Realisation of Economic Cooperation between Socialist and Developing Countries', *Narody Azii i Afriki* no.4 (1968), p.13.

[23] R. Ulyanovsky, 'The Developing Countries: Economic Front', *New Times* no.34, (Moscow, August 1976), pp.18-22.

[24] Weinstein and Henricksen (eds.), *op. cit.*, p.19; and see J. Mulira, 'Soviet Bloc Trade, Economic, Technical and Military Involvement in Independent Africa – A Case Study of Uganda, 1962-1979' *Geneva Afrique* vol. XIX, No.1 (Geneva, 1981), pp.44-5.

[25] Roger E. Kanet, 'The Soviet Union and the Developing Countries: Policy or Policies, *The World Today* 31 (1975), p.338.

[26] V. Romanov and I. Tsriklis, 'Ekonomicheskie Sviazi USSR Razvivai Usisisa stranami', *Ekonomicheski Nauki*, no.3, 1978, quoted in R. Kanet *et al.* (eds.), *The Soviet Union and Developing Countries*, p.32.

[27] See Table 7.1.²

[28] *ARB*, 1-31 December 1971, p.2225.

[29] See Table 7.2.

[30] Warren Weinstein and T.H. Henricksen (eds.), *Chinese and Soviet Aid to Africa*, p.259.

31 *Africa Diary* (New Delhi, 12-18 November 1979), pp.9384-5.

32 P. McPherson, 'Ethiopia: US aid next year *Africa News* (London, November 1983), p.4.

33 *Ethiopia Herald*, quoting the Soviet Ambassador to Addis Ababa in *Africa Diary*, 8-14 October 1978, pp.9204-5.

34 *ARB*, 1-31 July 1981, p.6122.

35 *ARB*, 1-31 July 1979, p.5355.

36 See Table 7.1.

37 *ARB*, (Economic and Technical Series), 14 January - 15 February 1982, p.6324.

38 A.U. Pritvorov, 'The Economics of Angola', *Narodny Azii i Afrikii* (Moscow). See Valenta, op. cit. p.107, and S. F. Soremekun, *Angola: Road to Independence* (Ife, University of Ife Press, 1983.).

39 Weinstein and Henricksen (eds.), *Chinese and Soviet Aid to Africa*, p.70.

40 Bruce Handler, 'South Atlantic Pact Rumoured', *Washington Post* (Washington), 29 November 1976.

41 P. Smaldonein, 'Soviet and Chinese Military Aid and Arms Transfer to Africa: A Contextual Analysis', in Weinstein and Henricksen (eds.), *Chinese and Soviet Aid to Africa*, p.77.

42 CIA, *Communist Aid to the Less Developed Countries of the Free World*, 1976, ER-77-10296, (Washington, DC, 1977).

43 Weinstein and Henricksen (eds.), *Chinese and Soviet Aid to Africa*, p.21.

44 See Table 7.3.

45 'Countering Invasion and Insurgency in Angola', *Africa News* no.35, (London, March 1984), pp.22-3.

46 US Navy, Office of the Chief of Naval Operations, 'Understanding Soviet Naval Development', in Weinstein and Henricksen (eds.), *Chinese and Soviet Aid to Africa*, pp.10, 15-22 and 100.

47 See Table 7.4.

48 See Table 7.4.

49 See Table 7.5.

50 *ARB*, 1-28 February 1978, ppp.4743-4.

51 *ARB*, 1-31 January 1980, p.5541.

52 *ARB*, 1-31 October 1980, p.5830.

53 *Africa Today* (London, December 1981), p.539.

54 *ARB*, 1-31 December 1982, p.6688.

CHAPTER 8

AFRICA'S STRATEGIC RELATIONSHIP WITH WESTERN EUROPE:
THE DISPENSABILITY THESIS

Jinmi Adisa and Adigun Agbaje

The nature of the strategic relationship between
Africa and Western Europe is difficult to determine.
About two decades after the European flags went
down, Europe's influence is still pervasive in the
continent via the multinationals, paratroopers, the
jeans and Coca Cola culture, the Commonwealth and
Franco-African summits. Africans would like to
believe that the presence underlines the strategic
importance of their continent to Europe, a tendency
which Europeans, in turn, are inclined to ridicule.
The controversy is partly political. Europeans are
hard pressed to accept a notion which may imply that
denial of African resources would 'bring Europe to
its knees'. Africans on the other hand cannot accept
the concomitant inference that they are dispensable.
They demand to know why, if this were so, the French
paratroopers, for instance, continually come
calling. In essence, the issue is one of definition.
The dispensability thesis intermingles the problem
of 'need' and 'want'. Thus it mixes up the question
of why Europeans remain in Africa with whether they
can do otherwise.
    The themes are interrelated and cannot be
easily separated, but it is none the less worthwhile
to seek further clarification. What is the character
of Europe's relationship with Africa? Is it an
imperative or a function of profit or social
preference? Is such a distinction in itself
realistic? This kind of analysis demands two
premises. First is a need to identify priority areas
of relationship and second an exploration of their
motive and character with a view to determining the
merits. Therefore the basic presumptions of the
dispensability thesis would be isolated and
evaluated.

Africa's Strategic Relationship

A.   WHY ARE THEY STILL HERE?

The instinctual response of the African to the
argument that his continent is dispensable is to ask
why, in that case, Europeans remain here. The retort
is banal in the sense that it confuses desire with
need. The individual like the state is involved in a
number of relationships that, at times, are not in
its own interest or which in the long run it can do
without. At the same time, the strength of
relationship is underlined by the time factor.
Durability bespeaks value to the extent that in
certain enduring cases it is hardly conceivable that
relationships could be broken. This places a premium
on Africa's relations with Europe which has lasted
and grown stronger over centuries. The length of
that relationship alone implies that there are basic
advantages to be had: things that one party obtains
from the other and wants to continue to get.
     Requirements have changed over time. Currently,
however, one can discern three major reasons for
European presence. First, for the purpose of
resource security as a source of strategic metals;
second, for reasons of commerce, trade and
influence; and third, as an arena of East-West
ideological competition. The first is extractive,
direct and almost bilateral; the second and third
derive their vigour from the character of the
international system or the global setting. The
three are inevitably intertwined and each has a
bearing on the other, as would be discovered on
closer examination.

B.   RESOURCE SECURITY AND STRATEGIC MINERALS

Africa is known to possess vast reserves of natural
resources in forms of minerals.[1] According to 1977
estimates the continent's share of the world's total
is as follows: coal 7 per cent, petroleum 8 per
cent, natural gas 12 per cent, uranium 30 per cent
of non-communist world, radium (the chief source),
thorium 20 per cent, iron ore 3 per cent, cobalt 90
per cent, copper 20 per cent, lead 8 per cent, zinc
5 per cent, tin over 15 per cent, bauxite 20 per
cent, titanium (the deposit at Sherbro in Sierra
Leone is greater than any yet found in the world),
antimony about 7 per cent, gold 50 per cent,
platinum 40 per cent, tantalum 80 per cent,
germanium (the bulk of the world's reserves), lithium
over 50 per cent and diamonds (the bulk of the
world's reserves).[2] The figures for important

130

minerals have not varied significantly since then (see Table 8.1).

More importantly, the continent of Africa accounts for a significant portion of the resources currently available to the countries that make up the European Economic Community (EEC) (see Table 8.2). Indeed, the continent's position assumes greater significance when it is realised that several of these minerals are essential for the production process of the highly industrialised countries of Western Europe and its defence. Some examples will suffice to illustrate this.

Uranium is necessary for nuclear power programmes. Cobalt, titanium and tantalum are useful for specialised steels. Chrome, manganese and vanadium are also vital elements of the same process. Chrome, extracted from the ground as chromium ore, is used principally in its alloyed form as ferrochrome. Ferrochrome in combination with nickel produces stainless steel, which is able to withstand heat and corrosion and is thus critical for the manufacture of jet engines, petrochemical and power plant equipment.[3] Chromium is also used to make other high resistant, high strength super alloys in the defence, aviation and power generation industries.

Similarly, vanadium is used as an alloying element for the manufacture of light weight, high strength steels for jet engines, airframes, transportation equipment and the construction of oil and gas pipelines. Titanium is important for the aerospace industry, while manganese, because of its de-sulphurising and de-oxidising properties, is an essential hardening agent used in the manufacture of dry cell batteries and the production of chemicals. The platinum group metals (platinum, palladium, rhodium, ruthenium, iridium and osmium), which are found and mined together, also have vital industrial and aesthetic uses. They are a key element in the anti-pollution technology and moreover they serve as catalytic agents, facilitating important chemical processes, such as platinium refining and production of nitrogenous fertilisers. Also, the corrosion-resistant properties of platinum make it popular for use in medical and dental supplies, electronic equipment, glassware and ceramics.

The fact of European dependence on African minerals is therefore indisputable. The argument is whether or not this dependence can be described as 'strategic'. The concept of 'strategic metals' is a relatively new one. According to David Hargreaves

TABLE 8.1: AFRICAN SOURCES OF UK AND EEC MINERAL IMPORTS (%)

Metal	UK		EEC	
Aluminium	Ghana	7	Ghana	3
			Cameroun	3
Antimony	n.a.		South Africa	9
Asbestos	South Africa	16	South Africa	13
	Swaziland	13	Swaziland	2
Bauxite	Ghana	72	Guinea	18
			Ghana	4
			Sierra Leone	4
Cadmium	South Africa	9	Zaire	4
Chromium	South Africa	39	South Africa	31
			Mozambique	5
Cobalt	Zambia	57	Zambia	33
	Zaire	1	Zaire	24
			South Africa	7
Columbium	Nigeria	1	Nigeria	2
Copper	Zambia	29	Zambia	19
	Zaire	2	Zaire	20
			South Africa & Namibia	4.5
Iron Ore	Liberia	3	Liberia	1.6
	Mauritania	9	Mauritania	6.5
Lead			Morocco	6
			South Africa	4
Manganese	South Africa	31	South Africa	52
	Gabon	18	Gabon	24
Nickel			South Africa	5
Phosphate	n.a.		Morocco	44
			Togo	13
			Tunisia	4
Platinum Group	South Africa	41	South Africa	24
Silver	South Africa	3		
Tin	Nigeria	15.5	Zaire	6.5
	South Africa	5	Nigeria	6
			Rwanda	2
Tungsten	Rwanda	5	Rwanda	3
Uranium	n.a.		n.a.	
Vanadium	South Africa	55	South Africa	42
Zinc			South Africa	2
Zirconium			South Africa	2

Source: Margaret Cornell (ed.), Europe and Africa: Issues in Post-Colonial Relations, op. cit., p.80.

TABLE 8.2:   AFRICA'S SHARE OF WORLD MINERAL RESERVES
              AND PRODUCTION (1981)

Minerals	% Share of World Reserves	% Share of World Production
Diamonds	92	70
Cobalt	42	63.4
Gold	64	53
Platinum	71	46
Chrome	97	40
Uranium	28	35
Manganese	50	29
Phosphates	70.1	23.4
Copper	13	16.7
Bauxite	33	15.5
Iron	17.25	7
Tin	7	4.7
Coal	3.8	
Silver		4
Lead	5.8	2.5

Source: Africa Research Bulletin (1983), p.6777.

and Sara Fromson, authors of the World Index of
Strategic Minerals, the concept was born in 1978
when guerrilla incursions into Zaire temporarily
halted supplies and triggered the price of cobalt
from US $4 to US $40 a pound.[4] Two-thirds of the
world's cobalt comes from just four African
countries - Zaire, Zambia, Zimbabwe and Botswana -
with Zaire alone providing 60 per cent. The only
main alternative source was the Soviet Union, and
the danger that was implicit in this situation
motivated American politicians and industrialists to
begin to lobby seriously for stockpile holdings,
while the need to accommodate vulnerable supplier
countries became a principle of US foreign policy,
as was made evident in American provision of support
facilities for French paratroop operations designed
to stabilise the Mobutu regime in Zaire. The
incident may well be regarded as having underscored
the strategic importance of African minerals, except
that this position has been queried by a prominent
European strategist, Colonel Jonathan Alford, the
Deputy Director of the prestigious International
Institute of Strategic Studies (IISS) in London.

C.   THE DISPENSABILITY THESIS

The Colonel confesses to having as much difficulty
in applying the term 'strategic' to minerals as he
does in applying it to Africa.[5] The problem is
partly one of definition:

> If by strategic minerals we mean those which
> are important in some way or another to the
> economies of the developed world, it is of
> course true that all minerals are 'strategic'.
> However, if we mean those whose denial in the
> short run would bring the West to its knees,
> there are hardly any.[6]

He adds that Europe needs uranium, chromium,
etc., for industrial processes but then European
states 'could go on functioning as societies for a
very long time without any of these things': they
could   recycle   or   salvage,   encourage   local
production, use alternative minerals for existing
industrial processes, switch processes altogether or
build stockpiles (as the US does) to cushion
themselves from short run interruptions.[7] Apart from
this, African countries are not in a particularly
strong position to play the mineral card 'although
it is very likely that the mineral market will
exhibit considerable nervousness if stability of
parts of Africa is threatened'.[8]   Thus he sums up:

> It is obvious that producers would wish us to
> believe that what they produce is in some way
> vital to our security. <u>We</u> should not
> necessarily take those claims at face value.
> Steadiness under fire is a traditional military
> virtue, which can also be a distinct political
> asset.[9]

Hence, Europe's interest in Africa is primarily
economic or commercial, rather than strategic.[10]
     The argument is partly persuasive: partly not.
The latter part, for instance, embraces a touch of
the political crusade which undermines earlier
certainties. If indeed the Colonel is so sure that
Europe can dispense with African minerals and that
Africans are too weak to play the mineral card, then
one wonders why, in the final analysis, he exhorts
Europeans to be 'steady under fire'. Surely the
'fire' metaphor in this regard has to be misplaced.
After all, the ability to put others under 'fire' is
an attribute of those who can shoot to wound or

kill. If Africans have this attribute vis-a-vis
Europe in regard to strategic minerals, it must be
the case that the continent is not as helpless as
the Colonel makes out. One is therefore left with a
sneaking suspicion that the Colonel's thesis had one
primary purpose all along - to secure the 'distinct
political asset' which he so clearly favours.

Political advantage apart, there are aspects of
the Colonel's argument that merit closer attention;
particularly his recipe for 'bail-out' prospects,
i.e. propositions for alternative sources and
stockpiling. Other Western governments apart from
the US have found it wise to take out such an
insurance policy against the prospect of denial or
extortion. The lesson of history as underlined by
the Arab oil embargo of 1973 is that such stockpiles
are valuable. Yet the logical difficulty of the
stockpile proposition is that, while it buttresses
the Colonel's position on the one hand, it short-
changes it and exposes a contradiction on the other.
This analysis is best expressed with references to
the individual. Individual insurance policies are
commonplace nowadays. It is a standard component of
the budgets of average middle-class families. As
such, it provides little evidence that a serious
threat is envisaged. Yet the same can hardly be said
for governments. When several governments in the
same hemisphere suddenly begin to take out the same
premium almost simultaneously, as the West is
currently doing with strategic minerals, it provides
some sort of indication that they view the threat as
viable. In other words, the Colonel's position in
this regard would appear to be at variance with that
of his 'home governments'.

This is not to overlook the possibility that
those governments may have chosen to err on the
side of caution and thus decided to make allowance
for mere probabilities. None the less, even this
measure of caution warns that the balance of
probability in this case may be positive or negative
and one could choose to err on one side or the
other. The Colonel in this case is too positive. He
has chosen to be extremely optimistic and is thus
euphoric on mere possibilities: Europe 'could
recycle, salvage or stockpile, etc.' His argument
ignores Karl Popper's dictum that it is impossible
to calculate effects beforehand. The unintended and
unforeseen often follow. As a result, the
prophylactics which the Colonel offers so
enthusiastically may turn out to be insufficient or
inappropriate on occurrence of the event.

There are other difficulties associated with the Colonel's 'instant' remedies. Europe may wish to emulate the US (as the Colonel proposes) by devising substitutes and increasing local production, but it is not certain that it can do it as creditably for two reasons. First, the character of politics and the nature of political elites differ significantly in kind if not in form. European leaders like their US counterparts are most often liberal-democrats, yet they are more pragmatic and rarely adhere to cold war images with the same intensity. Thus the penchant for political crusades is less ardent in Europe. Even if it were not, the mineral resources of Western Europe are not as great or diverse as those of the US, and the technology, though similar, is hardly of the same sophistication.

In any case, the dispensability thesis is disputed even among European scholars. Arthur Gavshon maintains, for instance, that 'without access to Africa's uranium there would have been no credible <u>force de frappe</u>,[11] the French independent nuclear deterrent. It is even more interesting to compare Colonel Alford's position with that of Robert M. Price, a prominent American Africanist.[12] Price contends that the four most significant minerals which southern Africa supplies to the West (chrome, vanadium, antimony and the platinum group metals) have four main attributes: they are essential in a core industrial activity; they are found in insufficient quantity or not at all in the industrial countries; there are no known feasible substitutes for them, and the major reserves outside southern Africa are to be found in the USSR, except for antimony, which exists in substantial quantities in China. In consequence, if the US and its allies were to be cut off from access to southern African minerals, the only alternative source for the West would be the two communist powers.

The situation, he notes, poses a two-fold strategic risk.[13] The first is an obvious one: that a traditional rival would be in a position to withhold vital resources to achieve political ends. The second, less obvious but perhaps more important, has to do with the structure of the communist economies. Since both Soviet and Chinese economies are not export-oriented economies, government investment policies cannot be relied upon to expand production of the minerals in question to keep up with demand (the assumption here being that the political will to do so would exist - a remote possibility). As such, there is a real danger of insufficient productive capacity to meet external demands, should the Western industrial world become solely reliant on the Soviet Union or China for supplies. This need not be the function of malevolent political design, but a mere function of the internal logic of the political economies of the two communist states. This realisation underlines two propositions. First is that the national interest of the US and west European countries emphasises the necessity for continued importation of material essential for the production of specialised steel from sources other than two communists. Second is that there is thus essential complementarity between the ingredients of modern industrial production and the mineral resources of southern Africa. It would, therefore, seem that, if there are circumstances in which these mineral endowments may be denied, there is a real possibility that the West would be 'on its knees'.

Colonel Alford's retort would probably be that Africans are too weak to do anything in any case. This assessment is valid on the surface. The continent is one of the poorest in the world. Most of the countries within it are dependent on primary products and, unlike the communist economies, theirs are export-oriented. 'Throughout the region, balance of payment crises, rising debts and increasing food imports have led to continual decline'.[14] Public debts rose from $5 billion in 1970 to over $65 billion in 1982, while the gap between export receipts and import expenditure had risen from $1.8 billion to $10.7 billion between 1973 and 1980.[15] Simultaneously, the population growth rate, which had been about 2.1 per cent per year since the 1950s, rose to 2.7 per cent in the 1970s and is expected to reach 3 per cent in the 1990s.[16] Moreover, according to a World Bank Development Report, 'there is now a real possibility that the per capital income' for low income countries in the area, 'would be lower by the end of the 1980s than in the 1960s'.[17] Certainly this does not augur well for muscle-flexing or bids for self-assertion on the part of Africans. The Colonel's optimism on this score would thus seem warranted.

This impression must be mitigated on two grounds. First is that the mineral basket in this case is southern African, and particularly South African, and the condition of states in that belt is not exactly the same as the continental average. South Africa, the bastion of white-minority rule,

has for example developed a siege economy with the
benevolence of the West. Thus, should any regime in
power there decide to lend succour to associated
states in an enterprise to strangle the West, its
ability to withstand stress would be much higher.
Political differences within the sub-region make
this possibility unlikely, but desperation to force
overt Western support in the face of biting
guerrilla attacks, aided by the Soviet Union and the
East, may entice white South Africa to do this
alone. Similarly, a black majority victory in the
face of covert Western support for apartheid and
Moscow's aid to insurgents could make the previous
scenario an open possibility, since it would give
the Soviet Union a pervasive belt of socialist
states willing perhaps to act in concert with the
former's will to deny or increase the cost of
Western access to their resources. These are tenuous
political scenarios (some would consider them far-
fetched), but they serve to demonstrate that, given
the volatile political circumstances of the mineral
basket of South Africa, the West may find itself
against options unrestrained by Africa's catalogue
of economic and political weaknesses. In retrospect,
optimism about Africa's ability to play the mineral
card may be ill-conceived.

In the long run (which the Colonel was careful
to exclude), his proposition would amount to
inclinations of autarchy. Ironically, his
proposition may be sound in this respect. Europe
could do without Africa at some cost to European
living standards, but then so could Africa do
without Europe. The continent existed long before
the Europeans became aware of it. Prior to that, it
was content to interact with other parts of the then
known world. Thus, if one pushes the criteria
further, then it is true to conclude that every
continent can exist without another. This
perspective may seem facile. Yet there is a
substantial group of African scholars which contends
that following the Chinese example of closing
borders and living within one's resources is the
ideal solution for Africa, since it is the only way
that it can evolve towards auto-centred development
and escape from the clutches of an international
capitalist order, where it remains perpetually in
peripheral status to cater for the European centre.
There is a great deal of sense in this position.
However, it is not easily conceivable, because Europe
and Africa have inter-penetrated each other so
deeply that the withdrawal pains involved in such an

enterprise would hurt seriously. The dispensability thesis minimises this cost, and yet it is the seriousness of it that underlines the strategic character of Euro-African relationships. The threat of separation is fatal in mental conception as in physical substance, and this notion of mental mortality is reinforced by post-colonial presence, as exemplified by the case of France, and the demands of the East-West ideological rivalry.

D. POST-COLONIAL PRESENCE

Nothing illustrates the strength of colonial links so much as the Portuguese experience in Africa. Long after the wave of African independence, Portugal clung on to her African colonies. There was a feeling that the metropole would be impoverished without them. Africans in these territories were thus offered only one option – to become 'assimilados' of the Portuguese culture and thus qualify to be full Portuguese citizens. The rejection of this proposition and the ethnocentric presumptions that underlined it resulted in arduous wars of national liberation. In fighting that war Portugal had the support of her Nato allies, but it was an expensive war and one she could not win. The burden of war impacted heavily on Portugal until the 'group of captains' led the Armed Forces Movement to overthrow Caetano's dictatorship on 25 April 1974 and subsequently dismantled the Lusitanian empire. The aftermath was independence for the African territories of Mozambique, Angola and Guinea Bissau, which saw the emplacement of Marxist-inclined regimes. Since the Eastern countries were the main supporters of the guerrillas in their difficult days, Portugal's influence in the post-colonial situation was reduced considerably. However, the extent to which she had gone to ensure that the colonies remained part of Portugal demonstrated the value that the Portuguese placed on their African territories.

Britain was wiser. She prepared her colonies for independence but managed to ensure that the preparatory process emplaced pro-British, liberal-democratic leaders who soon became part of the 'neo-colonial' arrangement of the Commonwealth. For several years after independence Britain remained the main trading partner, political overseer and principal investor in several of her colonies. She also signed bilateral defence pacts with some, in addition to a general Commonwealth understanding

which obligated her to come to the aid of such
territories in time of emergency. In addition
Sandhurst, Shrivenham, Mons, etc., served as
training grounds for the various armed forces which
relied mostly on British weapons and instructors.

Britain's relationship with her erstwhile
colonies was thus sustained in a new form, even if
it was not as institutionalised as the French. The
annual forums of the British Commonwealth served as
a platform for co-ordination and political
discussion to ease friction and enable the
consolidation of individual ties among the
leadership hierarchy. The good will that was
nourished upheld a framework of cultural, economic
and political linkages. Britain's influence in these
territories was recognised, if not always respected,
by external powers. The influence has waned over the
years, as anglophone territories broadened their
contacts with the outside world and became more
Afrocentric, while critical political differences
arose over the British attitude to de-colonisation
in Zimbabwe and the struggle aginst apartheid in
South Africa (see Chapter 4). Similarly, import-
export linkages were reduced by Britain's
integration into the EEC. Still, British influence
is being diluted not nullified. Her colonies remain
an obvious zone of influence: a position which helps
to nurture and support a global role for a declining
world power. The element of prestige is even more
crucial to France, which has contrived to obtain and
sustain a deeper and more significant relationship.

France has an organic relationship with her
former African territories. For her they represent a
significant sphere of influence, knotted together by
a complex of socio-economic and military ties. The
strength of this linkage is underlined by two
interrelated factors, namely close economic
relations and military co-operation agreements (see
also Chapter 9).

Within the economic sphere, the francophone
family is cemented together by the Franc zone,
French budgetary aids and the extent of trade
relations. Most francophone states are members of
the Franc zone. The CFA Franc guaranteed by France
is thus the currency of international transactions,
while foreign exchange earned by exports is kept by
the French treasury. This, along with credits
offered by France, gives the French metropole fiscal
and economic control over its former African
colonies. In consequence, French firms have almost
unlimited privileges. They could move capital freely

and repatriate all profits from their African investments, while the African countries have little power to ensure that such investments were correspondent with national purposes. The companies themselves are guarantors of French interests with regard to strategic minerals, and their activities have facilitated the exploitation of uranium in Niger, Gabon and Central African Republic to aid the expansion of the French energy programme and its nuclear capability. The companies may also be an arm of French foreign policy. Thus it has been asserted that French business groups are responsible for encouraging Gabon and the Ivory Coast to foster commercial ties with South Africa and for the South African penetration of the then Central African Empire through a $250 million loan to build its railway link with the sea in 1978.[18]

Aid is the second instrument of domination. France operates through two main bodies: the 'Fonds d'Aide et Coopération' (FAC) and 'Caisse Centrale de Coopération Economique' (CCCE). FAC is a state budgetary agency, while the CCCE is a public financing body on commercial lines. The latter offers credits to French firms for developmental projects, and its activities cover the whole of francophone Africa, concentrating particularly on the relatively rich territories of the Ivory Coast, Gabon and Cameroon, which also have close relations with France. Between 1974-77 the CCCE percentage of French aid value rose from 2 to 20 per cent.[19] In contrast, FAC is responsible for about 25 per cent of the budget of the Ministry of Co-operation which handles the affairs of France's African family.

The volume of the total aid package is enormous and it has risen from $660 million in 1982 to over $800 million in 1984.[20] A logical corollary of the aid package is the infusion of French technocrats into these territories. By 1977 there were about 4,000 French 'assistants techniques' in the Ivory Coast alone, and this is merely a reflection of the situation in key ministries of most francophone countries.[21] Consequently, the presence of Frenchmen in sensitive positions is a typical hallmark of francophone Africa. Beyond this the economic linkage is consummated by the extent of trade relations. France alone accounts for about 60 per cent of the external trade of these territories. Moreover, though their status of association with the EEC, through the Yaounde and ACP agreements of 1963 and 1969, and 1975 and 1980 respectively, have provided them with access to a bigger market, France is still the major purchaser of most of their products.

More significant is that France and the various territories are joined by a series of bilateral military accords. The agreements are of two varieties.[22] The first consists of defence treaties covering the whole gamut of military activity, including the use of French institutions for training military personnel, weapons' supply, the intervention of French troops to restore order and defend governments during crises, and a wide spectrum of military aid facilities. Such agreements, which have endured, include those signed with the Central African Republic and Gabon in 1960, Ivory Coast in 1961, Comoro Islands in 1973 and Senegal and Cameroon in 1974.

The second variety consists of military technical cooperation agreements, and the basic difference between this and the former is that it does not cover direct French military involvement. Agreements of this nature exist in respect of seventeen African countries including Burkina Faso, signed in 1961, Algeria (1967), Burundi (1969), Madagascar, Morocco and Tunisia (1973), Congo, Brazzaville, and Zaire (1974), Benin and Rwanda (1975), Chad and Mauritania (1976), Mali and Niger (1977), Libya (1978) and Mauritius and Seychelles (1979).[23]

However, the distinction between the two forms of agreements often exists only on the surface. France has had no qualms (in complicity with local regimes) to stretch even the second variety to include direct military activity. Thus Zaire and Chad, in which it was conspicuously involved in recent years, do not have defence treaties with her. Indeed, France has since 1964 developed a mobile interventionist force, on call at short notice in southern France to serve as reserve in case of emergency. This force, known as the 'Eleventh Airborne Division, complete with paratroop, marine, infantry and artillery brigades, had seaborne, amphibious and armed elements plus about 220 aircraft at its disposal. It also maintained a forward element on permanent alert in Senegal.'[24]

Along with this, France stages annual concerts in the guise of Franco-African summits, where her political designs for the continent are enumerated and reinforced or supported by the concurrence of her African protégés. 'Thus in the French scheme of things the economic structures ensure economic rewards for France, while the summits add the personal touch. The military presence then guarantees the perpetuation of friendly regimes and a continuation of that relationship.'[25] The visible consequence is that France has an active military disposition on the continent, as reflected in a policy of intervention. France has intervened at various times in Chad since 1968, Gabon (1964), Cameroon (1960 and 1961), Zaire (1977 and 1978), Niger (1963) to save regimes. Her paratrooop formations have also become memorable for their interventions in the 'coup' in the Central African Empire, which replaced Emperor Bokassa with his nephew, David Dacko (Operation Barracuda), in the Shaba crises of 1977 and 1978 to prop up Mobutu's regime (Operation Verveine) and in Chad in mid-1983 to check the advance of Libyan-backed Toubou guerrillas (see also Chapter 9). Understandably then, the French have acquired a reputation as the gendarmes of Africa, and the basic question is why they invest so much militarily in the continent. In this regard it is axiomatic that serious military involvement presumes strategic interest. Thus French military activity is a sore problem for the dispensability thesis: it has to be explained away.

One such explanation is that France is in these territories as part of its 'civilising mission'. This explanation does not in itself explain why it is considered necessary to sustain cultural influence with military investment. It also ignores the substantial benefits accruing to France via this enterprise and implies unconvincingly that the French mission is selfless. The issue could also be tackled from a comparative perspective. As such it could be argued that French military presence in and around Africa - 'exceeding 15,000 soldiers, sailors and airmen' is 'modest compared with Cuba's 35,000-strong force'.[26] As Gavshon points out, such surface comparison is misleading because it does not include the 'specialist <u>force d'intervention</u>' in southern France.[27] More importantly, it simply relates the question to the issue of East-West rivalry in Africa, which in any case is a strategic objective.

Colonel Alford's position is more clever. It assigns the value of French military activity to 'an equation of military involvement with access to material resource'[28] - in other words it is simply a function of a perceived need for resource security. He then proceeds to argue that this perception is misplaced (i) because it is impossible to demonstrate conclusively that a particular deployment has ensured that a particular resource continues to accrue to France; (ii) that a more powerful reason for these countries to trade with France is common sentiments derived from shared language, cultural and political ties and assured markets, and finally (iii) that in any case, the record of French military intervention is distinctly mixed.

> Chad is a demonstrable failure. The Polisario have effectively neutralised Mauritania, despite French military support. There are serious misgivings in France about the French role in the Central African Republic. Only in Zaire is it possible to argue that France (along with Belgium and the United States) did something useful in the short run, but if there is any permanence to the solution of the problem in Shaba it is more likely to be because Zaire and Angola have agreed not to de-stabilise each other than because of the intervention of 1978.[29]

The argument is interesting but problematic on two accounts. First, it is selective in its choice of examples and interpretation. France's record of intervention may be mixed, but not distinctly. There are examples galore. Alain Peyrefitte, the French Foreign Minister, listed several instances between 1960 and 1963 alone.[30] Since then there have been others; yet France's record of success has been clearly disturbed in only two places, i.e. Chad and Western Sahara, and these are places where certain external powers with military capability to oppose French designs, such as Algeria, Libya with the aid of the Soviet Union, are also directly involved. It is certainly no basis for France to consider its record of success, and she has shown no inclination so to do. The case of the Central African Republic (CAR) is even more interesting. It may be true, as the Colonel alleges, that it is causing misgivings in certain quarters in France, but one wonders to what extent it has done so in official circles.

The fact of the matter is that 1,000 French troops flew into Banqui to overthrow the regime of Bokassa and transfer power to David Dacko.[31] Since this was naked imperialism, they preferred to keep their part in the affair silent, but then Dacko in his press utterances contradicted Paris' portrayal of events by disclosing that he had flown in with the French takeover contingent. This embarrassed the Elysée, whose officials had tried to obscure French participation in formal explanations to the National

Assembly. The incident did not, however, motivate the French to relax their grip on the country. Indeed, the CAR episode on reflection was a remarkable success. It impressed upon African clients the element of the protective military cover by France and thus gave them a sustained basis for accepting their dependence on France and the latter's continued access to their resources. By implication, the CAR episode also stressed the dangers of risking France's displeasure. In this way, it reinforced 'the equation between deployment of military power and continued access to military resources' which the Colonel was seeking to downgrade.

More significantly, the 'extractive' material focus of the Colonel's thesis in this regard ignores the position of the Third World and Africa in particular in France's global policy. As one analyst has pointed out, France's African role is, in part, a bid to escape Anglo-Saxon domination in Western Europe. 'France in this sense seeks to consolidate its "national" sphere of interest in order to compensate for unaccustomed mediocrity and obsolescence in Europe.[32] The humiliations suffered at the hands of Germany during the Second World War, followed by a post-war context 'organised around two dominant centres of power, France could not achieve hegemony in Europe, much less the world.'[33] The French recognised that in this bipolar context only the US could guarantee West European security in the conflict with the Soviet Union. They could not challenge this, so they sought some measure of accommodation from the US.

However, de Gaulle's attempt to impress upon the United States the need for France to be a power failed woefully. The United States had a special relationship with Britain, which relegated France to a second fiddle and this was easily evident in the sphere of nuclear collaboration. In response, de Gaulle tried, and failed, to get the US to accept France along with Britain as a member of a three-power directorate to coordinate and develop Western strategy. Failure also attended similar efforts to constitute the primary states of Western Europe into a Third Force under French leadership to arbitrate between the Soviet and Anglo-American camps. The consequence was that France struck out for a role in the Third World to give itself a world role and validate its spiritual conception of itself. Africa provided the most suitable outlet for this energetic drive. Thus, to paraphrase Stanley

Hoffman, 'France is in Africa in "Search of France"'. This explains the position of the noted African scholar, Ali Amin Mazrui, that French civilisation has become primarily bi-continental.[34] 'French global pretensions are now reduced to relations between Paris and her former colonies. France would defend those residual global pretensions to the last franc but one.'[35]

Along with this, France's hold on Africa serves NATO's strategic interest. France uses established colonial links, post-colonial agreements and knowledge and experience of Africans to pursue Western interests without inviting local opposition. In this way France, an erstwhile metropolitan power, serves as a 'medium through which Africa has become cemented culturally to the Western security system'.[36] It is thus 'a significant factor in depoliticising Pan-Africanism among French-speaking Africans' in contrast to 'their English-speaking counterparts'.[37] The overall effect, maintains Bassey Ate, is that France, through the unique character of its presence in Africa, legitimises NATO involvement in the continent. The record, he adds, shows that particularly since the beginning of the seventies neither the USA nor Britain could intervene militarily in Africa without provoking an avalanche of reaction among Africans or risking counteraction by the Soviet Union.

> France on the other hand could despatch troops to Gabon, Mauritania, Chad or Central African Republic under the cover of some bilateral security agreement or on the pretext of legitimate invitation. Whereas the real purpose was one of insuring the survival of a Western-protected regime against radical insurgent forces or the need to protect continued Western access to some strategic real estate - witness the retention of 4,500 French troops in Djibouti since independence in 1977, and interventions in Shaba.[38]

Francophone African complicity inevitably mitigates the scale of African protests that accompanies such enterprises, reducing them to barely 'a murmur', while from the viewpoint of East-West global rivalry 'the French conduct with its aura of normality is less likely to be regarded in Moscow as de-stabilising than if the United States itself had undertaken direct involvement, as was the case in Angola in 1975.'[39] The consequence is that one can hardly escape the conclusion that French military policy in Africa serves the strategic purposes of the West in its global confrontation with the Soviet Union and her Eastern allies.

E.   EAST-WEST RIVALRY AND AFRICA'S PLACE IN THE NEW COLD WAR

The importance of Africa in the context of East-West rivalry is well documented.[40] Yet it is significant to stress that Western leaders have themselves acknowledged this reality. Thus, for example, Lyndon Johnson, the former US President, remarked that the continent was perhaps the 'greatest field of manoeuvre in the world-wide competition between the Communist and non-Communist bloc'.[41] The claim is perhaps an overstatement, but the regard is evident. It implies, in any case, that, if Africa is undervalued, it is not a function of its intrinsic worth. Rather it is because, for a long time, it has remained a Western sphere of influence and the West could take it for granted.

Part of the reason for this is that the Soviet Union was historically disadvantaged in the competition for African loyalty. The fault initially was its own. Stalin's two-camp image had no place for the newly independent states. Its leaders were regarded as Western lackeys. Khruschev altered this with his radical conception of alliance with the leaders of the new countries in a broad anti-imperialist front. He was perceptive enough to recognise that Russia, because it was not tainted by the colonialist brush, could secure certain advantages. Simultaneously, he came up against Soviet disadvantages. Largely because it was never a colonial power, Russia had no previous connections to build upon. Its adversary, the US, could use those of its Western allies. Similarly, the long period of association with the West had imbued several generations of African leaders with values and norms antithetical to Marxist ideology. Hence the creed did not find much root.

When Russia penetrated Africa, it was largely as a consequence of Western blunders and misjudgements, as in Nasser's Egypt and the Nigerian civil war. Even then, the Soviets stumbled partly by mischance and partly because they did not really understand Africa. Pro-Soviet leaders like Nkrumah in Ghana, Ben Bella in Algeria, and Modibo Keita of Mali, were overthrown. Others, like Sadat in Egypt,

Nimeiry in Sudan and Siad Barre in Somalia, were impelled towards an anti-Soviet line by exigencies of conflict and personal predilections, Sekou Toure's Guinea, the outcast of the francophone family, sought rapprochement with France, perhaps because of cultural obligations and to reduce dependence on Moscow. Liberation and nationalist movements helped by Moscow to leadership of new states soon discovered that, while the Soviet Union could offer arms, it had yet to prove its mettle as a mentor in socio-economic development. The Soviet Union was a late comer to the industrial revolution and thus could not provide consumer items, such as electronics, vehicles or luxury items which Africans desire. Inevitably some of its ardent friends still turn to the West.

Yet the Soviets have managed, or are grappling successfully, with these disadvantages. The time factor has improved their experience of Africa. They are learning well. Time has also impressed on African leaders the dangers of absolute dependence on the West. The policy of non-alignment, which most Third World countries profess fidelity to, has forced diversification of contacts, and Moscow and its Eastern allies are the beneficiaries. Moscow has also made rapid advances in recent years, which would in time over-compensate for her losses. In the aftermath of the Portuguese revolution she has gained a belt of friendly socialist states in Mozambique, Angola and Guinea Bissau, extending her political influence and physical presence from the Mediterranean littoral southwards to subcontinental Africa. This adds a serious dimension to her transformation from a continental to a global power, particularly if it is related to her other acquisitions in the continent. Moscow's new position of primary influence in regard to Ethiopia allows her serious influence in regard to the Red Sea, and this is in addition to naval and aerial staging facilities which she has acquired in Guinea Bissau, Equatorial Guinea and the offshore islands of Sao Tome and Principe. She also has some leverage with Algeria and Libya to which she supplies arms, and Benin, which acclaims itself as Marxist. Along with this are shipping and fishery accords with Mauritania and Sierra Leone.

Indeed, Moscow's biggest asset is the conflict in South Africa and in particular the related factor, the elimination of the white minority regime there, which is the prime interest of Africans. The US and its Western allies are entangled with the 'racist' government by enormous economic investments and associated 'kith and kin' fellowship. Moscow is on the right side of the conflict in support of black liberation movements. The overall result is that subsequent black victory with her help could secure a consolidated belt of socialist states from the Indian Ocean and the Atlantic and thus Moscow could deny the West access to what this chapter has already established as vital strategic minerals. Indeed, the process of the conflict itself could give Moscow primacy. A notable instance in this regard is the issue of South African nuclear capability. African states are too weak technically and financially at present to build a counter-force. In the circumstances, Moscow's nuclear umbrella could look very attractive, when and if circumstances demand it, to break the threat of South African nuclear blackmail.

The situation should inform a reconsideration of Western strategy. The new 'cold war' initiated by the Reagan administration in response to debacles in Angola and Iran have placed criticial emphasis on the decline of American power. Bases and staging posts are sought in Africa mainly as support facilities to the Rapid Deployment Force, in view of the proximity of certain parts of Africa to the Gulf area, which America desires to police to assure vital oil supplies. The focus is restricted and may be misplaced. If the US and its Western allies refuse to align their interests with African priorities, they may find themselves in a situation in which Moscow achieves continental primacy because it has studied and understood the Africa that the West has learnt to take for granted.

F. CONCLUSION

In conclusion, the basic problem of the dispensability thesis is that it is counter-factual. As such it can be as easily sustained as disproved. All that needs to be done is to adduce evidence on the side of one probability or the other. This chapter and that thesis have taken different directions. However, it must be affirmed that the postulate here would seem to be a better one. The dispensability thesis is erected solely on the foundation of probabilities, and it seeks to mitigate fundamental or existing realities. This leads it to underestimate the character of Euro-African relationship, which is one of strategic interdependence. Similarly, it makes artificial distinctions. Colonel Alford sums up, for instance, by stressing that Europe's interest in Africa is primarily economic or commercial, forgetting that military investment is normally to secure economic needs. The strategic and commercial or economic is thus not easily separated, as the case of France amply demonstrates. That example also reaffirms the strength of interlocking factors between Africa and Western Europe, especially their strategic interdependence. It would be a tragic error to undervalue this aspect after it has been entrenched by a century of close relationship after the partition in Berlin in 1885.

NOTES

1   ECA and Africa's Development 1983-2008: A Preliminary Perspective Study, 1983.
2   New African, (London, August 1977), cited in Alan P. Morris, 'Africa: A New Reality for Japan', paper submitted to the International Studies Association, 25th Anniversary Convention, 27-31 May 1984, p.3.
3   'South Africa: Time Running Out', The Report of the Study Commission on US Policy Towards Southern Africa (California, Los Angeles, 1980).
4   South (London, October 1983), pp.73-4.
5   Colonel Jonathan Alford, 'The Strategic Relationship' in Margaret Cornell (ed.), Europe and Africa: Issues in Post-Colonial Relations (London, Overseas Development Institute [ODI]), p.44.
6   Ibid.
7   Ibid.
8   Ibid., p.45.
9   Ibid.
10   Ibid., p.59.
11   Arthur Gavshon, Crisis in Africa: Battleground of East and West (Middlesex, Penguin Books, 1981), p.177.
12   Gwendolen M. Carter and Patrick O. Meara, International Politics in Southern Africa (Bloomington: Indiana University Press, 1982), p.61 ff.
13   Ibid.
14   Jennifer Seymour Whittaker, 'Africa Beset', Foreign Affairs, vol.62, no.3, 1983, p.748. See also Carol Lancaster, 'Africa's Economic Crisis', Foreign Policy (Fall, 1983).
15   Whittaker, 'Africa Beset'.
16   Ibid., p.749.
17   Ibid.

[18] Cedetim, L'Impérialisme Francais (Paris, Francois Maspero, 1978), p.127, translated by Oluseye Davis (University of Ibadan Postgraduate Seminar Series, 1985).

[19] Ibid., pp.127-8.

[20] Concord Weekly (Lagos, 6 June 1985), p.19.

[21] West Africa, 8 August 1977, p.1632.

[22] Concord Weekly, op. cit.

[23] Ibid.

[24] Gavshon, op. cit., p.175.

[25] Concord Weekly, op. cit.

[26] Gavshon, Crisis in Africa, p.175.

[27] Ibid.

[28] Colonel Alford, 'The Strategic Relationship', p.47.

[29] Ibid.

[30] See Waldemar A. Nielson, The Great Powers and Africa (London, The Pall Mall Press, 1969), pp.118-19.

[31] Details of the CAR episode are abstracted from Gavshon, Crisis in Africa, pp.168-9. Its credibility is backed by various other sources.

[32] Bassey Eyo Ata, 'The Presence of France in West Central Africa as a Fundamental Problem to Nigeria', Millenium: Journal of International Studies, vol.12, no. 2, (LSE, Summer 1978), p.115.

[33] Ibid.

[34] Extracts from Ali A. Mazrui, 'Nigeria in the Nuclear Age', NIIA - Lectures, 1980.

[35] Ibid.

[36] Bassey Ate, op. cit., p.116.

[37] Ibid.

[38] Ibid.

[39] Ibid.

[40] See Gavshon, Crisis in Africa.

[41] 'Africa: Guidelines for US Policy Operations, 1963', Washington Notes on Africa, Summer 1978, p.2.

CHAPTER 9

THE OAU'S RESPONSES TO EUROPEAN MILITARY
INTERVENTIONS IN AFRICA

Amadu Sesay

A.   INTRODUCTION

That externally-sponsored military intervention in
Africa - whether by European or non-European
states - contravenes one of the cardinal objectives
of the OAU is never in doubt. The aim of this
chapter, then, is to examine critically the OAU's
attempts over the last two decades or so at blunting
European military incursions in the continent. We
do recognise, of course, that European powers are
not the only intervenees in Africa. However, the
focus of the chapter is limited by the perspective
of the book, which is concerned with Afro-European
relations since the Berlin Conference in 1884. In
that respect the Soviet Union is included in our
study, not because it was present at Berlin in
1884 - America was also present - but because it is
a European power.
     Intervention[1] itself, especially military
intervention in African states, is an important
subject in contemporary international relations for
a variety of potent reasons. First, it would shed
light on the continent's political evolution.
Secondly, it would provide a litmus test for some of
the neo-functionalist theses which, among other
things, hold that regional international
organisations like the OAU are better equipped to
tackle regional problems. Thirdly, intervention
poses serious threats not only to the security and
territorial integrity of African states, but also
for the continent generally and the international
system at large. This point is rather salient and
relates directly to the other reason why
intervention is an important issue today in Africa.
This is that it violates both the rhetorical
commitments of the non-African powers to observe

152

Africa's neutrality, which would enable it to cope with the immense task of economic development and nation-building, as well as the principle of 'try the OAU first', which is enshrined in the OAU Charter.

Finally, intervention violates the Charter of the UN. Besides, it is against the tenets of the non-aligned movement, to which all the independent African countries subscribe - except South Africa. The phenomenon of European military intervention in Africa is therefore worth studying.

Intervention in the domestic affairs of one state by another state in whatever form is not a new development in international politics.[2] There are numerous historical examples whereby states have interfered in the internal affairs of others to effect favourable economic, political, socio-cultural and, indeed, strategic changes. As Barnett has rightly observed, 'there is nothing exceptional about powerful countries asserting their imperial prerogative of using force and coercion on the territory of another without its consent'.[3] But Barnett's position is simply echoing the famous saying of the Anthenian Empire that the 'strong do what they can and the weak do what they must'.[4] This maxim is as true today as it was true at the time of the Anthenian Empire.

In contemporary international politics, the small developing states of the Third World are helpless in the face of the preponderant economic and military might of the great powers of the East and West, whenever they are bent on interfering in their domestic affairs to effect changes in their (intervenees') favour. A number of examples can be cited in support of the contention that intervention has been a popular instrument of foreign policy in the international system for a long time. In the 18th and 19th centuries, the European powers intervened militarily in the domestic affairs of African states and kingdoms to overthrow 'legitimate authorities' in those states and replace them with pliant leaders. This development, which eventually led to the partition of the continent and European colonialism, has been ably discussed in Chapters 1 and 2. In Asia, the British and Americans intervened in China during the Opium Wars to effect changes in leadership in that country which would be favourable to them. And in Europe, the Europeans and Americans intervened in Russia in 1917 on the side of counter-revolutionary forces, the 'White Russians' in order to overthrow the newly-ceated socialist regime in

that country, led by V. I. Lenin. And in more recent
times America intervened in the Dominican Republic,
Cuba and Guatemala in the 1960s, Iran in the late
1950s and Grenada in 1983. The Russians intervened
in Hungary in 1956, Czechoslovakia in 1968 and
finally in Afghanistan in 1979.

Africa has not been spared either. First was
the Franco-British intervention in Suez in 1956.
Then in 1960 America and Belgium sent their troops
into the Congo, now Zaire, ostensibly to rescue
their nationals resident in that country. In 1964
France intervened in Gabon to restore to power
President Mba, who had earlier been overthrown in a
coup d'état by his soldiers. The early 1970s and
1980s also witnessed numerous cases of external
intervention in Africa. First was the Portuguese-
led invasion in Sekou Toure's Guinea, in November
1970. In 1975, the Soviet Union and Cuba intervened
in Angola on the side of the MPLA, which was
fighting a civil war with rival liberation movements
who were backed by China and the US.

A number of significant points emerge almost
immediately from the above examples. First, as far
as Africa is concerned the modes of intervention by
the great powers have scarcely changed much from
what they were in the 18th and 19th centuries (see
Chapters 1 and 2). Secondly, the motives for
intervention have remained almost the same over the
centuries. Behind every act of intervention are
economic, political and strategic considerations
from the perspective of the intervenee. US
intervention in a Third World country, for instance,
could be provoked if 'a constitutionally elected
regime demonstrated sympathy for communist ideology
or dependence on communist governments or had taken
or threatened some action inimical to US business
interests in the country'.[5] Thus, it could be argued
that one of the major reasons why the US intervened
in Grenada in 1983 was because the government of
Maurice Bishop was perceived as communist and
dependent upon the Soviet Union and Cuba, a
development which threatened American interests in
the Caribbean. The socialist policies of the Bishop
government were enough to 'convince the State
Department that the government in question is
"subversive" and that it is fair game for "counter
subversive" operations from our side'.[6]

In Africa, external military intervention has
been motivated by neo-colonial economic and
political interests. There is no doubt that the
major reasons behind the numerous rescue operations

mounted by European states and the US to prop
Mobutu's government in Zaire are neo-colonial. As
ably argued in Chapter 8, African countries,
particularly Zaire, are very rich in strategic
mineral resources. It 'may be that the struggle for
African resources is only just beginning. Cobalt and
platinum are rare minerals, along with uranium,
diamonds, gold, iron and copper, they are vital to
the industrial world.'[7] Zaire possesses many of
these rare and vital resources. It would therefore
be in the interest of the capitalist West to ensure
easy and cheap access to them. This would only be
assured if a pliant and puppet leader is installed
in that country.

The third point that emerges from the pattern
of intervention in the world generally is that it
has now become an accepted form of inter-state
relations, an instrument of foreign policy. To that
extent, it has not only become a permanent feature
of 20th century international relations, it is also
notable that its range has increased, as has the
variety of the methods used. Today, states make less
and less use of crude military force in their
relations. Instead, various other means are now
available for influencing the behaviour of other
states, unlike the situation in the 19th century.
Force remains a major option to be utilised by
states and it is in fact being used by them. None
the less, it is being increasingly put under control
through the UN system, international law and so
forth. But, as the various interventions cited in
this chapter show, the great powers can use force to
bring about favourable changes in other states
whenever they perceive that their vital economic or
political interests are in jeopardy.

There are important reasons why intervention
has become such a popular mode of inter-state
relations in the contemporary international system,
and particularly with reference to Africa and the
Third World. These reasons could be divided into two
broad categories: (i) factors external to the
African states, and (ii) those that are internal. We
shall examine each of these factors in some detail
below.

B.   EXTERNAL FACTORS

The post-1945 era has witnessed the globalisation of
the international system. Many small, weak and
barely viable states, especially in Africa, have
since 1945 emerged into statehood and have taken

their 'rightful' places amongst others in the most representative global organisation, the UN. In the UN, sovereign African 'mice' are regarded as equal with sovereign 'elephants', like the United States and the Soviet Union. Unfortunately, however, such theoretical parity is a far cry from the real world situation in which these states live. Thus, most of them, if not all, are heavily dependent in various ways - economic, political strategic, technical and financial, to name a few - either directly on their erstwhile colonial metropoles and their friends or on the Eastern bloc of states and China. This situation makes it easier for foreign powers to interfere in the affairs of African states, either unilaterally or at the request of the African countries themselves.

A second factor is the emergence of two dominant economic, political and ideological centres represented by the US and the USSR, both of which are also superpowers with world-wide political, economic and ideological interests. Besides, each superpower represents one of the rival universal ideologies, liberal democracy in the case of the US and socialism/communism in the case of the USSR. This has made it possible for the two states and/or their friends to intervene in third parties either for ideological or economic/strategic reasons. We have already pointed out cases of intervention involving the protection of one or all of these interests.

Third, is the unprecedented availability of weapons of mass destruction in the hands of the superpowers and other great powers - nuclear weapons. The advent of such lethal weapons of war has made war, especially one between the two dominant powers, 'unthinkable'. Thus, other means have to be devised in order to achieve their national interest objectives, especially in areas which they consider as strategic, i.e. Angola or Zaire. Consequently, they have perfected other means of influencing states in the international system short of using force, whenever possible. All this has made intervention, either directly or by proxy, a popular instrument of great power foreign policy.

Fourth, is the nature of the international system itself - highly decentralised and made up principally of sovereign independent states. Every one of them is expected under normal circumstances to be his own keeper. And, in striving to look after their national interests, states try to accumulate power with which they hope to advance such interests vis-a-vis those of others in the system. As states sometimes pursue conflicting interests, they occasionally use force to influence the behaviour of others. The various cases of intervention cited in this chapter clearly illustrate this phenomenon in contemporary international politics.

C.   DOMESTIC FACTORS

As noted earlier, Third World countries present an especially tempting target for great power military intervention. Because they are economically weak and politically unstable, African states have been particularly vulnerable to external military action. Africa is strategically the weakest of all the continents. Apart from that, most African countries have weak political economies, being heavily dependent on either the capitalist West or the socialist East for markets for their raw materials and for their import needs. Intra-African trade is negligible, less than 3 per cent of their total world trade.[8] This situation has left African countries very much at the mercy of their trading partners in two ways. First, they have no control over the price they receive for their raw materials and secondly they do not have control over the price of the finished goods that they import. The only instance of a very effective cartel of raw resource producers is OPEC. However, since the early 1980s, OPEC has not been able effectively to dictate the price of oil.

Dependence, whether economic or political, is however not without strings: increasing incorporation into the dominant political or economic system. More important is the propensity for the dominant partner, especially the countries of the West, to interfere in the domestic affairs of African countries to protect their economic or political interests which dependence breeds. This is because, after enticing an African government or leader to pursue dependent political and economic policies, which would guarantee their control over the African states, the capitalist West would be reluctant to see African states diversify their links and/or embark upon self-reliant economic policies. Leaders who dared to diversify their international linkages or pursued inward-looking policies have had to pay the price, either with their lives or their political power, i.e. Nkrumah, Lumumba, Obote, to name a few of them. On the other hand, France did not hesitate to engineer the replacement of Emperor Bokassa, of the former Central African Empire, who had become a personal embarrassment to the French President, Giscard d'Estaing, with a pliant David Dacko in 1980.

A second domestic factor concerns the African political environment. This is very dynamic and is characterised by rapid leadership turnovers, as well as political instability. In Africa, there is as yet to emerge a set of well-established rules of political succession. Thus, every so often, we witness succession conflicts within governments and between governments and opposition elements.[9] The resultant power tussle/political vacuum provides an ideal setting for great power intervention. This could come about in a variety of ways. First, an incumbent African leader may call upon his external friends for assistance, either by invoking a treaty commitment or simply asking the state concerned to come to his rescue, i.e. as Mobutu did in 1977 and 1978 during the two Shaba crises. Secondly, opposition elements could call upon their external backers to help them overthrow the incumbent government. This is normally done through the coup d'état. For instance, Ghana in 1966 and Liberia in 1980, and since 1976 Joanis Savimbi has called upon the US and other Western countries to come to his aid in his war against the MPLA government in Luanda.

Thirdly, intervention could be triggered by domestic strife in an African country. This could either lead to guerrilla warfare, as in Ethiopia and Uganda, or to open civil war, as was the case in Sudan for many years and in Nigeria for thirty months. Such wars have invited intervention, not only from European powers but also from the United States and China. Closely related to such conflicts are frontier disputes (see Chapter 3). The most popular case has been the long-standing territorial irredentist claims of Somalia against Ethiopia and Kenya. This claim led to open war between Somalia and Ethiopia in 1978, in which the Soviet Union intervened openly, first on the side of Somalia and later on the Ethiopian side, which eventually defeated the Somalis.

A fourth domestic explanation for external intervention is the existence of military defence pacts or military cooperation agreements between African countries and extra-continental powers, especially with the erstwhile colonial powers in Europe. However, and as Mulira pointed out in his chapter, African countries have also entered into defence agreements or military cooperation treaties with the Soviet Union. And, as Adisa and Agbaje have pointed out in their chapters, some of these defence agreements - especially those between France and some of her former colonies - have been in existence for decades. What is important from our point of view is that these agreements have been invoked several times by African countries to get military support abroad. Besides, they have also been used by foreign powers as the raison d'être for stationing their troops in African countries. African leaders have argued that, in the absence of a Pan-African military force, defence agreements with external powers are an insurance policy against domestic and external threats to the integrity of their persons and their regimes. This argument is however shallow. Such neo-colonial defence arrangements, as Nkrumah pointed out over two decades ago, enable the 'metropolitan powers ... to support their neo-colonialist controls by direct military involvement in the internal affairs of African countries'.[10] This is the most crucial point, which is often lost on those African leaders who embark upon such pacts with former colonial masters.

Before we end this discussion, we should point out that there have been cases of external military intervention that are not covered by the factors we have identified above. The most important case was the abortive invasion of Guinea by Portugal in 1970. Sekou Toure, then President of Guinea, was not only an outspoken anti-colonialist but was also a Pan-Africanist, who offered his country's territory for use as rear bases by the liberation movement in Guinea Bissau (PIAGC), which was then fighting Portuguese colonialist forces. One of the objectives of the invasion, then, was to topple the 'progressive' government of Toure and to replace it with one which would be pliant to Lisbon. Understandably, also, such a regime would not have assisted the guerrillas of Amilca Cabral in his liberation war.

D. TYPES OF INTERVENTION

European powers have adopted various modes of intervention in Africa. First we have what we can call direct military intervention, using the troops of a European country either at the invitation of an African state or unilaterally. Such direct military incursions could also be carried out in the form of coup d'état or 'rescue' missions. But intervention could also be indirect, using proxies, i.e. the secret services of European powers or African opposition elements based inside or outside their state. Again, this type of intervention could also take the shape of a coup. The coup in the former Central African Empire, that in Ghana against Nkrumah and that in Liberia against President William Tolbert are just a few examples of such interventions.

Finally, intervention could be carried out by the citizens of European countries acting in their private capacities. These are the mercenaries. The activities of mercenaries should not however be totally divorced from their governments. This is because, apart from the love of money and adventure, mercenaries come to Africa because they sometimes believe that their actions are furthering a cause which would enhance their countries' national interests in the continent. Examples of such interventions are numerous: the Congo, now Zaire; Nigeria/Biafra war; Angola; the Republic of Benin, and most recently the Seychelles, 1981.[11]

E.   OAU'S RESPONSES

All international organisations, be they universal or regional, political, economic or military, are set up by states to achieve their collective as well as their individual national interests. Thus their constitutions or charters normally spell out how these interests are to be achieved and/or protected in the international system. In the case of the OAU, the relevant sections of the charter for our purpose are contained in Articles II and III. Under Article II(a), member states pledged to 'defend their sovereignty, their territorial integrity and independence'. This was to be done through the harmonisation of their policies, especially in the following areas: (i) political and diplomatic cooperation, (ii) cooperation for defence and security. A Defence Commission was consequently set up to achieve this objective.

Article III(ii) and (iii) also deals with a security-related objective. Among other things, it legislated against interference in the internal affairs of other members and urged each of them to respect the sovereignty and territorial integrity of the other, as well as its inalienable right to independent existence. The clauses did not

specifically mention interference in the affairs of
African states by non-African powers. It is
reasonable to suppose, however, that the framers of
the clauses had in mind not only member, but also
non-member, states, especially the ex-colonial
masters and the superpowers, the US and the USSR.
If the Charter was not specific, the second annual
summit, held in Accra, Ghana, in October 1965,
categorically urged members 'not to tolerate
subversive activity directed from outside Africa
against any member state'. They were also to 'oppose
collectively and firmly by any means at the disposal
of Africa every form of subversion conceived,
organised or financed by foreign powers against
Africa, the OAU, or against its members
individually'.[12] Thus the continental organisation
clearly has a policy which seeks to eliminate extra-
continental military interference from Africa. This
position is to be expected because, after all, the
coup in Togo in January 1963, a few months to the
founding summit in Addis, was already a good pointer
to what the newly-independent African states could
expect in the future.

The rest of the chapter is devoted to an
examination of the OAU's attempts to blunt external
military intervention in the continent. The main
objective is not to give a blow by blow account of
external interventions in Africa but rather to look
critically at those factors which have been
responsible for the Organisation's inability to
respond effectively to external military incursions
into the continent.

States and/or international organisations can
respond in any of three ways to a military
intervention situation: rhetorically, i.e. verbal
condemnation of the invasion; they could offer
material/financial support to the victim, or they
could offer direct military assistance. That is,
they could send troops to the victim of the
intervention to enable it to repel the invading
forces. However, the OAU's responses to external
military intervention in Africa, where it responded
at all, have by and large been limited to our first
category, that is they have been largely rhetorical.
To be sure, the Organisation has made offers of
material and financial, as well as military,
support. But, given the peculiar circumstances of
African states and their continental organisation,
as we shall see later, the last two categories of
response have been mainly symbolic gestures to the
victim. We should point out also that even the

collective diplomatic/rhetorical responses have not been unanimous, that is the Organisation has never been able to come out with one voice on the issue of intervention. This is to be expected. After all, the OAU is a conglomeration of a variety of interests, as well as alignments.

The OAU has identified three categories of intervention in the continent: (i) to promote legitimate African and OAU positions/objectives, such as the liberation of territories still under colonial and racist minority domination, (ii) intervention, whose sole objective is to promote neo-colonialist links/relationships between an external power and a particular African country, and finally (iii) intervention at the behest of a 'constituted' African authority, i.e. an African president or prime minister, as the case may be. What is very important for our purpose, however, is that the responses of African countries or for that matter the OAU as a collectivity, depend very much on the type of intervention we are dealing with on the one hand, and on the other the identity of both the victim and the intervenee.

These crucial points came out clearly in General Olusegun Obasanjo's speech to the 15th summit meeting in Khartoum, in July 1978. He told his colleagues that they had to be quite clear about what they:

> mean by external intervention in the context of contemporary political developments in Africa. Typical examples of the kind we have in mind ... are the criminal mercenary-led aggressions against the Republic of Guinea in 1970, and the externally-organised invasion of the Republic of Benin ... These are operations purposely mounted in order to protect foreign interests and to subvert the stability and sovereignty of specific African states.[13]

The Nigerian Head of State however made it clear that African leaders need to make a clear distinction between the above interventions and others:

> in the struggle for independence and freedom the only source of effective support was the Eastern bloc countries. The Soviets were therefore invited in Africa for a purpose and that purpose was to liberate the countries to which they were invited from centuries of

cruelty, degradation, oppression and exploitation. Unless we wish an undesirable situation to remain in Africa, we should not be overconcerned by the presence of those we invited to fight for specific causes and no more.[14]

What the Nigerian leader is saying in effect is that there are certain types of intervention which are quite acceptable to the OAU and to the majority of African countries because of the objectives such intervention hopes to achieve; and there are types of intervention which should not be tolerated in the continent because their objectives do not tally with those of the OAU. This is a very crucial point because it explains why the OAU can never adopt a uniform position on intervention. As an association of independent states, each of which has specific interests to cater for, members have not always adhered to the strict Pan-African ideal in arriving at judgements with regard to intervention. Their ideological colours or sympathies are sometimes allowed to influence the way they react to specific cases of intervention in the continent. Some examples would suffice here.

In July 1978, shortly before the Nigerian leader's speech at Khartoum, the Senegalese President, Leopold Senghor, admitted in an interview that he was 'disappointed in the West, which has behaved illogically by letting the Soviet-backed Cubans establish a foothold in Angola'. Soon, he said, the Cubans and the Soviets 'would be followed by East Germans' in that strategic part of the continent. He then concluded that 'the forces of communism are intent on waging an ideological struggle in Africa' to which the West should respond in kind, if not more.[15] In our second example, the Nigerian Permanent Representative to the UN, Leslie Harriman, supported the presence of Cuban troops in Angola, arguing that they 'never attacked a sovereign state or crossed forcibly internationally-recognised boundaries. On the contrary, what they have done is to assist oppressed peoples to regain their self-determination from their colonial masters.'[16] Finally, the Ivorian leader, Houphouet-Boigny, contended in an interview that the francophone countries, which were heavily criticised by anglophone countries for supporting the French idea of a Pan-African peace force which would be directed from Europe, should 'have no complexes at all about it, since the European

163

nations of NATO call on the United States in case of attack, and the Eastern European nations call on Russia'.[17] We shall in the following paragraphs examine critically the OAU's responses to three specific cases: (i) the Portuguese invasion of Guinea (1970), (ii) the Angola civil war (1975-76) and finally (iii) the two Shaba crises. We include the Shaba invasions, although the OAU did not respond directly to them, because they provided the backdrop against which the Khartoum summit was held.

The Portuguese invasion of Guinea was perhaps the boldest attempt by an external power to influence the behaviour of an African state. It was also the most dramatic demonstration of the danger to which African states were exposed from neo-colonial powers. The abortive invasion brought home to every African state the point that each of them could be the target of neo-colonial military adventures, as long as external powers saw any of them as an obstacle to the realisation of their national interests in Africa, be they economic, political or strategic. It was hardly surprising, then, that the episode drew bitter venom from the OAU and its members, at least at the rhetorical level.

At an emergency conference held in Lagos in December 1970 to consider the invasion, African states were united in their vilification of Portugal. The resolution at the end of the meeting '(i) vigorously condemns the treacherous aggression committed by Portugal against the Republic of Guinea ...', and 'all mercenaries who invaded the Republic of Guinea, as well as those forces which participated in planning the aggression; (ii) condemns in particular the North Atlantic Treaty Organisation powers which allow, through their complicity and assistance, various attacks by Portugal against several African states and territories; (iii) calls upon all member states of the OAU to prevent the entry, passage, or any activity by any mercenary or by organisations of individuals who use them against African states;' and finally '(iv) requests all member states of the OAU to immediately outlaw, arrest and hand over all mercenaries to the country against which they are active'. As far as help for Guinea was concerned, African states were to provide 'immediate financial, military and technical assistance to Guinea and invites all African states to contribute to this fund'. Furthermore, and as if the call for assistance so far was not enough, the Ministers asked members to make what they described as 'immediate and complete assistance to the Republic of Guinea so as to enable it to face the consequences of aggression'. Finally, the resolution requested the Defence Commission to meet and 'study ways and means of establishing an adequate and speedy defence of African states and the implementation of the present resolution ...'[18]

A number of points are worth making straight away. The first is that the resolution marked one of those rare occasions when the OAU as a body, and African states individually, spoke in unison in condemning external military intervention in the continent. The second point is that, in spite of its rhetorical vehemence, the resolution was, in practice, very illusory. Its recommendations did not seem to have taken into consideration the peculiar circumstances of the OAU or its members. It could be argued that in some ways the OAU's weak position was evident in the resolution, which also called upon the UN 'to put an end to the criminal acts of Portugal'.[19] The illusion in the resolution is evident in the section calling for financial, material and military assistance to Guinea by member states.

Although on paper the resolution seemed to have addressed itself adequately to almost all the needs of Guinea: material, financial, technical and military assistance, the gesture was basically symbolic. First and most importantly, the ministers met two weeks after the invasion. Thus, the OAU clearly demonstrated that it could not be relied upon by members in times of emergency. If the Guinean people had not gallantly repelled the invading Portuguese force, the OAU, the entire African continent, and indeed the world, would have been treated to a <u>fait accompli</u> by the Portuguese. There would, under such circumstances, have been little or nothing that the OAU could have done to reverse the situation. Secondly, the OAU asked members to give complete assistance to Guinea. This call, coupled with the request to them to make available military and technical assistance to Guinea, meant that the Organisation had a military option in mind at the time. But this was hardly a realistic position in view of the fact that the 'war' had already been fought and won at the time the OAU decided to raise its own army. Besides, the OAU did not say how such a force was to be raised. This is very important, given the total absence of a

Pan-African interventionist force, either at the time or now. Furthermore, it is difficult for us to believe that the OAU was serious about its offer of military assistance to Guinea. In the first place, the resolution was merely a request to member states. OAU resolutions, even those of the AHG, the highest authority, do not have the force of law. Thus, in the case of Guinea, members quietly forgot about the resolutions immediately after the conference.

But, even if we assume that members states were indeed disposed to help, such help would not have made much difference to the objective situation at the time. The invading troops had long been withdrawn. Besides, African states are known to be militarily weak. Many of them would have hesitated to send in their troops. But even if their troops were to be sent to Conakry, who was to command them? And who was to finance such troops? Finally, what about the logistical support - who would have provided it? These are all very important questions because, as the OAU debacle in Chad in 1982 has shown, it is one thing for the Organisation to call for troops from its members, it is another thing entirely to work out its command structure, financing and the logistical support system. We are tempted to say that Nigeria could have provided the answers to some of these questions in 1970. However, Nigeria had just concluded a thirty-month civil war. We are not sure if it would have had the political will to mount another military operation elsewhere. Besides, as the Nigerian experience in Chad in the late 1970s and early 1980s demonstrated, it could not be relied upon for logistical support, even for short distances where the target was a neighbouring state. In short, then, we could safely dismiss the military option in the resolution as the pious hopes of an impotent organisation.

The resolution also called for technical assistance, but did not specify the sort of assistance that was expected from members. Besides, we are all aware of the technological bankruptcy of African states. Most of them depend on external sources, mainly European and American, for their military hardware. It is also true that these same countries are members of the NATO Alliance to which Portugal also belongs. As such, the West would not have been happy to see African states using their military hardware against an alliance partner. It is not inconceivable, therefore, that the West would have imposed an arms embargo on African states if they had sent in arms and equipment to Guinea to fight the Portuguese. Such a scenario would have been especially plausible if the invasion had led to a conventional war between Guinea and Portuguese forces. All this points to the inevitable conclusion that the OAU was in no position to render effective help to Guinea in 1970.

There was a brief lull in the interventionist activities of European and non-European powers in Africa after the 1970 abortive invasion of Guinea. Then in 1975 Portugal decided, after an unexpected coup d'état in Lisbon, to grant independence to all its former African colonies: Angola, Guinea Bissau and Cape Verde Islands and Mozambique. The last two achieved their independence without incident (in the sense that there was no domestic strife in the two). In the case of Angola, however, the Portuguese authorities did not hand over power to a united party of nationalists but only to the invisible 'Angolan People'. Not surprisingly, a civil war ensued immediately among the rival liberation movements, the MPLA, UNITA and FNLA. The Russians and Cubans quickly came to the aid of the MPLA with massive military and technical assistance (see Chapter 7). Cuban troops fought side by side with MPLA forces in the civil war. For their part, the FNLA and UNITA were supported by West European countries and the United States. The West also encouraged South Africa to send its troops into Angola and to fight side by side with UNITA forces.[21] The OAU was therefore constrained to wade into the conflict.

Two attempts were made by the Organisation to find a lasting solution to the civil war and so end external intervention in the country. First, by the Council of Ministers and later by a special summit of the Heads of State and Government, both in January 1976. On the surface, the issues involved were clear. The MPLA was undoubtedly the most progressive of all the liberation movements in the country. Besides, the other movements had committed a mortal sin by teaming up with South Africa, the continent's foremost enemy. Furthermore, it was plain that the Russians and Cubans were advancing one of the OAU's fundamental objectives, the liberation of colonial territories. Clearly, then, the West, which had intervened on the side of the MPLA's rivals, was on the wrong side of the fence. But this was reflected neither in the debate nor in the resolution. Indeed, it became evident at the meeting that there was a fundamental ideological gap

between the majority of francophone African states
and some of the conservative anglophone states on
the one hand, and the 'progressives' on the other.
It was evident that, whilst the conservative group
indeed acknowledged in private that the
participation of South Africa on the side of the
FNLA and UNITA alliance had discredited the
alliance, they were nevertheless reluctant to do so
in the open. Rather, they were more concerned with
Cuban and Russian presence in Africa.

Apart from these ideological reasons, some
states had particularistic considerations for not
wanting to take positions. For instance, although
Zambia has been in the forefront of the activities
of the Front Line States in southern Africa[22] and
the anti-colonialist crusade in the continent,
President Kaunda was nevertheless uneasy with the
Soviet and Cuban presence so close in Angola. He was
also not unaware of the ethnic and linguistic
affinity between some of his subjects and the people
of southern Angola, which was still controlled by
Savimbi. Finally, as a landlocked state, which had
in the past depended heavily upon the Benguela
railway line for its exports and imports, Zambia was
also sensitive to the fact that the line ran through
territory controlled by Savimbi's UNITA forces.

Another country which was particularly
interested in the outcome of the Angola civil war
was Zaire. Apart from the fact that Mobutu had
very close links with the West which made it
imperative for him to take anti-Cuban and anti-
Soviet postures in his country's foreign policy, he
also had blood ties with the FNLA's Holden
Roberto.[23] This was one of the reasons why Zaire
allowed the FNLA to use its territory as a base both
before and after Angola's independence from
Portugal.

The split within the ranks of the OAU was
reflected in the fact that the emergency summit
meeting broke up in disarray after two days, with 22
states voting in favour of a government of national
unity, whilst 22 were in favour of recognising the
MPLA as the sole government of the people of Angola.
In the meantime, the civil war continued and so did
external intervention in the conflict. It could not
have been otherwise. We have already indicated that
the OAU was split down the middle over the issue of
which government to recognise. Besides that, the OAU
was neither the biggest financier of the liberation
movements in the country, nor was it their biggest
arms supplier. The most decisive actors in the

Angolan drama were consequently extra-continental powers: the USSR, Cuba, the USA and Europe. As it was, it was the massive involvement of the Russians and Cubans with arms and men on the side of the MPLA that ensured the movement's victory over its rivals. But it was only after Nigeria had recognised the MPLA government in February 1976 as the sole legal government of Angola that the diplomatic scales in Africa and elsewhere were tilted in favour of that government. It is significant to point out that European countries as well as the US have continued to aid Savimbi's rebel UNITA guerrilla forces against the MPLA government in Luanda, OAU protests notwithstanding.

Between 1977 and 1978 there were important developments in the continent with regard to external military intervention. First was the invasion of the Republic of Benin, in January 1977, then in March that year the first Shaba invasion by exiled Katangese was launched. To re-establish his tenuous hold over the mineral-rich territory, President Mobutu called upon his former colonial power, Belgium, and France to his rescue. They intervened in Zaire, both with men and equipment, and ensured the successful expulsion of the invading force. Then in May 1978, another attempt was made to unseat Mobutu with the second invasion of Shaba province. As in 1977, the Zairean leader again appealed for external assistance from the West: France, Belgium and the United States. And for the second time he was able to re-establish his authority with their help.

Throughout both crises, the OAU remained silent. For instance, although a summit of the Organisation was held in Libreville, Gabon, in July 1977, a few months after the first Shaba incident, no mention was made of the episode throughout the meeting. The Organisation was also silent over the second invasion which took place two months before the Khartoum summit, which in fact discussed the issue of external military incursions in Africa.

The reasons for the OAU's silence are not too hard to see. First, the interventions were at the behest of the government in power. Besides, the interventions did not threaten the integrity of the neighbouring states. Thirdly, the OAU's silence was a reflection of a deep-seated dilemma in which it had found itself over the issue of external intervention. On the one hand, it was opposed to such incursions which, as we have indicated earlier, provided one of the reasons for creating the

Organisation in the first place. On the other hand,
however, given the existence of the non-
intervention clause, coupled with the weak political
and military base of its members and its own
inability to protect them, it was left to every
member state to make adequate arrangements for its
own defence and security. Finally, we could argue
that the Shaba invasions were not the typical neo-
colonialist arch-type that General Obasanjo of
Nigeria described in his Khartoum speech, as they
were both the result of 'invitations' from an
incumbent African leader.

The Khartoum summit addressed the issue of
external military intervention but left the matter
open-ended. The substantive resolution strongly
condemned 'the policy of force and intervention in
Africa, regardless of the source, and opposes all
plans to recolonise the continent as well as any
attempts or acts incompatible with the principles
and objectives of the continent'. It further
denounced the 'attempt to control and make trouble
in Africa'.[24] More importantly, though, the OAU also
'upheld the right of every independent African state
to call upon friendly countries outside the
continent to come to their assistance if they
perceived that their security and sovereignty were
under threat'. With this last proviso, the
Organisation unwittingly legitimised external
intervention in the continent. What was responsible
for this confusing state of affairs?

First, was the realisation by the OAU that it
was not in any position effectively to protect its
members if they were threatened by external military
action. It was an admission of impotence on the
part of the Organisation. The second reason was
ideological. In that regard, the OAU positions on
intervention merely highlighted the divergent
ideological and political commitments of its
members. As we have argued earlier in the chapter,
that divergence has constrained African states/
leaders to take contrasting positions on the issue
of intervention in accordance with their
perceptions, not only of the motives for
intervention but also the identity of the
intervenee. A few examples from the Khartoum
summit would suffice. For instance, President Machel
of Mozambique, a progressive, paid warm tributes to
what he called the Cuban interventionist force for
their assistance in defeating South African troops
and 'other imperialist puppet forces' from Angolan
territory during the civil war in 1976. On the other

hand, he condemned the Western powers for collaborating with the white racist regime of South Africa against the MPLA. He concluded by observing that 'the interventionist sacrifice of the Cuban people is exemplary. The African people', he said, 'also prize the exemplary sacrifice of the Soviet Union and other socialist countries and of the world's democractic and progressive forces as a whole in building the Angolan people's victory.'[26]

The appreciative speech of the Mozambican leader contrasted strongly with that of the Zairean Foreign Minister, who castigated Algeria and Libya for leading the attack against France for proposing a Pan-African peace force. 'They tried to steal the show as they always do', he noted, 'but the silent majority is coming alive.' For his part, President Senghor of Senegal expressed surprise that African states had shown what he called greater interest in and concern about the presence of the 10,000 French troops in Africa than about the 50,000 Cubans scattered across the continent.[27]

Although it could be argued that, in the absence of an effective Pan-African arrangement, African states have the right to seek protection elsewhere, it is worrying none the less that, in giving its blessing to the right to invite 'friends' in time of need, the OAU also gave blanket support to the repressive policies of African states. It would have made some difference, for instance, if the Organisation had qualified its resolution by stating that external support could be sought only in cases involving external threats. Otherwise African leaders would use the clause to request support in repressing legitimate demands for reforms by their citizens. This would in the long run breed only resentment, political instability and, of course, external intervention.

This danger was recognised by President Nimeiry, the Chairman, in his speech: 'Each invitation for intervention is followed by another counter-intervention.' African leaders, he warned, must not use the right to invite their friends for help as a pretext for political oppression. 'If the call for intervention is to silence some minorities asking for the attainment of legitimate aspirations instead of negotiations to solve their differences, this might increase the problems of our countries.'[28] External intervention would by itself not solve the long-term problem of how African states could evolve a tradition of peaceful political succession. This point was poignantly captured by the Nigerian Head of State, Obasanjo, thus:

'for as long as we neglect the true interests of the generality of our peoples so long will other powers find it easy to interfere in our internal affairs and divide our peoples. There is no better defence against external forces than the government which endeavours to carry the majority of the population along with it and treats its peoples fairly decently.'[29]

Sadly, however, most African states do not heed such advice. Indeed, the majority of the OAU's leaders remain virtually the sole determinants of what is 'good' for their peoples. Hence, they do not tolerate popular participation in policy-formulation. They also do not tolerate dissent from orthodox government positions on matters of policy. Finally, since the concern of almost all African leaders is with their survival and that of their governments, irrespective of their performance, it stands to reason that they would continue to ask their friends abroad for support whenever they perceived a threat, either from domestic or external sources, to their integrity or that of their regimes. The above reasoning, however, accounts only partially for the inability of the OAU effectively to come to grips with the problems of external military intervention in Africa. It is to these that we now turn.

Besides those that we have already identified, there are also other important reasons for the OAU's failure. These can be divided into two broad categories: (i) those that are institutional and (ii) what we can call structural problems, as they relate to the political economy of African states. We shall examine each of these categories in detail below.

F. INSTITUTIONAL PROBLEMS

These relate mainly to the shortcomings of the Charter in terms of what was left our or what it actually contains. The first constraint that must be mentioned is the absence of an African High Command, although the issue has been debated several times within the OAU. It was the hope of Nkrumah that an African High Command would form the nucleus of an African army and that such an army would be used to promote African objectives, such as the liberation of colonial territories. It would also be used to blunt external military actions against African states. There is no doubt, then, that an African High Command would be highly functional if it were to be set up. This has not been possible, more than twenty years after the Charter was signed in Addis Ababa.

Several reasons have been suggested for the inability of the OAU to raise an African force. The first relates to the lack of political will on the part of Africa's leaders. The second point has to do with the various barriers that now divide the African countries: ideological, linguistic, cultural, etc. It is argued that it would be difficult to put such a force together, given the diversity of the continent. For instance, what would be the linqua franca of such a force? Besides, given the different military traditions of African countries, how would such a force be integrated? There is the financial aspect; where would the money for such a force come from? Would African states be prepared to pay for such a force, given the present reluctance of African countries to meet their financial commitments to the OAU? If past experiences are anything to go by, it is unlikely that African countries would be prepared to finance an African High Command. This doubt is strengthened by the current economic squeeze which has adversely affected the activities of every African state.

Another problem relates to the raison d'être of such a force. This is rather crucial, because many people are convinced that the force would be misused: to smother internal dissent, for instance. In that regard, we could argue that the force could be called out only to tackle external aggression against African states. But, since such aggression would not be an everyday occurrence, what would the force do when it was not actively engaged in combating external aggression? Perhaps it could be engaged in agricultural development schemes. But would not that dull its fighting capability? These are just a few of the many questions that would have to be addressed, if such a force were to be established.

But, even if we assume that there is such a force, there would still be no assurance to a victim of aggression that the force would automatically come to its aid. This is because it is very likely that the force would come under the supervision of one body of the other. In that case, the relevant body would have to meet and give the go-ahead signal before the force could be sent to the troubled spot. If the latter, however, would political considerations not influence the decision to move in or not to move in? Such a danger would always be there and could affect even the most clear cut case of neo-colonialist intervention. As the examples of Angola and Shaba have shown, African states do take political considerations into account with regard to the issue of external intervention in the continent. Given the obvious attendant uncertainties in such political decisions, African states would continue to rely on external friends, even if the High Command were to be established, unless, of course, such arrangements were completely forbidden. Proscription would however work only if African states could rely on the Pan-African force in times of need. This means that the force should be seen to be able to move in as and when needed by OAU members.

One other important weakness of the OAU relates to its financial status. Although the Organisation is the biggest of it's type in the world in terms of its membership, it is also the poorest in terms of its financial resources. Indeed, the OAU is a poor resource organisation in whatever way we may want to interpret resource to mean. Isebil Gruhn has, for instance, described it as 'ill-financed and ill-staffed'.[30] We shall however consider only the financial aspect of its resources here.

In a comparative study of African and non-African international organisations and their rankings in terms of their financial endowment, John Clark noted that:

'especially revealing are the relative rankings of the regional ADB, a broad socio-economic organisation, and the OAU, an organisation with political plus broad socio-economic purposes. While the ADB ranked only behind the EAC, Entente and UDEAC among the possible competitors listed, the OAU generated less financial commitment than all the major sub-regional organisations except the Maghreb organisation, less than the global UN, and less than the inter-regional Arab League. The only major organisation other than the Maghreb to score lower than the OAU on financial support index was the Commonwealth ...'[31]

The OAU has been living on a shoe-string budget since its creation in 1963. As the interim

Secretary-General, Peter Onu, revealed in 1984, members' dues were in arrears of $34m. that year. By April of that year, also, only five states had fully paid their financial commitments to the Organisation. The majority, 35 of them, had not made any payments since 1970.[32] The situation had not improved by 1985, either. In February that year, the Organisation was owed over $38m. in unpaid membership dues. For the 1984/85 financial year, only about 20 per cent of the projected $25m. in contributions had been received by the secretariat.

Obviously the parlous state of the OAU's financial resources has contributed in no small measure to its ineffectiveness. This was pitifully manifested in the case of the Guinea invasion and in its attempt to mount a peace keeping force in Chad in 1981. In both cases, the Organisation could not successfully go through with its initiatives - giving financial assistance in the case of Guinea and maintaining a military presence in Chad to separate the warring factions in the country - for lack of funds. Whilst no assistance was offered to Guinea, the OAU peace force in Chad had to be withdrawn prematurely in 1982 because there was no money to finance it.[33] But why should African states refuse to bail out their own creation?

A number of reasons can be suggested to explain this situation. The first has to do with the fact that support for international organisations is a 'state of mind'. Thus, whether to give or not to give financial support to an organisation is a political decision, and it could be one way or the other dependent upon the extent to which leaders are satisfied that the organisation is, or is not, responding to the needs of their state. After all, institutions are set up to serve the needs of their members. In that vein, the OAU members are probably not facing up to their financial responsibilities because they are disillusioned with the performance of the Organisation. According to this reasoning, the African states are much more committed to extra-continental bodies, such as the UN and its agencies, simply because they are seen to be 'delivering the goods', whereas the OAU has not been able to do so. But how valid is this argument? Such a view is obviously short-sighted. In fact, the argument could be easily debunked. What it fails to take into cognisance, for instance, is that the OAU has not been able to perform exactly because of the lack of commitment on the part of its member states. Thus, members should pay their dues regularly and on time and see if the OAU does not 'deliver the goods'. Then, and only then, would they have cause to blame the Organisation. This does not mean, of course, that members should pay only to erect new obstacles in the way of the OAU's effective execution of its policies and objectives.

As for their support or preference for the UN, such a policy is misguided because the UN encourages the creation of regional inter-nation organisations like the OAU precisely because it believes that they are in a better position to respond to their peculiar regional needs. It is in this regard that the attitude of African states towards the OAU is disappointing. After all, their half-commitment to the OAU is a contravention of the idea to 'try the OAU' or 'try Africa first', which is implied in the UN encouragement of regional arrangements like the OAU. The concept of 'try Africa first' will have no practical meaning if African states continue to give priority to extra-African security arrangements. Such a position is also unrealistic. After all, the OAU is Africa's baby, and it is up to the Africans to ensure that it not only survives but also grows up to be useful and important in future.

The final factor in explaining the OAU's poor responses relates to the ideological divisions among African states. The OAU's ideological map is a variegated one. It ranges from semi-democratic states with multi-party systems like Senegal, to sit-tight, one party, one man dictatorships like Sierra Leone, through military dictatorships like Benin, to self-proclaimed Marxist-Leninist regimes like those in Angola and Mozambique. The different ideological colours have influenced the way in which African states interpret and/or react to developments, not only within the continent but also to world events, as we have demonstrated. As long as such preferences continue to divide Africa, there will never be agreement on the issue of external intervention among African states. Unfortunately, there seems to be no end to such ideological factions as yet in the continent. The prospects of a unitary government for Africa are very remote.

G.   THE   STRUCTURAL   PROBLEMS

These relate on the one hand to Africa's increasingly asymmetrical links with the developed world, especially the capitalist world, and on the other hand to the increasing inequalities among and within African states. African countries are heavily dependent upon extra-African powers for the sale of their commodities, aid, technical assistance and for their imports. For instance, in 1981 only a few countries had significant imports from Africa: Burkina Faso (26 per cent), Burundi (16.9 per cent), Senegal (12.9 per cent), Seychelles (16.8 per cent) and Zimbabwe (35.2 per cent). For the majority of African states where statistics are available, intra-African trade accounts for very small percentages of their total imports, an average of between 2-3 per cent.[34] More distressing, however, is the fact that 'many African countries do not appear to have a definite policy on the development and expansion of intra-African trade'.[35] What this means in effect is that for the foreseeable future the majority of African countries will continue to depend on extra-African sources for their imports. Consequently, African countries will continue to exhibit divided loyalties to, and sympathies for, their 'friends' from Europe or elsewhere, from whom they get their imports and/or send their exports.

African states could not, under the circumstances, act together as a trade union against the European powers, given the fact that their 'economies are controlled by and large from these very European capitals from which favours are solicited'. Unfortunately, there is no end in sight to such dependency. As Nkrumah pointed out in 1963, Africa 'as a continent emerged in a difficult age with imperialism grown stronger, more ruthless and experienced, and more dangerous in its international associations'.[36] Such neo-colonialist associations include the Commonwealth, the francophone summits, the EEC/ACP, and a host of others. Their objectives are all the same; to continue to control Africa remotely. It has worked in the past, it works now and will work in the future unless African countries consciously devise self-reliant and self-sufficient policies that will enable them to extricate themselves from the external economic stranglehold.

H.   CONCLUSION: THE FUTURE OF EXTERNAL INTERVENTION

As we have argued elsewhere,[37] the future of external military intervention in the continent looks rather bright. This conclusion takes into consideration a number of important indicators. First, there seems to be no end in sight to the continent's debilitating economic plight, coupled with the devastating drought which has affected over twenty African countries.[38] And as long as this poor economic situation and natural disasters continued to plague the continent, African countries would continue to be incorporated into the capitalist political and economic periphery in the absence of an effective African response. Besides, the weak political economies of Africa would continue to generate domestic unrest and threats to the integrity of both the African states and their leaders. Such a scenario would, as in the past but perhaps much more so now, compel African leaders to adopt draconian measures against their populations, especially the dissenters.[39] Opposition elements would be forced to go under ground and would subsequently seek assistance from extra-African powers in their fight against the 'constituted' authorities. On their part, the African states would use such opposition to justify their continued linkages with external powers, especially in the military sphere. In the event, intervention would occur either on the side of the constituted authorities or on that of the opposition. Whatever the case might be, intervention under such circumstances could lead only to counter-intervention.

A second point that has to be taken into consideration is that for the foreseeable future the African continent would not be able to undertake self-reliant and self-sufficient economic schemes that would take it out of the clutches of the capitalist world. So far, the Lagos Plan of Action has been a total failure, as the majority of African countries has not bothered about its implementation either at the national, regional or continental levels.[40] Africa should pursue the Lagos Plan vigorously, after divesting it of all its neo-colonial trappings.[41] After that, each state should strive to create what we can call a stable domestic economic and political order, which is an indispensable pre-condition in the fight against external intervention. A regime which was impervious to the demands of its citizenry could not expect them either to defend it or to be satisfied with their lot. Before then, however, the continent would continue to depend in various ways on European powers and the United States.

The creation of an African military command, or the High Command as it is commonly called, would also go a long way to tackle the problem of intervention in Africa. However, African states do not have the political will to create such a force at the moment. Apart from that, the deepening economic crisis facing the continent also militates against such a move. For most African states, the immediate concern is with survival; other issues are accordingly secondary. In other word, 'African states have just enough problems on their hands to cope with, without adding the complicating factor of the High Command'.[42] For the time being, then, African states would remain at the mercy of extra-African powers.

The future of external intervention is also tied to the emergence of a viable OAU. We envisage here a structural reform of the Organisation to make it more virile and inward-looking. The prospects of this are however slim. The Organisation would continue to be debilitated by inter-state ideological rivalries, inter-state conflicts and, of course, financial neglect by its members. In any case, we should not expect the OAU to be inward-looking when its members are pursuing dependent policies with regard to the countries of the West.

Besides, as presently constituted the OAU serves the interests of African leaders. Thus, they are unlikely to 'sponsor efforts to change the status quo and will support each other by and large, against those who seek such change'.[43] It is instructive to note in that regard that the Organisation's Council of Ministers, at a meeting in Addis Ababa in February 1985, rejected the creation of a 'mini' security council as 'a principal permanent forum, capable of responding with the required promptness and efficiency to crises which occur in the political and security sectors on the African continent' as 'premature and ill-timed'.[44] The creation of such an organ would have no doubt improved the Organisation's ability to respond to crisis situations in the continent: inter-African disputes, civil strife and, of course, external intervention. Surely, if such a body had been in existence in 1970, it would not have taken the OAU two weeks to respond to the Portuguese invasion of Guinea.

Finally, the revival of cold war rivalries between the East and West would make African countries targets of cold war politics and would increase the prospects of external intervention in the future. This point is rather significant, given the fact that Africa commands a lot of strategic mineral resources, which are in high demand in the developed East and West and over which each of them may want to secure control. This point has been treated very well in Chapter 8. Already, we are witnessing the damaging effects of the present (1985), American adminstration's cold war perception of African events in Namibia, Angola and South Africa. It was such calculation that also brought the Americans into the Chad conflict in 1982.

In summary, then, it looks as though for the foreseeable future there would be no effective continental approach to the issue of external military intervention. In the circumstances, African states would have to rely on the old and tested methods of either inviting friends for protection or signing military defence pacts with extra-continental powers for the same purpose. We do not also expect African states to be unanimous in their condemnation of external military intervention for reasons which we have already given in other paragraphs.

NOTES

[1] The literature on intervention is growing. For details see, Richard J. Barnet, Intervention and Revolution (London, Granada Publishing Limited, 1972); Ayoob, M. (ed.), Conflict and Intervention in the Third World (New York, St. Martins, 1980); Ekstein, H. (ed.), International Wars: Problems and Approaches (London, Macmillan, 1964); Gurtov, M., The United States against the Third World: Anti-Nationalism and Intervention (New York, Praeger, 1974); R. Little, Intervention (London, Martin Robertson, 1975), and J. Rosenau.

[2] For an historical survey of intervention see Ola Balogun, 'A History of Intervention', in Guardian (Lagos, 30 November 1983), and Boon Fawehinmi, 'Super Powers: Licensed to Kill', Guardian, 16 February 1985.

[3] R. J. Barnet, Intervention and Revolution, p.258.

[4] Quoted by R. J. Barnet, in Intervention and Revolution, pp.258-9.

[5] Barnet, Intervention and Revolution, p.243.

[6] Ibid., p.225.

[7] Dennis Austin, 'Things Fall Apart?', in Orbis, 25(4), Winter 1982, p.941.

[8] E/ECA/CM.11/64 Domestic and Intra-African Trade and Finance (Addis Ababa, 29 March 1985).

[9] See, for example, the abortive coup in Guinea on 4 July 1985. For details see the Guardian, Concord (Lagos) and Daily Sketch (Ibadan), all of 5 July 1985.

[10] United We Stand, an Address by Kwame Nkrumah

at the Conference of Heads of State and Government in Addis Ababa, Ethiopia, on 24 May 1963, (Accra, Government Printer), n.d. (henceforth simply United We Stand), p.4.

[11] For details, see ARB, 1-30 November 1981, pp.6254-6.

[12] ARB, 1-31 October 1965, p.379.

[13] Address by Lt. General Olusegun Obasanjo, Head of State of the Federal Republic of Nigeria, to the 15th Ordinary Session of the OAU Assembly of Heads of State and Government in Khartoum, Sudan, July 1978, in New Nigerian (Kaduna, 25 July 1978) (henceforth simply, An Address).

[14] An Address.

[15] Daily Times (Lagos), 6 June 1978.

[16] Daily Times, 6 June 1978.

[17] ARB, 1-31 May 1978, p.4860.

[18] ARB, 1-31 December 1970, p.1948.

[19] ARB, 1-31 December 1970, p.1948.

[20] ARB, 1-31 December 1970, p.1948.

[21] For more on this see Richard Leonard, South Africa at War (Westport, Lawrence Hill, 1983).

[22] For details of the roles of the Front Line States, see Amadu Sesay, 'The Role of the Front Line States in Southern Africa', in Olajide Aluko and Timothy M. Shaw (eds.), Southern Africa in the 1980s (London, George Allen and Unwin, 1985), pp.19-40.

[23] They are brothers-in-law.

[24] ARB, 1-31 July 1975, p.4839.

[25] See Amadu Sesay, 'The OAU and Continental Order', in Timothy M. Shaw and Sola Ojo (eds.), Africa and the International Political System (Washington DC, UPA, 1982), pp.168-225.

[26] ARB, 1-31 July 1975, p.4912.

[27] Ibid., p.4913.

[28] Ibid., p.4912.

[29] An Address.

[30] Isebill Gruhn, in Christian Science Monitor (Mass., 4 November 1982).

[31] John F. Clark, 'Patterns of Support for International Organisations in Africa', in Timothy M. Shaw and Albert Heard (eds.), The Politics of African Dependence and Development (London, Longman & Dalhousie University Press, 1979), p.326.

[32] Concord, 6 April 1984.

[33] See Amadu Sesay et al, The OAU After Twenty Years (Boulder, Westview Press, 1984).

[34] E/ECA/CM.11/64, p.4.

[35] Ibid., p.5.

[36] United We Stand, p.4.

[37] See Amadu Sesay and Orobola Fasehun, 'Possible Futures of the OAU in the World System', in Olajide Aluyko and Timothy M. Shaw (eds.), <u>Africa Projected</u> (London, Macmillan, 1984), pp.

[38] E/ECA/CM.1129 <u>Africa's Food and Agriculture Crisis: Prospects and Proposals for 1985 and 1986</u> (Addis Ababa), 1 April 1985.

[39] See Philippe Lemaitre, 'Who will rule Africa by the Year 2000?', in H. Kitchen (ed.), <u>Africa: From Mystery to Maze</u> (Lexington, Mass., D.C. Heath, 1976), for more scenarios on this issue.

[40] E/ECA/CM.1137, <u>Evaluation of the Implementation of the Regional Food Plan for Africa 1978-84 and Preliminary Assessment of the Food and Agriculture Aspects of the Lagos Plan of Action</u> (Addis Ababa, February 1985).

[41] See Amadu Sesay and Orobola Fasehun, 'Possible Futures of the OAU in the World System', in Olajide Aluko and Timothy M. Shaw (eds.), <u>Africa Projected</u>.

[42] Director of the National Institute for Policy and Strategic Studies, Jos, Nigeria, in <u>Punch</u> (Lagos, 5 June 1985).

[43] Thomas M. Franck, 'Afference, Efference and Legitimacy in Africa', in El Ayouty and H. C. Brooks (eds.), <u>Africa and International Organisation</u> (The Hague, Martins Nijhoff, 1974).

[44] <u>West Africa</u> (London, 11 March 1985), p.454.

CHAPTER 10

AFRICA AND EUROPE: COLLECTIVE DEPENDENCE OR
INTERDEPENDENCE?

S.K.B. Asante

A.   INTRODUCTION

> 'The ACP states do not wish to remain always
> dependent upon the industrialised
> countries ...'
>> Ambassador Josua D.V. Cavalevu of Fiji,
>> Chairman of ACP Committee of Ambassadors
>> (1983)

> 'We view, with disquiet, the over-dependence of
> the economy of our continent ... This
> phenomenon had made African economies highly
> susceptible to external developments and with
> detrimental effects on the interests of the
> continent.'
>> (OAU, Lagos Plan of Action, para.9)

> 'The industrialized countries and the ACP states
> know that they are very interdependent on each
> other ...'
>> Ambassador Cavalevu (note 21)

> 'The Lome Convention cannot be viewed in
> isolation; it is not independent of earlier
> developments. The very relationship between the
> EEC countries and the ACP countries has a long
> history and is necessarily conditioned by it -
> for better or for worse.'
>> Laurens Jan Brinkhorst, Dutch State
>> Secretary for Foreign Affairs (note 25)

    The interactions and images of the European
Community (EEC) of ten and the now sixty-four
African, Caribbean and Pacific (ACP) states would
for long remain an irresistible field of study, not
just because they raise central questions about the

behaviour of rich and poor in the world, but also
because they offer the opportunity, first to reflect
on the impact of the historical antecedents on the
Africa- EEC relationship dating back to the Berlin
Conference of 1884-85, and secondly to analyse the
key provisions of the Lome scheme in relation to the
concepts of 'dependence' and 'interdependence' which
have been variously used to describe this
relationship. The historical context of the ACP-EEC
Lome Conventions is obviously vital. For Lome cannot
be understood outside this context. The form and
substance of the Conventions which shape the
relationship between Europe and Africa have their
origins in an historical framework. While the
Berlin Conference established the undisputed sway of
colonialism in Africa, the Treaty of Rome, which
gave birth to the EEC, marked the advent of neo-
colonialism and dependency in Africa.[1] To this
extent, therefore, the Brussels conference of
1973-74, which created the Lome regime in 1975, is
the ultimate successor to the Berlin meeting.
　　This heritage of colonial domination by Europe
and its perpetuation since the post-colonial period
in a variety of disguised and direct forms,
culminating in the Lome agreement, has produced a
continuing debate among scholars, some commenting
favourably on the benefits that will accrue to the
African countries from 'the willingness of EEC
member states to pursue policies helpful to these
countries'. To such observers, Lome is 'an unmixed
blessing', establishing a radically new
relationship, based on partnership in place of the
old, unequal ties. Hence, William Zartman, for
instance, describes Lome as 'a welcome development',
and as the latest step in a slow historical process
from colonial domination towards mutual cooperation
and equality.[2] Similarly, Isebill Gruhn sees Lome as
a progressive document which constitutes 'an inching
towards interdependence'.[3] While attempting to offer
a somewhat balanced evaluation of the Lome regime,
Ellen Frey-Wouters would tend to reflect a similar
view in her recent study when she remarks that the
Lome system is 'more than an enlargement of old
colonial links', as it marks a step forward towards
a new system of relations between the EEC and ACP
countries. This relationship, she concludes, 'can no
longer be characterised as neo-colonialist'.[4] These
observers quickly point to the improvements agreed
upon in trade relations, stabilisation of export
earnings, industrial cooperation and financial aid.
　　On the other hand, a growing number of critical

scholars has sought to mute such enthusiasm by
arguing that, whilst Lome may appear to be
progressive to the EEC, in the ACP countries its
impact and image are more problematic: it has tended
to generate further inequalities rather than
development. These critics tend to see the EEC as
the latest manifestation of metropolitan domination
and hence a primary cause of under-development.
Lome is therefore described as a neo-colonial
device to maintain a relationship of dependence
between Europe and Africa or another machinery for
updating dependence of the African countries on
their former colonial powers. To critics like David
Wall, Lome is not only neo-colonial in tone but it
also perpetuates the client status of Africa; at
best it pays compensation or reparations for
previous exploitation.[5] Viewed globally, Michael
Dolan asserts that Lome is essentially neo-
colonialist and representative of traditional
spheres of influence and bloc politics,[6] while Lynn
Mytelka argues that Lome preserves the role of the
African countries 'as producers of raw materials and
agricultural products ... permitting the emergence
of a new international division of labour'.[7] Thus,
to these critics Lome constitutes a new and subtle
kind of subjugation of the African states, making it
difficult for them to industrialise and achieve the
much needed diversification of the economies.
Mytelka and Dolan thus conclude that Lome, like the
Treaty of Berlin, seeks to keep Africa safe for
European interests, especially corporate ones,
against non-European challenges: in particular it
reflects the interests of specific states and
sectors.[8] Seen from this perspective, then, Lome
does not make any fundamental inroads into the
dependency relationship between industrial and non-
industrial countries. Although it reflects efforts
to devise a new type of relationship between
countries of most unequal economic development, the
important question is to what end - the perpetuation
of collective dependence or the initiation of steps
towards balanced interdependence or collective self-
reliance?

From a stance of structural change, the meaning
of Lome depends on the extent to which it attempts
to transform the forms and structure of the former
traditional dependence on the metropolitan powers by
all the African countries into some kind of mutually
beneficial interdependent relationship. From this
perspective, we may be tempted to ask: has Lome
created a qualitatively new relationship between

Europe and Africa based on partnership in place of the old inequalities? Does the scheme structurally alter the old colonial trade patterns? Or is Lome the EEC's brand of neo-colonialism? To what extent does Lome constitute an 'inching towards interdependence' rather than a shift in the nature of imperialism? If, on the other hand, the Lome scheme is not a progressive document, what, then, are the various African counter-strategies to the problems of collective dependence or neo-colonialism in the quest for beneficial interdependence or a greater degree of economic independence?

This chapter attempts a critical overview of the Lome regime in the light of the question posed by the title of this study. Throughout the emphasis would be placed on Africa, not only because nearly all the 51 independent African countries are signatories to the Lome agreement, but also because it is the African continent which historically has been tied to Europe at the political, economic, social and cultural levels ever since the fifteenth century. This relationship is what Guy Martin has recently termed the 'ideology of Eurafrica', that is a body of thought originating in the colonial period, according to which 'the fate of Europe and Africa is seen as being naturally and inextricably linked' together.[9] As expressed in the relationship between the EEC and African states, Eurafricanism consists of 'modified, multilateral linkages between the old colonial metropole of Europe and the African periphery'. It is a symbol of the continuity of the unequal division of labour between Europe and Africa. Hence, specifically, the chapter focuses attention on the extent to which the original Lome and its 'child', Lome II which expired in February 1985 - exactly a hundred years after signing the Berlin Treaty - attempts to put right the historically evolved imbalance in the relations between industrialised Europe and the developing African countries. The question of balance or symmetry is one of the principal criteria according to which the Lome system should be judged. Does it retain, not to say reinforce, one-sided dependence and vulnerability? Or does it correct the asymmetry, either by increasing the EEC's dependence or by reducing that of the African countries, or both? Before considering some of these issues, it would seem appropriate to set the stage with a brief review of the key concepts of this study.

B.   THE KEY CONCEPTS

The literature on 'interdependence', 'dependence' and the more commonly used term in recent years 'dependency' or dependencia is vast, sophisticated and controversial.[10] The latter terms, 'dependence' and 'dependency', for example, have sometimes been labelled identically and often treated indiscriminately for analytical purposes. It is not intended to review the literature on these concepts in any detail. What is done here is just to have a cursory look at them.

In an interesting documentary study, Timothy Shaw has noted that the concepts, 'interdependence' and 'dependence' have come 'to characterise and symbolise rather different world views and visions'. While the former tends to be proposed 'as both approach and ideology' by individuals and institutions in the advanced industrialised states, the latter is seen by many in developing countries 'to be their major problem and constraint, resulting in under-development rather than development'.[11] In recent years, however, the concept of 'dependence', whether mutual or otherwise, has generated a sustained but lively controversy among social scientists. Robert Keohane and Joseph Nye,[12] for example, view it as helpful in explaining the distribution of power in the world, whereas Sanjaya Lall[13] condemns it as an 'unhelpful' and 'misleading' analytical category. Again, scholars like Richard Rosecrance and Arthur Stein[14] also complain about the lack of conceptual clarity, and some even deny that there is any generally accepted definition of the term.[15]

Two basic meanings of the concept of 'dependence' may be distinguished. In conventional economic parlance, 'dependence' would mean a state of being determined or significantly affected by external forces. A country may, for example, be described as being 'dependent' on foreign trade or foreign technology. In such a usage there is no hint of anything undesirable, nor is there any implication of a process of causation: dependence is defined with reference to some particular objective economic fact and says nothing in a descriptive or causal sense about the condition of the economy as a whole. A number of advanced countries 'depend', sometimes heavily, on either foreign investments or foreigners for their industrial technology.

On the other hand, the term 'dependence' may be used to refer to the recent experience of developing countries. Here it is essentially directed at the post-colonial era when direct forms of colonial subjugation had ended and new forms of 'imperialism', by various means which ensure dependence rather than open domination, had supervened. In this sense, 'dependence' is meant to describe certain characteristics of the economy as a whole and is intended to trace certain processes which are causally linked to its under-development and which are expected to affect adversely its development in the future. As used in this study, then, 'dependence' refers to a relationship of subordination in which one thing is supported by something else or must rely upon something else for fulfilment of a need. Hence Ambassador Josua Cavalevu's remark in the first opening citation that the 'ACP states do not wish to remain always dependent ...'[16]

In this usage, 'dependence' is closely related or similar to the concept of 'dependency', which has recently emerged as a distinct school traced to the writings of the <u>dependencia</u> economists from, or working on, Latin America.[17] Indeed, scholars like Guy Martin would prefer using the concept of 'dependency' rather than 'dependence' to describe the relationship between Europe and Africa under the Lome scheme.[18] James Caporaso and Raymond Duvail have, however, suggested that a fundamental distinction should be made between 'dependence' and 'dependency'. For 'dependency' involves a more complex set of relations centering on the incorporation of less developed, less homogeneous societies into the global capitalist system and the 'structural distortions' resulting therefrom.[19] The components of dependency are the magnitude of foreign supply of important factors of production (technology, capital), limited development choices and domestic 'distortions' measures. This process has shaped the political economies of the peripheral countries in Africa in such a way as to subject their development to the needs of the European capitalist countries at the centre. Although both Caporaso and Duvail admit some similarity between 'dependence' and 'dependency', they emphasise the differences.

The other concept of this chapter - 'inter-dependence' - has so many and varied meanings that it is no longer fully clear what investigators intend to signify when they use the term.[20] During the first Lome negotiations, for instance, both the EEC and ACP negotiators bandied the term 'interdependence' about to suggest the kind of objective they were aspiring to achieve. As indicated in the third opening citation, the ACP states were wont to share the view that they and the EEC countries 'are interdependent on each other'.[21] In this respect, one tends to agree with Hedley Bull that the term 'interdependence' has become a 'cant word' that serves to rationalise relations between a dominant power and its dependencies, in which 'the sensitivity is more one-sided than it is mutual'.[22] But in a very loose and general sense, one can say that interdependence is a state of affairs where what one nation does impinges directly upon other nations. Specifically, then, 'interdependence' may mean the direct and positive linkage of the interests of states such that, when the position of one state changes, the position of others is affected, and in the same direction.[23] Precisely, therefore, 'interdependence' suggests a system in which states tend to go up or down the ladder of international position (economic strength, power, welfare, access to information and/or technology) together. Thus the concept does suggest a kind of 'connectedness'. It does presume a strong relationship of interest. But it does not indicate whether that relationship is positive or negative.

Also, interdependence can itself constitute a controversial problem and give rise to tension and conflicts. This is the case when interdependence is 'particularly unbalanced or asymmetrical, that is when the dependence of one party is much greater than that of the other party'.[24] In such a situation there is no equality, no even distribution of costs and benefits and hence no harmony of interests. A strategy of interdependency thus calls for an optimal balance of dependencies. Only in this way will it be possible to arrive at joint management of the interrelationship which is mutually acceptable and beneficial.

In this chapter, therefore, by 'interdependence' I mean an attempt to make adjustments and to provide for basic restructuring in order to put right the historically evolved 'imbalance' in the relations between Europe and the African countries, particularly the ex-colonies of the EEC member states. Our basic hypothesis, therefore, is that, although the Lome regime attempts to offer possibilities for restructuring the cooperation system, the record of Lome I, coupled with the adjustments, advances, innovations and implementation of Lome II, does not appear to give one the assurance of the creation of a mutually acceptable and beneficial interdependence between Africa and Europe.

C.   YAOUNDE: A CONTINUITY OF DEPENDENCY STRUCTURES

As Laurens Brinkhorst correctly stresses in the fourth opening citation,[25] we cannot deny Lome its historical antecedents. Specifically, the EEC-ACP 'interactions and images' cannot be separated from the 'historical relationship between Europe of colonial capitals and an Africa of colonial outposts'. This is evidenced in the inauguration of the new association in 1958 between the European Community of Six and the colonial territories of France, based on a special section (Part IV) of the Treaty of Rome. Basically, the association was a convenient device for accommodating European colonial trading interests in Africa with the newly formed European Community. It was hardly an association arrangement that provided for basic restructuring, tailored as it was to the wishes of some to continue the old relations on the old basis.

Established as a temporary expedient of the colonial era, the association proved to be a remarkably durable and adaptable kernel from which the Community gradually extended its influence in Africa. For the association regime was succeeded by the two Yaounde Conventions of June 1964 and July 1969, following the independence of the associated states and territories. The Yaounde Conventions were multilateral agreements between the Six and Eighteen successor states to the Belgian, French and Italian colonies in Africa. These were clearly neo-colonial arrangements by dint of their terms, the manner in which they were implemented, and the mercantilist ethos underpinning them. The second Yaounde Convention in particular, 'retreated from the Eurafrican model but retained the basic nature of a set of paternalistic relationships "given" by the EEC and "accepted" by the Associates'.[26] Although both parties so earnestly stressed their equality and parity, the manifest inequality between the EEC and Eighteen in terms of wealth and influence underlined the fundamental imbalance.

Thus, despite what Carol Twitchett would seem to suggest,[27] the Yaounde regime actually bolstered colonial structures: 'There was no pretence to equality - supplicants not masters. Nor was structural change on the agenda.'[28] As an unequal relationship, it ensured Europe's continuing

economic domination of Africa even after formal
decolonisation. Hence the Yaounde association is
seen as a machinery for reinforcing 'a dependency
relationship' between the EEC and the francophone
African countries. Although the over-dependence of
the former French Africans on France, in terms of
both aid and trade, existed before the inauguration
of the Yaounde regime, the Yaounde Conventions did
not only reinforce this type of relationship;: they
also widened and greatly internationalised it to
include the other EEC member states, who were eager
to share the 'spoils' which had previously accrued
solely to France and hence 'keen to perpetuate
intimate links' between the Community and its
Associates. There is thus a large measure of truth
in Reginald Green's remark that:

> This history is not one of a European quest for
> interdependence based on equality but of
> technocratic paternalism in Brussels allied to
> governmental interests dominantly (not solely)
> concerned with the profitable transformation of
> colonial mercantilism into a more modern
> material supply-market provision system
> lubricated by appropriate financial and
> technical transfers.[29]

It is ironical that the Commonwealth African
countries did not think seriously of their relations
with Europe until the British accession to the Rome
Treaty. They suspiciously viewed the Yaounde new
association as the multilateralisation of former
bilateral dependency ties, whereby six powerful,
developed countries were virtually annexing 18 of
the poorest, most under-developed and powerless
countries of Africa.[30] It was, typically, an
association of the rider and the horse, in which the
former had all to win and the latter all to lose. In
short, the Common Market was seen as:

> ... a European scheme designed to attach
> African countries to European imperialism, to
> prevent the African countries from pursuing an
> independent neutral policy, to prevent the
> establishment of mutually beneficial economic
> ties among these countries, and to keep the
> African countries in a position of suppliers
> of raw materials for imperialist powers.[31]

Furthermore, the economic advantages offered by the
Yaounde-type arrangement were designed to induce

them to accept certain conditions which they regarded as inconsistent with their economic under-development and political independence.[32] On the whole, Yaounde was considered 'a kind of colonial anachronism', which had helped to perpetuate the division of Africa originally imposed by the imperial powers at the Berlin Conference.

The British accession to the Treaty of Rome in 1972 and her subsequent entrance into the European Community in 1973 offered the Commonwealth countries in Africa and the Caribbean an opportunity to re-examine critically the Yaounde scheme and to explore the possibility of joint negotiation in order to obtain better terms of trade from the EEC. They subsequently put into motion a series of meetings, first among themselves, secondly with all the other African countries, and finally together with the ACP countries they entered into eighteen months of negotiations with the EEC, culminating in the creation of the original Lome Convention in February 1975. Following its expiry in February 1980, Lome II was concluded in October 1979 and entered into force in March 1980. Lome III has been negotiated for the period 1985 to 1990. It has been noted that the Yaounde regime did not fundamentally alter the position of imbalance between Europe and Africa. To what extent, then, did the Lome Convention change this position of imbalance? Put differently, to what extent was Lome III less neo-colonial than its predecessors? Did it introduce new departures to help the African states to move towards the achievement of a sustained growth, improve their capacity for exploiting and developing technology, and to bring about some balance or symmetry between Europe and Africa?

D. LOME: A NEW DEPARTURE FROM ASYMMETRICAL INTERDEPENDENCE?

The Lome regime was inaugurated on 28 February 1975 with a 'fanfare of self-congratulation'. The Convention was intended to symbolise a new era in relations between the industrialised countries of Western Europe and the Third World - an era in which there would be a real cooperative partnership between the two parties. Hence, Lome has been hailed by many observers as a prime example of successful North-South cooperation: an encouraging example of development assistance, heralding a new era of Euro-African cooperation and constituting a model for economic development at the global level. The EEC described it specifically as a pioneering model of cooperation between equal partners. The preamble of the Convention expressed a desire by the contracting parties to safeguard the interests of the ACP states whose economies depend to a considerable extent on the exportation of commodities, while efforts would be made to promote their industrial development.

Lome no doubt possessed valuable features. For, besides its multilateral package of measures covering aid, trade and industrial cooperation, Lome established a set of consultative fora, with the 'promise of a continuing, effective and productive dialogue' between Europe and Africa. It must be added, however, that the proof of the pudding is in the eating. Much depends on the will and effort with which the scheme is implemented. In other words, the key to a dynamic and evolutionary Lome lies not in the texts but in the attitudes of the implementers and the institutional ethos of which they are part. A critical analysis of the Lome I and II agreements, and especially their implementation, would tend to suggest that, although the scheme is unique in some respects, as Adrian Hewitt and Christopher Stevens, of the Overseas Development Institute in London, have recently concluded, 'much of the euphoria greeting it was quite misplaced!'[33] From a stance of structural change, in particular, Lome was in no sense 'a road to Damascus' conversion for either Europe or Africa. The continuity from the age-old colonial patterns of dependency, as enshrined in the Yaounde II arrangement, is as evident as the change. But the question that remains to be tackled is whether the practical measures inaugurated by the Lome regime can effectively correct the asymmetry inherent in post-colonial relations between Europe and Africa.

The primary objective of the Lome scheme was to facilitate inter-regional trade and other economic exchanges between the EEC and ACP. However, as Timothy Shaw has remarked, in view of the international division of labour designed and established by 'the states and corporations of Europe' during the period of colonialism after the Berlin Conference, any increase in exchange would mean 'more of Africa's raw materials being traded for Europe's manufactured goods'.[34] Having inherited this unequal exchange, Africa's main interest in the Lome ageement was first to 'guarantee its traditional markets in Europe', and secondly to 'restructure its exports' to include more processed and manufactured goods. Specifically, Africa had

sought to exclude alternative sources of raw
materials for Europe and 'to secure access for its
own manufacturing industries in Europe'. On the
other hand, the paramount interest of Europe in
entering the Lome 'deal' was to ensure a 'reliable
flow of cheap primary products' and to retain her
already established markets in Africa for
manufactured and capital goods.[35]

E.   CONTINUITY OF COLONIAL PATTERNS OF TRADE

The essential incompatibility of EEC and African
interests is seen more clearly in the agreement
covering trade cooperation than perhaps in any other
part of the Lome scheme. A careful analysis of EEC-
Africa trade flows since the inauguration of the
Lome regime in 1975 shows that the Lome Conventions
have had a relatively limited impact on African
exports to the EEC. Statistically, during the Lome I
period, only 38.4 per cent of ACP exports went to
the Community, as compared with 45.6 per cent before
Lome. The free access to the EEC markets under the
Lome trade regime is not enough to ensure a rise in
the ACP's exports, which to a large degree depend on
the need to increase trade promotion with regard to
ACP products by improving external trade structures,
extending schemes and implementing a marketing
policy. Thus, although in principle, the Lome system
is 'committed to take positive action to ensure
effective access to EEC markets for the exports of
the ACP countries', in practice market promotion for
these products has so far proved to be
disappointing.[36] The ACP-EEC trade relations have
thus become a source of concern, as forcefully
expressed by President Kaunda at the ACP council
meeting in Lusaka in December 1977, when he claimed
that the ACP states:

> ... negotiated the Lome Convention in the
> belief that would confer on (their) exports
> terms and conditions more favourable than those
> granted to the products of other countries.
> After some two years of implementation of the
> Convention, (they) now have many reasons to
> doubt that this is the understanding and policy
> of the Community.[37]

Generally, the African states 'clearly fear'
that their vaunted special relationship with Europe
has yielded few tangible results, especially in the
area most important to them - boosting their exports

to Europe. The frustrations experienced by the African states are also well reflected in a 'Draft Report for the Joint Committee of the ACP-EEC Consultative Assembly', held in March 1978 at Brussels. In it, M. Guillabert of Senegal, the rapporteur, expressed the African states' disappointment over the implementation of Lome, pointing out in particular that, under the Lome Convention, 'their trade balance with the Community has passed from surplus to deficit ... that, in real terms, their exports to the Community are lower now than in 1974.'[38] This trend is of course inconsistent with the aims of the Lome Conventions. Indeed, an extensive research into more detailed patterns of ACP-EEC trade might well reveal that the principal beneficiaries of the Lome trade provisions are the main European community exporting companies. Moreover, despite the Lome scheme, non-ACP developing countries have had a much more dynamic export record with the EEC than the ACP states.[39]

But it is to the spheres of market access of manufactured and semi-manufactured exports from Africa that one should look for hard evidence of Lome's contribution to longer-run economic development in the African countries. Although under the scheme industrial products are accorded free access to the EEC markets, the trouble is that the trade concessions do not have the effect of encouraging the development of processing and manufacturing industries in the African countries. There are cases where, when an African country is able to 'take advantage of its theoretical rights' (to export manufactured goods to the EEC markets), it runs the 'risk of administrative action to discourage it'. For, although Lome is a contractual agreement, it is substantially subject to interpretation by the EEC. A case in point is when the Community had to lean on the Ivory Coast in 1977 to discourage it from developing an export capacity in clothing and cotton textiles. The experience of Mauritius has been even more severe.[40]

Briefly stated, the EEC member states are in no way prepared to encourage African countries to take a fuller advantage of Lome's free access provisions. The prevailing economic recession has fed unsubstantiated European fears of 'cheap labour' products from developing countries threatening jobs throughout the Community. Although the competing products come from such non-ACP countries as South Korea, Taiwan and Singapore, the EEC members appear to be more seriously concerned with the few industrial products - which is less than 3 per cent of the volume of total ACP exports - coming from the ACP states. Hence, for example, in submissions to a House of Commons Committee considering the original Lome Convention's renegotiation, the British Department of Industry stressed 'the need to prevent disruption of our domestic industries through low-cost imports', while the then Minister of Trade, Edmund Dell, suggested that there was very little prospect of African exports having a significant impact on British industry.[41]

Besides, the apparent liberality of the trade provisions is circumscribed by a number of significant restrictions. One of these relates to Lome's rules of origin, which broadly specify a minimum 50 per cent of value added to products in the exporting country (or cumulatively in the ACP as a whole) if they are to qualify for duty-free access into the European Community. Given the very low level of industrialisation in most African states, this appears to be highly restrictive and a particularly onerous requirement. In most African states manufacturing adds on only some 25-40 per cent of value and the rules of origin constitute an almost impossible hurdle. Recent investigations by the Commonwealth Secretariat suggest that 'few manufactured mineral products from Commonwealth Africa reach the required 50 per cent of value added'. Most of their processed and manufactured products do not benefit from the Lome Convention's free access provisions 'because they have only between 20 and 48 per cent of value added as a proportion of their gross value'.[42] The rules of origin are thus too stringent to confer much benefit on the infant African industries while, on the other hand, a direct advantage is given to EEC firms in setting up assembly or processing industries because EEC materials, like African inputs, are considered to be 'originating products'.[43] This undoubtedly creates an unfavourable bargaining position for the African countries. More directly, the rules of origin requirement in many cases cancels out the benefit of preferential access to EEC markets and discourages the essential expansion of the value and range of manufactured goods from the African countries. Put differently, these rules virtually eliminate any actual or potential advantage from the trade cooperation provisions of Lome. Not surprisingly, the profile of African exports to Europe remained broadly unchanged in the

1970s, with little evidence of diversification.

Furthermore, a final safeguard clause exists whereby imports arriving through the preferential system under the Lome scheme, which threaten to disturb a sector of the European economy, may have their free access to the European market prohibited. The presence of this clause introduces considerable uncertainty into the trade relationship. The Community threatened to impose this clause in 1979 in order to force Mauritius to agree to voluntary limitations on its textile exports.[44] Thus, throughout, Europe has been concerned about maintaining its historic hegemony in African import markets as suppliers of manufactured and consumer goods. By the same token, retaining African countries as suppliers of raw materials is important. Hence the traditional trade patterns set since the Berlin Treaty remain unchanged. As James O'Neil Lewis has correctly noted:

> Traditional business links with the former metropolitan countries, and long-established financing, shipping and marketing arrangements, all help to maintain the previously existing patterns ... Thus, while the traditional commodity exports of the developing countries tend to continue to go to the traditional markets, the products of their new manufacturing industries often find great difficulty in entering those markets and, consequently, tend to be diffused in negligible quantities over a large number of relatively unimportant markets. This is a situation to which developing countries find it difficult to adjust. How ... are they ever going to improve their economic position if they are not able to sell the output of their new industries?[45]

In general, it is not only in the area of trade cooperation that the dominance of European over African interests, as in the old colonial era, is made evident; this is also revealed in the Lome aid and industrialisation programmes.

F.   HOW MUCH IS EEC AID AIDING?

The Lome aid programme, in spite of its innovations, does not appear adequately to meet the most pressing demands of the African countries. For, although the overriding aim of the Lome aid is to 'correct the structural imbalances in the various sectors' of the

African economies and that this is to be achieved by
financing projects and programmes which contribute
essentially to economic and social development in
'accordance with the priorities and objectives' laid
down by the African (ACP) states (Article 40 of Lome
I), in practice the contrary appears to be the case.
A closer examination of the projects to which aid
has been channelled reveals that the principle of
fostering the diversification of the African
economies has been neglected; that is, the
production of goods which might eventually compete
directly with European goods has not been
encouraged. Where industrial projects have been
favoured, these have been overwhelmingly to increase
energy supplies, and very little attention is paid
to the importance of local industrial development
linked to agricultural development. As a study of
European Development Fund (EDF) aid to Cameroon has
concluded, 'judged against the current criteria for
aid effectiveness - sustained economic development,
increases in local administration competence and
improvement in the lot of the poor - the EDF's aid
allocation mechanism seems to have missed the mark
...'[46] In this regard, Rajana's recent remark that
on balance the EEC aid under the Lome scheme has
'contributed to a measure of development in the ACP
states'[47] would seem to have been overstated.
Indeed, the use of the Lome aid funds in the
promotion of further raw material exports leaves
the African countries increasingly vulnerable to the
fluctuations in raw material prices and the vagaries
of the international market.

Besides, although Lome has been publicised as a
model agreement for the future relations between
developing and developed countries, aid is given to
the African states not on the basis of agreement but
on the sole decision of the EEC. The African
countries are not represented on the EDF Committee,
which is the decision-making body for the
allocation of aid moneys. In terms of aid
administration and management, as well as the
execution of EEC aid projects, national firms and
technicians from beneficiary African countries
continue to play a secondary role. All this seems to
indicate a continuity (of dependence) rather than a
substantially new departure.

G.   IS STABEX STABILISING POVERTY AND DEPENDENCE?

Even the STABEX scheme, one of the most notable
innovations in the Lome regime, designed to

compensate ACP states for loss of export earnings due to fluctuations in certain eligible commodity prices, is of questionable importance for the African countries so far as their economic development is concerned. STABEX no doubt expresses an institutional recognition on the part of the EEC that fluctuations in the level of export earnings are harmful to the developing African states. However, this generous language of the conventions does not add up to much in practice. Enhancement of the economic development in the African countries greatly depends on the encouragement of domestic processing of the products in which they have comparative advantages. On the other hand, the STABEX scheme applies, by and large, to primary commodities 'released for home use in the EEC' or brought under the inward processing arrangements in the EEC in order to be processed. Because processed materials are not included in the overall calculations, related domestic industry is not encouraged, nor is domestic consumption. A disincentive is thus being given to African countries to undertake the investment necessary to diversify their production, increase the proportion of value added locally, and thereby reduce their vulnerability to fluctuations in primary product prices. Instead, African states are being encouraged to engage in the production of products with a declining return in earning.

Indeed, several provisions of STABEX 'may actually constitute a disincentive' to African states to undertake additional processing. For instance, not only are many processed products not covered by the scheme but, as Joanna Moss has noted, a move to process a product domestically which 'leads to a reduction in its exports to the EEC could be interpreted as trade diversion, rendering the product ineligible for a STABEX transfer'.[48] Besides, while the scheme offers to stabilise export receipts for certain basic products, it does not deal with the much bigger problem of raising the prices for these products. And, moreover, STABEX is concerned with the stabilisation of nominal earnings rather than real earnings, and export earnings could, therefore, 'be stabilised at inadequate levels'. Persaud has stressed this defect of the scheme:

> An export earnings stabilisation scheme which has the broader objective of promoting economic development must be concerned with maintaining increases in import purchasing power and,

therefore, with preventing declines in export earnings, not only from nominal levels but also from real levels.[49]

Looked at in a wider perspective, STABEX is a disincentive to international economic diversification. It tends to bring the African countries under the firm grip of Europe and offers them an incentive to maintain traditional patterns of trade. The scheme aims at compensating African states for declines in earnings from those tropical products of import interest to Europe, and therefore encourages them to trade only with Europe. Exports to other destinations are not given similar protection. In this particular sense, STABEX has neo-colonial consequences because these limitations encourage the continuation of the traditional centre/periphery or dependency relationship with a double negative effect. First, for the possibility of STABEX compensation, the African states must export to the EEC. Secondly, they must export their traditional primary products which 'maintain the neo-colonial international division of labour'.

Briefly, then, STABEX provides no solution for the fundamental structural problems facing commodity economies. It is a scheme for 'short-term compensation rather than necessary long-term change and diversification'. In this regard, the STABEX scheme is designed to perpetuate inherited one-sided market structures – reconfirming the traditional role of the African states as the suppliers of primary products. As Johan Galtung has put it, STABEX, in an important sense, is 'paying the raw material exporting countries for remaining exporters of raw materials rather than turning to higher levels of processing ... becoming more self-reliant'.[50] To this extent, then, the STABEX scheme looks like stabilising poverty and African collective dependence.

Similarly, while the aims laid down by the Lome Convention in regard to industrial cooperation appear to be generous and ambitious, it has to be acknowledged that the actual results to date are very meagre or even non-existent. The fact that there are no special financial resources for industrial cooperation is certainly a major handicap. Furthermore, the principle of free access of technology has not been reflected in the facts, mainly because of difficulties associated with the system of the ownership of technology in force in the Community. Besides, Europe is not prepared to transfer parts of its technology - a major weapon of its superiority over developing countries - to African states, as this could weaken its leverage with these states and in the long run reduce the market for European goods. Hence, despite the promise of the Lome declaration under the industrial cooperation agreement, no effective measures have been undertaken towards the establishment of a sound base for sustained, self-motivated and self-reliant industrial development in Africa leading to a considerable reduction of the continent's dependence on Europe. Also, Lome makes no provision for a policy to promote and provide protection for foreign investments. The lack of favourable conditions has discouraged investment in the African states, thereby creating a further obstacle to their development.[51]

Of considerable significance to note, also, is the failure of the Lome system explicitly to recognise or sufficiently encourage full permanent sovereignty of the African states over their own economic activities and natural resources. Neither does the system attempt to regulate and supervise the activities of foreign corporations by taking specific measures in the interest of the national economies of the African countries where such corporations operate. The EEC has no binding code of conduct for European corporations in order to prevent their interference in the internal affairs of the African countries and to regulate their activities. Yet the question of controlling the negative effects of the activities of transnational corporations has found concrete expression, not only in the deliberation on the establishment of a New International Economic order,[52] but also in the two Brandt Commission Reports of 1980 and 1983 respectively.[53] It has also been recognised by a number of international organisations - OECD (1976), UNCTAD (1980), the United Nations Centre on Transnational Corporations,[54] and the Andean Foreign Investment Code, Decision 24 under the Cartagena Agreement establishing the Andean Group in 1970.[55] Significantly, too, in Title V, Chapter 2 of the Lome Convention, the European corporations operating in African countries are not prevented from repatriating their profits, while the African governments are to refrain from making any attempt to regulate direct foreign investment and technology transfer in the interests of domestic development. In this regard, the EEC has sought to protect and encourage the expansion of European multinational firms into the African states, which are restricted by the Convention in making independent decisions. The question then arises: to what extent does the second Lome agreement concluded in October 1979 attempt to tackle these various features of dependence of Africa on Europe in the Lome I Convention?

H.   LOME II: SELF-RELIANCE OR UPDATING DEPENDENCE?

Although the 1979 agreement introduces special sections on minerals, investment issues, agricultural cooperation and special provisions for least-developed, island and land-locked ACP countries, Lome II does not represent a radical departure from Lome I - just as Yaounde II was not significantly different from Yaounde I. The new Convention on the whole retains the features of dependence in Lome I, despite its introduction of some outstanding new features. Whilst no substantial modifications are made under Lome II in the areas of aid, trade and industrial cooperation towards some degree of African self-reliance, the new Convention introduces a scheme to promote African mineral production and assist in establishing export revenue derived from minerals. This is the so-called MINEX scheme which, like the STABEX, has some obvious limitations. For example, the nine minerals covered by the scheme are those which are of the utmost importance to Europe's industrial machinery. The ACP's demand that the scheme be extended to include eight additional minerals which are of considerable importance to many ACP states was rejected by the EEC on the ground that it did not consider them to be of any substantial importance to the Community. There can be no doubt that the principal beneficiaries of the MINEX scheme will be the EEC countries. For, by this scheme the Community has finally succeeded in subordinating the Lome agreement to its general scheme for alleviating its own pressing and chronic energy and mineral deficiencies. The provisions under the scheme are intended to increase investment by European firms in mineral exploration, which has declined dramatically since 1974.

It is worth noting, also, that the EEC insisted under the new Convention on maintaining the original Lome rules of origin - which is one of the major obstacles to self- reliant development - although conceding broader scope for derogations. Similarly, the ACP group was not successful in persuading Europe to dispense with safeguard clauses. Although the EEC undertook not to use safeguard clauses for protectionist purposes, the African states are justifiably sceptical about the likely effectiveness of machinery of consultation provided under the agreement, given the EEC's poor record on consultation regarding textiles, and 'they have no recourse to sanctions or compensation'. Moreover, as this safeguard has already been used against Maghreb manufactures in the agreement which the EEC has with those countries, one cannot rest assured that it will not be used against the African countries, when the expansion of their exports in time poses greater problems for the EEC economies themselves.[56] On the whole, then, although Lome II is a comprehensive Treaty containing eleven Titles, compared with seven in Lome I, this new agreement appears in many respects to reinforce the existing structure of production in the African states, in much the same way as the original Convention of Lome has been doing since 1975. This has in turn deepened their external dependence. Basically, therefore, Lome II is not a contribution towards self-reliance or balanced interdependence; it is mostly just an amended version of Lome I.

I.   THE LOME SYSTEM: AN OVERVIEW

Up to this point in our analysis we have attempted to examine the relevant provisions of the Lome Conventions in relation to the question of dependence or interdependence, as defined in this study. It is evident from this analysis that, in the areas of trade, STABEX, aid and industrial cooperation in particular, there is hardly anything suggestive of any structural change away from dependence and towards beneficial interdependence, as observers like Gruhn would have us believe. On the contrary, there is much evidence to suggest that these provisions perpetuate the existing structure of international division of labour and economic relations. This is particularly true in the area of trade which, undoubtedly, is one of the fundamental aspects of the Lome system and a real barometer of African-EEC relations. African states continue in their traditional role as exporters of raw materials, with little or no value added, except for petroleum. The Europeans for their part, have maintained their hegemonic position, albeit with a diversification of industrial goods suppliers. Thus Lome has been unable to initiate a transformation in

Africa's export composition. As Katharine Focke reinforced in her report to the sixth annual meeting of the ACP-EEC Consultative Assembly held in Luxembourg in September 1980, the structure of ACP-EEC trade, among others, still 'retains most of the features of colonial times'. It reveals 'an acute imbalance' both among the products exported, and among the ACP exporting countries no appreciable improvement has taken place since the Lome Convention entered into force.[57] Thus, one can hardly dispute Dolan's contention that:

> It is euphemistic ... to label a relationship interdependent, if manufactured goods flow primarily from the EEC and raw materials flow primarily from the ACP states ... some theories of development and economic imperialism ... suggest that such an international division of labour will ensure under-development for the ACP states and continued dependence upon the EEC.[58]

In the light of this, any suggestion that the Lome system has introduced 'new economic relations' between Europe and Africa,[59] or any idea that Eurafrica is now characterised by 'creeping interdependence', can hardly be sustained.

STABEX has not been able to provide an adequate answer to the deterioration in the terms of trade of the African countries either. The scheme does not directly address the many problems to which primary product exporters are exposed other than short-term foreign exchange shortages. Even here, the approach is patchwork. Studied in terms of structural change in the relationship between Europe and Africa, STABEX is a 'broken reed'. Confining the product coverage to materials which have undergone none or only limited processing serves as a disincentive to African states to diversify and to attempt more value-added production. To put it a little more cynically, therefore, STABEX is a bribe paid to the African states to retain their menial and traditional contemptible role of being the 'hewers of wood and drawers of water'[60] for the Europeans. The scheme is not conceived as one which might lead to a path towards balanced interdependence. Rather, it reinforces the asymmetrical relationship between Europe and Africa.

Similarly, it would be rather naive to take the Community's commitment to ACP industrialisation seriously,[61] because the industrial cooperation agreement of Lome 'lacked substance'. This was acknowledged by the former Community Commissioner for Development, Claude Cheysson, when he stated that the industrial cooperation provisions 'lacked operational content'. The transfer of industrial capacity from the EEC to the African countries will continue to be a difficult and slow process. The EEC's lack of commitment to industrialisation in Africa is evident also in the noted tendency for EDF aid under Lome I to focus more on human needs and infrastructure, somewhat to the neglect of manufacturing and related productive projects. Thus, the history of Lome is one of promises without fulfilment.

Viewed against this background, it is tempting to argue that the widely-acclaimed Lome partnership concept, the 'agreement among equals' idea touted by the EEC, emerges more as a child-parent relationship. Perhaps the horse and rider analogy noted above is even more fitting. For, as Chief Peter Afolabi, Nigeria's Ambassador in Brussels and Chairman of the Industrial Cooperation Working Group in 1983, has remarked, Lome continues to show 'signs of cracks and asymmetry'.[62] Although the Lome system was 'jointly negotiated, jointly agreed and jointly signed by two contracting parties', in practice, there 'is really no transparent' joint ACP-EEC interpretation of the texts whenever problems arise.[63] Studied from a globalist point of view, Lome is also not a viable vehicle for Africa to attain the objectives of the NIEO.

J. LOME AND NIEO

The Lome scheme no doubt contains a number of provisions that, taken together, make for a fresh impetus to international development cooperation in general on a global scale. Hence it was hailed originally by some observers as a constructive initiative in North-South relations and a first concrete step towards a new economic order. While the current immobility of the North-South dialogue[64] would tend to sustain this view, in practice Lome can hardly be viewed as a step which offers possibilities for a restructuring of the cooperation system and which contains assurances for the future. To a great extent it is an agreement which is incompatible with the NIEO.[65] As a trade-oriented scheme which, as noted above, perpetuates unequal exchange, despite some peripheral industrialisation in some African states, Lome is not a new departure from the traditional system of relations between the rich and the poor. Balaam thus concludes:

> In terms of the international system of the 1970s, the Lome Convention presents no radical departure from the tradition of North-South relations. The economics which fired the development schemes of the 1960s still lie at the base of the Lome Convention. The Convention is not a herald of a NIEO but a tribute to the ancien régime.[66]

The ungenerous EEC interpretation and implementation of the Lome scheme, which has led to a further widening of the gap between Europe and Africa, has made the NIEO remain a distant goal for the African states.

Closely studied, Lome leaves much to be desired when viewed within the context of the proposals enunciated in the Declaration and the Programme of Action on a NIEO. For the scheme does not touch, let alone adequately respond to, issues like indexation, long-term commodity agreements, buffer stocks and other important elements in the current discussion of NIEO. It may even interfere with the development of this new world order. It may weaken the motivation of African countries to join other developing countries in the strategy to press for international commodity agreements, general preferences, regulation and control of transnational companies, and the creation of producer organisations. It may even impede the attempts to achieve a better form of global cooperation, since Lome bypasses the international institutions through which the developing countries are exerting their effort for a more just international economic order.[67] Viewed also within the context of Africa's development, Lome is evidently incompatible with the development strategies strongly espoused in the Organisation of African Unity's Lagos Plan of Action (LPA).[68]

K.   LOME AND THE LAGOS PLAN OF ACTION

Africa's relationship with Europe under the Lome agreement and her subsequent adoption in April 1980 of self-reliant development strategy of the LPA would seem to have put African leaders in a state of quandary as to which 'correct' path to adopt towards the economic development of the continent. On the one hand, the fundamental objective of the Lagos document is the establishment of self-sustaining development and economic growth, based on the principles of collective self-reliance. This calls for a restructuring of the economy of Africa, implying among other things (i) the increasing dependence of economic growth and development on internal stimuli and the gradual substitution of domestic for imported inputs, (ii) disengagement, at least partially, of Africa's economy from that of the international economic system as a necessary step towards breaking the dangerous dependency syndrome which seems to be impeding Africa's development, (iii) reduction and alteration of traditional trade and investment relationship, (iv) the strengthening of collaboration among African countries and, finally (v) the re-orientation of development efforts in order to meet the basic social needs of the peoples of Africa.

On the other hand, as indicated above, the Lome scheme advocates a new regime of relationship between Europe and Africa, which has ensured the latter's collective dependence on the former through trade relations, industrial cooperation, economic development through EEC-financed aid, and consultation through a range of institutions. Thus, whereas the historic Lagos document advocates a departure from 'orthodox assumptions and prescriptions', the Lome regime updates and institutionalises, albeit in a comprehensive, generous language, the traditional post-Berlin conference and post-colonial dependence structures. But, while the Lome system is out of step with the LPA, it is to a large extent in conformity with the perceptions and development strategies of the widely-publicised Africa Report of the World Bank, An Agenda for Action, or the Berg Report.[69] From a stance of structural change, in particular, both Lome and the Agenda, unlike the LPA, chart no new path for Africa, break no new ground and offer no new perspectives. Rather, they accept the validity of the existing approach to African development and tend towards further capitalist penetration of African economies.[70] The LPA and the Lome scheme (and the World Bank Agenda) are therefore antithetical in character, objectives and content. To this extent, the statement by Edgard Pisani, EEC Development Commissioner, at the opening of the EEC-ACP Lome III negotiations in October 1983 that the aims of the Lome regime, 'bear a close family resemblance to the ones in the Lagos Plan of

Action[71] can hardly be sustained.

Apart from the incompatibility of Lome with the LPA, there is the question of African regional economic groupings, like the Economic Community of West Africa States (ECOWAS), Central African Customs and Economic Union (UDEAC) and the Southern African Development Co-ordination Conference ((SADCC), which are the major fundamental building blocks of the Lagos Plan. These groupings, within whose framework the economy of Africa is to be restructured, have adopted the strategy of self-reliant development aimed at reducing their dependency on the former metropolitan powers in Europe.[72] In this regard, the Lome agreement is also essentially incompatible with the development of African regional groupings. Furthermore, Lome represents a vertical Eur-African orientation, while ECOWAS, UDEAC and SADCC 'reflect an interest in horizontal South-South links'. For example, while African regional groupings aim at encouraging the growth of horizontal economic transactions among their members, the Lome arrangement is geared towards intensification or reinforcement of the existing pattern of vertical trade links between Europe and Africa. To this extent, Lome constitutes an important constraint, at least in the long run, on the degree of economic cooperation attainable within African regional groupings. Thus, although greater economic self-reliance is a necessity for the regional economic integration schemes in Africa, since it enables them to escape from the historic dependency on the industrial centres and facilitates their development, the successful implementation of this strategy within the Lome framework remains problematic.

L.   WHICH WAY AFRICA? SOME POLICIES

There can be no doubt that, from a stance of structural change, the Lome system is only a small step forward from the old post-Berlin conference links. Given the degree and nature of dependence on Western Europe arising from the structures of trade and technological relations inherited from the pre-emptive colonial intrusion into their body politic, the balanced interdependent idea touted by Europe would remain mere rhetoric. And what is more worrying, the Lome regime as a whole does not seem to give promise of a release from a state of dependence to a state of a mutually-balanced set of interests. There is, therefore, a paramount need on the part of the African countries to initiate various counter-strategies, both from within and outside the Lome system, in their quest for economic independence. This is particularly important because there is the fear that the Lome system, if prolonged unduly, will constitute the whole of Africa into a permanent appendaqe of Europe. A long period of close association with Europe within the framework of the Lome system may tighten the vertical relations between Africa and Europe far more extensively than in the past and create enclaves that may well have the result of strengthening the participation of foreign companies or European powers in the economies of African countries.

However, given the entrenchment of neo-colonialism in Africa and the extent of diversification of markets and sources of investment and technology among different metropolitan countries, any abrupt severance of Africa's intimate linkages with Europe is likely to inflict unacceptable pain upon the continent's fragile economies. Hence, any progress on designing and realising a more equitable and beneficial interdependent relationship between Europe and Africa is likely to be slow. It is not even likely that there would be any major changes in Africa's present relationship with Europe during most of the 1980s. But, while remaining within the Lome system, African countries should begin to adopt strategies geared towards a balanced and beneficial relationship with Europe. As Archibald Mogwe, Botswana's Foreign Minister and President of the ACP Council of Ministers, stated at the opening of the Luxembourg negotiations for Lome III, the ACP states are preoccupied with self-reliant development and their cooperation, through a new convention, must alter their present state of dependency 'and give support to our self-reliant development through the reinforcement of our indigenous cultures'.[73]

M.   TOWARDS A 'BALANCED INTERDEPENDENT' LOME REGIME

The foregoing criticisms of Lome I and II question seriously any future agreeement, unless Lome is substantially revised in the direction of creating a more balanced, reliable and genuine interdependence between Europe and Africa. The new Lome III and all other subsequent agreements should therefore provide an opportunity of making an effective and sustained progress towards the original aim of the signatories to create 'a new model' for relations between Europe and Africa, 'compatible with the aspirations of the international community towards a more just and more balanced economic order'. To attain this end, aspects of the key provisions of the Lome scheme would have to undergo a thorough reform. One crucial area which has been most disappointing to the African states is trade cooperation. This is all the more disturbing because the future economic development of the African countries will depend to a large extent on their successful participation in international trade. Since the bulk of their trade is with Europe, it would be necessary for them to obtain more specific EEC commitment regarding the promotion of their exports in the Community. In this regard, African countries should strengthen their powers of collective bargaining as regards imports from and exports to Europe, and increase the extent to which they can benefit from the possibilities offered by the markets of the EEC members. Importantly, too, efforts should be made towards improved access for manufactures and semi-manufactures from the African countries. As indicated earlier in this chapter, it is on this aspect of the trade agreement that the contribution of Lome to future economic development in Africa would ultimately be judged. Lome's highly restrictive rules of origin which govern the right to duty-free access for African products to European markets need thoroughgoing reform, so that they can be made more flexible and clearer for the African states, as they are at present 'hopelessly complex and unnecessarily restrictive'.[74] The revision of the rules of origin is necessary so as to take into account the very low level of industrialisation in most African states.

Furthermore, to achieve a genuine industrial development in Africa, Europe should eliminate the contradiction between free trade area and the safeguard clause system by providing for a long period of importation of African products. There is the need for a more restricted definition of the safeguard mechanism, which at present limits the potential for investment in the African countries. If the EEC is really committed to the economic development of the African states, then Europe must adjust its attitudes and policies accordingly. The STABEX scheme, for instance, has been left far behind by the 'reforms in the IMF's compensatory financing facility', and has been disappointing in its effects, even on its own terms. As STABEX would seem to have 'imprisoned' the African countries in export-oriented monocultures at the expense of the production of food and of finished goods, it would be necessary for the African states to focus attention, not solely on the need to inject far more massive financial resources into STABEX or the inclusion of new products in the system. Rather, African policy makers should seriously consider the impact which STABEX might have on the structural problems facing the agricultural sector of their countries. Put differently, the STABEX list should include Africa's first-stage processing products. Appropriately, too, the scheme should be 'globalised' - that is, to encompass all African products to all destinations, not just the EEC.[75] But, until a global scheme is established, the African states must continue to press for a more comprehensive and realistic STABEX, and greater involvement in the management of the scheme. Policy decisions must be made in respect of details in its management. Evidently, the continuing denial of a direct role by the African states in the decision-making process of STABEX flies in the face of the claim enshrined in the Preamble to the Convention that it represents equal partnership between Africa and Europe.

Similarly, since the primary aim of the EEC aid is to 'correct sectoral imbalance', Europe should bring the African states into partnership in the determination of broad policy and selection of projects. Specifically, African states should be clearly seen to be involved at a political level in decisions on the allocation of EDF resources, for example in the financial and technical cooperation agreement. This would give a greater feeling of involvement, participation, pride and independence by African states. Aid would then be directed to projects which have the potential for contributing to the diversification of African export products. Another area of major concern is related to the operation of European transnational corporations in the African states, which covers most of the sectors of importance in their economies. It is high time that the Lome regime introduced measures geared to dealing with the circumvention of the costs associated with transnationals, as already in force in various international and regional organisations, including the EEC itself. In broad terms, such measures should aim at controlling restrictive business practices arising out of technology transfer between Europe and Africa. Besides, it would be highly desirable for the African states to

set up appropriate institutions and also offer
suitable incentives for the development of
indigenous technology wherever possible.

Besides these specific measures, which are
required under the Lome regime in order to establish
a relationship based upon reciprocity and balance
rather than one-sided dominance and asymmetry, the
African countries might consider introducing some
other significant issues which would be vital to
their economic health. Among such negotiable matters
is the need for introducing into the Lome scheme
some special emergency provisions which may be
applicable to any economy in dire straits. Such
provisions should make it possible for the EEC,
among other things, to agree to remove all
restrictions on the exports of the 'ailing economy'
for a specified period. This would provide the much-
needed incentive to the afflicted state to enable it
to bring the economy back to normalcy, and possibly
within a reasonably short period. Emergency
measures of this type, quite apart from those
relating to aid from the EDF, are becoming
increasingly necessary in view of the frequent
fluctuations in the world economy. Again, with the
enlargement of the EEC to include the southern
Mediterranean countries like Greece, Portugal and
Spain, which produce many goods which compete with
African exports, particularly textiles, fruits and
vegetables, it is necessary that the African states
seek protection under the Lome regime against
adverse consequences of the EEC enlargement on their
products. They must unequivocally press for a
guarantee that their original agreements with the
Community of Nine would not subsequently be
threatened by the accession of new members to the
EEC. More specifically, a legal clause should be
inserted into the Lome arrangement which would
enable the African countries to negotiate the
effects of enlargement with the EEC, after the
enlargement negotiations have themselves been
concluded.

In addition, as a counter-strategy to the
exclusive dependence on the former metropolitan
countries of Western Europe, African countries
should diversify their external economic relations –
trading partners and sources of technology and
capital – to include countries like the United
States, Australia, Canada or Japan. This approach
has the potential for strengthening the bargaining
position of the governments of African states by
enabling them 'to play off' one developed economy

against another. Further, as an effort to tackle the problem of dependency on Western Europe, African countries may also develop closer economic relations with the industrialised countries of the socialist community, such as members of the Council for Mutual Economic Assistance (CMEA) or COMECON, the Eastern European Common Market. The importance of such a diversification of external economic links cannot be over-emphasised. Ali Mazrui has driven this point home in his BBC Reith Lectures, when he declared:

> ... there are occasions when freedom begins with the multiplication of one's masters. If one is owned and controlled by only one power, freedom is often particularly restrictive. But, if an African society cultivates the skills to have more than one hegemonic power competing for it, this has possibilities for liberation. To be dependent on two giants, especially when the giants have rivalries between them, is sometimes an opportunity to play one against the other - and maximise one's own options.[76]

Another option still available for African countries in the effort to strengthen the bargaining power of the continent vis-à-vis Europe is to join forces in mutual cooperation through the creation of sub-regional, regional and inter-regional schemes of integration evolving into an African Common Market, and ultimately leading to an African Economic Community, as espoused in the 'Final Act' of the Lagos Plan of Action. President Nyerere has said that 'small nations are like indecently clad women, they tempt the evil-minded'. Regional cooperation schemes would make smallness of individual countries slightly less vulnerable. And it is only through collective action that African states can, to an appreciable degree, free themselves from the present collective dependence on Europe and the international economic order, in which most of them appear doomed to a dependent role as perpetual suppliers on terms dictated by outsiders.

One other alternative available to African countries in the pursuit of economic independence is to develop preferential economic links with other developing countries in Asia and Latin America. In more concrete terms, this implies the promotion of economic cooperation among developing countries, 'the new imperative of development in the 1980s', to quote Elvin Laszlo. A vast realm is open for joint action by these countries in the fields of economic

and technical cooperation. Several conferences have
already been held on this issue, most notable in
Mexico City (1976), Colombo in the same year, Buenos
Aires (1979), Caracas (1980) and New Delhi (1981),
and several UN agencies have already established new
bureaucracies to handle the subject. Joint action by
developing countries can be crucial in enabling them
to defend the prices of their exports of raw
materials and to protect their sovereignty over
their natural resources. It can also encourage the
growth of indigenous capacities in science and
technology, facilitate the marketing of their
products, help to increase their industrial
capability and, above all, strengthen their
decision-making power in multilateral
institutions.[77] Indeed, by taking full advantage of
opportunities of mutual interdependence and
complementarity of their economies, the countries of
the South, as Adebayo Adedeji, Executive Secretary
of the Economic Commission for Africa, concluded in
an illuminating address, 'will sooner or later put
themselves in a position to seize the initiative and
assume the leadership for bringing about the
establishment of the new international economic
order'.[78]

All of these contacts would represent Africa's
desire to blunt the impact of its continuing
dependence on the industrialised nations by
diversifying that relationship beyond exclusive
reliance on Western Europe. These contacts would
furthermore enhance Africa's bargaining strength and
exercise its countervailing power, thereby creating
the compulsions which would make Europe willy-nilly
negotiate the desired changes in the Lome regime.
While all this may sound utopian to many readers, it
is important to stress that at this point our
concern is not so much with what is immediately
practicable as with what is ultimately desirable.

The final policy prescription for solving
Africa's continued dependence on Europe is based on
the proposition that any meaningful restructuring of
relations with Europe and indeed with the
international economic system as a whole, would
never be effective in the absence of what may be
termed 'new domestic economic orders' in many
African countries, that is, internal policy reforms.
After all, Lome is intended to be only an external
stimulus to modernisation within the African
countries. The acceleration of general economic
development and the modernisation of the economy in
the African countries are, however, determined by

socio-economic and political conditions at home. As Frey-Wouters rightly reminds us, the principal limits to sustained economic growth and accelerated development 'are political, social and institutional rather than physical'.[79] Long-term economic development basically depends on the extent to which 'it proves possible to mobilize limited social resources'. Far-reaching internal changes are necessary in the political, institutional and economic structures as essential bases for creating a balanced and beneficial interdependent Lome regime.

N.   CONCLUSION

Africa has undoubtedly travelled a long way - albeit difficult and bumpy - from the late nineteenth century Berlin conference era of Eur-Africanism to the late twentieth century Eur-African relations characterised by the Lome Conventions. What clearly emerges is that Europe is pursuing the same old policies but with new means. As a short-term, transitional arrangement, Lome should have been appropriate and beneficial to the African countries. Trade with Europe and aid from Europe are both necessary and unavoidable. But the dominant short-term gain has proved inadequate. Exports to Europe have grown rapidly in nominal but not real terms; and aid has lagged badly in disbursement. Contrasted to Yaounde II, the Lome treaty is an improvement: it is less unequal. But, studied against the background of the real needs of the African countries during this last quarter of the twentieth century, the Lome Conventions fall short of expectation. Although it is taking the interests of Africa into account in some respects, the Lome deal is also a compromise in which Europe is not restricted in pursuing its own interests.

It has been argued that, from a long-term perspective, close participation in the EEC system does not seem to be in the interests of the African countries. These countries, in response to the goal of the Lagos Plan of Action, should move towards greater autonomy and individual and collective self-reliance and should orient economic decisions around their national and regional political constituency rather than allow the locus of decision-making to gravitate towards the private and public sectors in the European countries. Thus, besides the diversification of economic relations aimed at reducing dependence, Africa must accept that no society can develop without becoming self-reliant and inward-looking. This, however, calls for self-discipline and sacrifice. We must accept the discipline that is required for establishing 'new domestic economic orders', if we ever hope to transform our relationship with Europe from one of permanent dependence to one of beneficial interdependence which can generate within the African society itself the engine necessary for sustained economic growth.

NOTES

[1] See Kwame Nkrumah, Address to the Ghana National Assembly (Accra, 30 May 1961).

[2] I. William Zartman, 'Europe and Africa: Decolonisation or Dependency?', Foreign Affairs, 54 (2), January 1976.

[3] Isebill Gruhn, 'The Lome Convention: Inching toward Interdependence', International Organisation, 30 (2), Spring 1976.

[4] Ellen Frey-Wouters, The European Community and the Third World: The Lome Convention and Its Impact (New York, Praeger, 1980), p.253.

[5] See David Wall, 'The EEC-ACP Convention: A Model for a New International Economic Order?', Halifax Conference on Canada and the New International Economic Order, Saint Mary's University, August 1975.

[6] Michael Dolan, 'The Lome Convention and Europe's Relationship with the Third World: A Critical Analysis', Journal of European Integration, 1 (3), May 1978.

[7] Lynn K. Mytelka, 'The Lome Convention and a New International Division of Labour', Journal of European Integration, 1 (1), September 1977, p.64.

[8] Lynn K. Mytelka and Michael B. Dolan, 'The Political Economy of EEC-ACP Relations in a Changing International Division of Labour', Institute of Development Studies (Brighton, May 1979).

[9] Guy Martin, 'Africa and the Ideology of Eurafrica: Neo-Colonialism or Pan-Africanism?', The Journal of Modern African Studies, 20 (2), 1982, p.222.

[10] For detailed discussion of these terms, see James A. Caporaso, 'Dependence, Dependency and Power in the Global System: A Structural and Behavioural Analysis'; and Raymond D. Duvall, 'Dependence and Dependencia Theory: Notes Towards Precision of Concept and Argument', both in International Organisation, 32 (1), Winter 1978, pp.13-44 and

51-78.

[11] T. M. Shaw, 'Towards an International Political Economy for the 1980s; From Dependence to (Inter)dependence'. (Halifax, Centre for Foreign Policy Studies, Dalhousie University, 1980), p.7.

[12] Robert O. Keohane and Joseph S. Nye, 'World Politics and the International Economic System', in C. Fred Bergsten (ed.), The Future of the International Economic System (Lexington, Lexington Books, 1973), pp.121-5.

[13] Sanjaya Lall, 'Is "Dependence" a Useful Concept in Analysing Underdevelopment?', World Development, 3 November 1975, p.808.

[14] Richard Rosecrance and Arthur Stein, 'Interdependence: Myth or Reality?', World Politics, XXVI (1), October 1973, p.2.

[15] See, for example, Hayward R. Almer et al., Analysing Global Interdependence, 4 vols. (Cambridge, Mass., Centre for International Studies, MIT, 1974), and Vol. 1: Analytical Perspective and Policy Implications, p.2.

[16] Josua D.V. Cavalevu, in The Courier, November 1982 - December 1983, p.4.

[17] For example, T. Dos Santos, 'The Structure of Dependence', American Economic Review (60), May 1970, pp.231-6; Samir Amin, 'Underdevelopment and Dependence in Black Africa: Origins and Contemporary Forms', The Journal of Modern African Studies, 10 (4), 1972, pp.503-24.

[18] Guy Martin, 'The Political Economy of African-European Relations from Yaounde I to Lome II, 1963-1980: A Case Study in Neo-Colonialism and Dependency', PhD. dissertation, Indiana University, Bloomington, 1982.

[19] James A. Caporaso, Introduction to the Special Issue of International Organisation on 'Dependence and Dependency In the Global System', International Organisation, 32 (1), Winter 1978, p.1; Duvail, 'Dependence and Dependencia', Ibid., pp.51-78.

[20] See, for example David A. Baldwin, 'Interdependence and Power: A Conceptual Analysis', International Organisation, 34 (4), Autumn 1980, pp.471-506; Kenneth Waltz, 'The Myth of Interdependence', in Charles P. Kindleberger (ed.), The International Corporation (Cambridge, Mass., 1970).

[21] Josua Cavalevu, op. cit.

[22] Hedley Bull, The Anarchical Society: A Study of Order in World Politics (London, Macmillan, 1977), p.280. Cited in Shaw, 'Towards an

International Political Economy', p.16.

23 See Alex Inkeles, 'The Emerging Social Structure of the World', World Politics, 27 July 1975, pp.477-86. See also, Gordon K. Douglass, The New Interdependence (Lexington, Lexington Books, 1979).

24 Laurens Jan Brinkhorst, 'Lome and After', in Frans Alting von Gensau (ed.), The Lome Convention and the New International Economic Order (Leyden, A.W. Sijthoff, 1977), p.6.

25 Ibid., p.7.

26 Reginald H. Green, 'The Lome Convention: Updated Dependence or Departure Towards Collective Self-Reliance?', Africa Review, 6 (1), 1976, p.43.

27 Carl C. Twitchett, Europe and Africa: From Association to Partnership (Farnborough, Saxon House, 1979), p.122.

28 Reginald H. Green, 'The Child of Lome: Messiah, Monster or Mouse', in Frank Long (ed.), The Political Economy of EEC Relations with African, Caribbean and Pacific States: Contributions to the Understanding of the Lome Convention on North-South Relations (Oxford, Pergamon Press, 1980).

29 Green, 'The Lome Convention', p.43.

30 Martin, 'Africa and the Ideology of Eurafrica', pp.228-9.

31 Text of Joint Communiqué by President Nkrumah of Ghana and President Brezhnev of the Soviet Union, 24 July 1961. Cited in Arnold Rivkin, Africa and the European Common Market: A Perspective (Denver, 1964), p.35.

32 See J. Pinder, 'The Community and the Developing Countries: Associates and Outsiders', Journal of Common Market Studies, XII (1), September 1973, p.53.

33 Adrian Hewitt and Christopher Stevens, 'The Second Lome Convention', in Christopher Stevens (ed.), EEC and the Third World: A Survey (London, Hodder & Stoughton, 1981), p.30.

34 Timothy M. Shaw, 'EEC-ACP Interactions and Images as Redefinitions of Eurafrica: Exemplary, Exclusive and/or Exploitative?', Journal of Common Market Studies, XVIII (2), December 1979, p.142.

35 Ibid., p.142.

36 Frey-Wouters, The European Community, p.43.

37 See ACP Council, ACP/365/77.

38 See M. Gullabert, 'Draft Report for the ACP-EEC Consultative Assembly Joint Committee' (Brussels, 1978).

39 Carol Cosgrove Twitchett, 'Towards a New ACP-EEC Convention', The World Today, 34 (2),

December 1978, p.475. For further details see her chapter on 'Patterns of ACP-EEC Trade', in Long (ed.), The Political Economy of ACP-EEC Relations, pp.145-82.

[40] For details, see Hewitt and Stevens, 'The Second Lome Convention', p.37.

[41] Second Report from the Select Committee on Overseas Development, Session 1977-8; Renegotiation of the Lome Convention, Vol.2: Evidence and Appendices (London, HMSO, H.C. 586-11, 1978).

[42] Twitchett, 'Towards a New ACP-EEC Convention', p.479.

[43] Abby Rubin, Lome II: The Renegotiation of the Lome Convention (London, Catholic Institute for International Relations, 1978), p.6.

[44] See Joanna Moss, The Lome Conventions and Their Implications for the United States (Boulder, Westview Press, 1982), p.31.

[45] See James O'Neil Lewis, 'Trade and Development', Association News, 25 (May-June 1974), pp.11-12.

[46] A. Hewitt, 'The European Development Fund as a Development Agent: Some Result of EDF Aid to Cameroon', ODI Review (2) (London, 1979), p.55.

[47] Cecil Rajana, 'The Lome Convention: An Evaluation of EEC Economic Assistance to the ACP States', The Journal of Modern African Studies, 20 (2), 1982, p.215.

[48] Moss, The Lome Conventions, p.96.

[49] Bishnodat Persaud, 'Export Earnings Stabilisation in the ACP-EEC Convention', in Long (ed.), The Political Economy of EEC Relations, p.100.

[50] John Galtung, 'The Lome Convention and Neo-Capitalism', The African Review, 6 (1), 1976, p.40.

[51] See Guillabert, 'Draft Report for the ACP-EEC Consultative Assembly'.

[52] See General Assembly Resolutions 3201 (S-VI) and 3202 (S-VI), 1974. For a detailed discussion of this, see S.K.B. Asante, 'The New International Economic Order and the Problem of Controlling Multinational Corporations'. Paper presented at the International Conference on the Future of Africa and the New International Economic Order, University of Ife, Nigeria, June 1982.

[53] See North-South: A Programme for Survival: Report of the Independent Commission on International Development Issues (Brandt Commission) (London, Pan, 1980), pp.187-200: and Common Crisis, North-South Co-operation for World Recovery (London, Pan, 1983), pp.82-3.

[54] For United Nations efforts, see UN Centre on Transnational Corporations, Transnational Corporations in World Development: Third Survey (New York, United Nations, 1983); and especially, Commission on Transnational Corporations, Report on the Special Session, March and May 1983, Economic and Social Council, Official Records, 1983 Supplement No. 7, E/1983/17/Rev. 1 and E/C.10/1983/S/5/Rev.1.

[55] For details of the Andean Investment Code, see Constantine V. Vaitsos, The Role of Transnational Enterprises in Latin American Economic Integration Efforts: Who Integrates and With Whom, How and For Whose Benefit? Report prepared for UNCTAD Secretariat, TAC/E1/SEM.5/2, March 1978.

[56] Carol Cosgrove Twitchett, 'Lome II: A New ACP-EEC Agreement', The World Today, 36 (3), March 1980, p.115.

[57] The Courier, 64 (November-December 1980), 'Yellow' page 2.

[58] Dolan, 'The Lome Convention', p.390.

[59] See 'Special Issue of The Courier - Lome Dossier', (31), March 1975, pp.2-3.

[60] Tom Soper, 'Africa and the Common Market', The Listener, 10 August 1961, cited in Omari H. Kokole, 'STABEX Anatomised', Third World Quarterly, 3 (3), July 1981, p.448.

[61] Moss, The Lome Conventions, p.134.

[62] Peter Afolabi, 'Lome Shows "Signs of Cracks and Asymmetry"', The Courier, 82 (November-December 1983), 'Yellow' page xvi.

[63] D.V. Cavalevu, Ibid., p.3.

[64] See Robert L. Rothstein, 'The North-South Dialogue; The Political Economy of Immobility', in John J. Stremlau (ed.), The Foreign Policy Priorities of Third World States (Boulder, Westview Press, 1982), pp.151-67.

[65] See notes 5 and 6 above.

[66] Hugh V. Balaam, 'The Lome Convention: Who Profits?', Workshop on the European Community and the Third World (Princeton, Princeton University, December 1976), p.12.

[67] For details, see S.K.B. Asante, 'The European Community, the Lome Conventions, and the North-South Dialogue'. Paper presented at the International Colloquium on Relations Between Europe and Africa in the Framework of the North-South Dialogue, Lome, March 1982.

[68] Organisation of African Unity, Lagos Plan of Action for the Economic Development of Africa 1980-2000 (Geneva, International Institute for Labour Studies, 1981).

[69] IBRD (World Bank), Accelerated Development in Sub-Saharan Africa: An Agenda for Action (Washington, DC, 1981).

[70] For detailed comparative analysis of the Lagos Plan and the Agenda, see Robert S. Browne and Robert J. Cummings, The Lagos Plan of Action vs. The Berg Report: Contemporary Issues in African Economic Development (Lawrenceville, Brunswick Publishing Co., 1984). See also, S.K.B. Asante, 'Expectations and Reality: Transnational Corporations and Regional Self-Reliance Objectives of the Lagos Plan of Action'. Paper presented at the International Conference on OAU/ECA Lagos Plan of Action, and the Future of Africa (University of Ife, Ife, Nigeria, March 1984).

[71] See The Courier, 82 (November-December 1983), p.vi.

[72] For the case of ECOWAS, see S.K.B. Asante, 'The Experience of EEC: Relevant or Impediment to ECOWAS Regional Self-Reliance Objective?', Afrika Spectrum, 3 (1983); Sam Olofin, 'ECOWAS and the Lome Convention: An Experiment in Complementary or Conflicting Customs Union Arrangements', Journal of Common Market Studies, September 1977, pp.53-72.

[73] Archibald Mogwe, 'A Crucial Moment in the Future of our Peoples', The Courier, 82 (November-December 1983),'Yellow' pages II.

[74] G. K. Helleiner, 'Lome and Market Access', in Long (ed.), The Political Economy of EEC Relations, p.186.

[75] Kokole, 'STABEX Anatomised', p.457.

[76] Ali A. Mazrui, The African Condition: A Political Diagnosis (London, Cambridge University Press, 1983), p.82.

[77] For further details, see Benno Engels, 'The Global Approach to South-South Cooperation', Development and Cooperation, 1 (January-February 1984), pp.14-16; Elvin Laszlo, Regional Cooperation among Developing Countries (New York, Pergamon Press, 1981).

[78] Adebayo Adedeji, 'Africa and the South: Forging Truly Interdependent Economic and Technical Links', a talk delivered at India International Centre on 19 May 1979, published in Africa Quarterly, XX (1-2), p.13.

[79] Frey-Wouters, The European Community, p.142.

CHAPTER 11

THE DIALECTICS OF REGIONALISM: EURAFRICA AND WEST AFRICA*

Timothy M. Shaw

The centenary of the Berlin Conference is both symbolic and instructive: symbolic because it marks a century of change from colonialism to neo-colonialism and now post-neocolonialism; and instructive because it reveals how little has changed despite national political independence and global economic interdependence. The interrelated dialectics of politics and economics and of levels of integration come together in any discussion of EurAfrica and African regionalism: regionalism as North-South dependence, and regionalism as South-South interdependence respectively. The degree of compatibility and incompatibility between these became apparent in 1985 as Lome III was being negotiated between the EEC and ACP and as ECOWAS attempted to advance regional cooperation along the West African coast in an area of diverse colonial and neo-colonial relationships.

A.   REVISIONISM, REGIONALISM AND THE CONTINENTAL CRISIS

Contemporary contradictions between regionalisms take place in a world system characterised by recession, inflation and transition. The demise of the post-war Bretton Woods order of relative expansion and diffusion has resulted in a more anarchic, unyielding world of general contraction and highly uneven patterns of growth and decline, from the resilience of South Korea and Singapore to the stagnation of Senegal and Zambia, and the decay of Ghana and Tanzania, i.e. the new division between Newly Industrialising Countries (NICs) and Least Less Developed Countries (LLDCs), between 'Third' and 'Fourth' Worlds.
    The last decade, then, has seen a relatively

homogeneous continent become considerably heterogeneous, with myriad implications for cohesion and regionalism. It has also witnessed a growing tension between the political and the economic, as well as an emerging set of contradictory responses symbolised by the OAU's Lagos Plan of Action, on the one hand, and the World Bank's Agenda for Action on the other. If the latter advocates extroverted growth, compatible with EurAfricanism, then the former advances African self-reliance, compatible with continental regionalism.

In short, the present conjuncture of global and continental crises has stimulated a variety of responses at the levels of politics and economics on the one hand and of EurAfrican and continental regionalisms on the other hand. Given the new diversity of political economies on the continent, these alternatives, and not necessarily compatible policies and preferences, are advocated by different states, classes and fractions. The myth of Pan-Africanism is thus under attack from both extra and intra-African forces of either disinterest, division or dominance. Regionalism a hundred years after Berlin is a controversial ideology and policy because of a multiplicity of interpretations, interests and implications. Its tendency to manipulation and ambiguity is a reflection of the range of contradictions generated by the current crisis and the intensity of competition for scarce resources in a period of no growth. Regionalism becomes more problematic and antagonistic as growth is elusive and projections are unpromising. Hence the willingness of diverse interests to define it in different ways to maximise their prospects of renewed growth, if not development.

Therefore, regionalism has had a rather chequered history in Africa. An approach to African development and unity that has its origins in post-Berlin colonial practice, regionalism has been based on the premise that several states can prosper together more than a single state. In pursuit of development and unity, declarations of intent to advance regional integration have become commonplace on the continent over the last two decades. However, the results have been less spectacular than the resolutions: decay has been as frequent as development. And African plans have been advocated along with EurAfrican raising questions of compatibility.

Nevertheless, despite many cautionary tales, optimism abounds over the latest effort at

regionalism in the continent; the Economic Community
of West African States (ECOWAS). In many ways a
'second-generation' institution, ECOWAS is, despite
the subsequent appearance of SADCC, both bigger and
more ambitious than previous experiments in either
Africa or elsewhere. Nevertheless, its prospects
remain problematic, and its aspirations remain
ambiguous. Its tenuous situation and support lead to
a set of questions about its future that are posed
in the concluding section, (E), although the
turbulent future of Southern Africa - the
conjuncture of racism and repression,
destabilisation and disengagement - may yet spill
over to affect ECOWAS.

Regional development and unity are likely to
remain elusive in Africa in the mid-term future
because of changes in the global political economy
as well as because of related shifts in the
continental system. If regionalism was difficult in
previous decades, notwithstanding prior schemes in
the colonial period after Berlin, it is likely to be
even more so in the 1980s because of interrelated
changes in the global and continental divisions of
labour and economic priorities. Until the mid-
1970s, international growth was sufficiently large
for the marginal redistribution of surplus and
opportunity from the centre to the periphery to be
neither impossible nor controversial. However, in
the less benign and more calculating world of the
1980s - world of recession and inflation still
trying to live with fluctuating exchange and
interest rates and with ineluctably higher prices
for energy - Third World regional development at the
expense of metropolitan growth is most unlikely.
Internatiional economics are once again zero-
rather than mixed-sum; the environment for
regionalism is no longer tolerant, let alone
supportive. If ECOWAS fails, the causes may well be
extra- rather than intra-African; and, if it
succeeds, the benefits may well flow outside
rather than inside the region. Yet, despite the
problems of regionalism in Africa over the last
twenty years, many of which arose in less difficult
times than today, West African leaders retain the
faith that ECOWAS will be exceptional. Given the
lack of visible, viable options, such faith may be
the lack of any alternative: regionalism and self-
reliance by default.

This chapter attempts to explain and evaluate
the elusiveness of regionalism in Africa by contrast
to the seeming resilience of EurAfricanism, by

224

situating it in the context of the changing global political economy. The prospects for unity and development on the continent in the 1980s are profoundly affected by pressures on the international division of labour elsewhere. Likewise, any projections for regionalism in Africa in general and West Africa in particular, cannot exclude world trends and forecasts: the ambiguity of dominance, especially of EurAfrica. In short, given the global capitalist system, dependent regions, like dependent states, are conditioned by external interests and institutions:

> To understand dependence as a conditioning context of certain kinds of internal structure is to understand development as a world-wide historical phenomenon, as a consequence of the formation, expansion and consolidation of the capitalist system.[2]

B. AFRICAN UNITY IN THE 1980S: BEYOND BERLIN?

International capitalism has evolved considerably in the two decades that Africa has been formally independent. This evolution - from liberalism to protectionism, from American hegemony to 'trilateralism', and from growth to recession - has important implications for the African continent. If most African states failed to grow before the mid seventies, their prospects have since deteriorated.[3] And any improvement that has occurred - before but especially after the mid-seventies - has been unevenly generated and distributed, both between and within countries.

Growing inequalities in Africa have important implications for unity as well as for development. In response to the elusiveness of growth, the 'development strategies' of states have diverged away from a consensual form of 'African socialism' and towards various types of 'state capitalism' and 'state socialism'. And these alternatives tend to be related to differences in international position and potential. Uneven development in terms of both empirical and ideological orientation is not new to Africa.[4] However, the emergence of a small group of 'middle powers' is unlikely to be a transitory phenomenon. Rather, their position at the 'semi-periphery' - by contrast to the peripheral position of most African states - is structural, not just political or ephemeral, encouraged by continued EurAfrican relationships. Independence did not bring development for all but it did facilitate growth for some.

African unity has always been something of a myth. But its mythical qualities have multiplied as the continent has become more unequal. In particular, the uneven impact of recession and inflation in the mid-seventies exacerbated inequalities: a minority of 'Third World' states weathered the storm, whereas the majority of 'Fourth World' states were further depressed and impoverished economically. The Third World of Newly Industrialising/Influential Countries (NICs) includes the major centres of manufacturing and communications - Algeria, Egypt, Ivory Coast, Kenya, Nigeria and Zimbabwe - whereas the Fourth World of the real periphery is increasingly marginalised. The latter, Most Seriously Affected States, can hardly afford to import enough food, let alone capital, so that their economic prospects continue to dim, rather than brighten. By contrast, the NICs have adjusted to OPEC more readily and positively and they have captured most of the (inadequate) increase in the regional product that has been generated in the last decade. In Africa the 'middling rich' get somewhat richer, while the poor get even poorer. And EEC interests concentrate on the former at the expense of the latter, disclaimers of North-South dialogue notwithstanding.

The NICs have so far been able to benefit by adopting orthodox economic policies of incorporation within the world system; their relative structural proximity to OECD members has enabled them to take advantage of shifts in the international division of labour. The production of oil and gas in Algeria and Nigeria, of manufactures in Egypt and Zimbabwe, and of primary products and services in the Ivory Coast and Kenya have enabled this set of relatively affluent countries to grow further. The logic of 'trickle-down' seems to work for them: the semi-periphery[5] and centre countries continue to share positive growth, even at the cost of negative growth in the periphery itself. Despite EEC aid, STABEX and MINEX, the semi-periphery was drawn closer to Europe, whereas the periphery has drifted away.

By contrast, then, the majority of African states has become increasingly impoverished as the terms of trade have moved against them. Growing dependence on foreign food, as well as capital, markets and technology, has led them into indebtedness. In response this periphery has sought to disengage and to satisfy Basic Human Needs (BHN) rather than to meet international market demands. Strategies of national and collective self-reliance may be a necessity for them rather than a choice. So, not only in empirical but also in ideological terms, African states are diverging: the periphery wants to move away from the centre, while the semi-periphery needs to move towards the centre. This divergence tends to retard African unity at both continental and regional levels and is reflected in distinctive attitudes towards regionalism, whether it be EurAfrican, continental and/or regional.

The different interests of middle and minor powers - Third and Fourth Worlds respectively - undermines the prospects for either unity or development in Africa: dependence on or disengagement from the centre countries, especially from the pervasive EEC nexus affect both unity and development. At the continental level, the NICs are the major actors in the OAU system, while at the regional level they are the 'core', the catalysts to integration. Moreover, paradoxically, although the middle powers can dominate the OAU regional systems, their outwards, extroverted orientation may make them disinterested in doing so: for them Africa is still primacy. Conversely, the Fourth World may have more to gain from and so be more insistent upon regional cooperation, providing it is defined in appropriate ways; for them continental or regional integration is the only option. For the latter, then, collective self-reliance, in addition to national disengagement, may be a question of survival rather than of choice.

These alternative orientations towards regionalism - disinterest versus determination (but see sections (C) and (D) below on the tension between structural position and development policy) - are quite similar to the alternative approaches apparent in the literature: orthodox versus radical. In the case of the former, orthodox position, incorporation in the world system is taken to be normal and advantageous, whereas in the case of the latter, radical position, dependence on the world system is assumed to be involuntary and deleterious. The former takes it for granted that decolonisation has begun to occur and is effective, whereas the latter believes that dependence is a continuing inheritance and constraint.[5] So the Third World - the more affluent among the Group of 77 - tends not to need and so may be disinclined to support regionalism other than EurAfrica, whereas the Fourth World - the more impoverished of the 77 -

both needs and welcomes it, providing it is redefined as self-reliance. Therefore, unity is elusive in both conceptualisation and implementation.

Indeed, African unity is more of a myth in 1980 than it was in 1960 because the old ideological cleavages have been superseded by new structural divergencies: the Monrovia-Casablanca divide was more personal and pliable than the current Third World versus Fourth World tension, with its structural roots in EurAfrican incorporation. The distinctive positions and policies of the NICs compared with the Least Developed Countries cannot be transcended by an Addis Ababa summit, particularly in a period of growing recession and competition in continental and global economies. Although consensual African and non-aligned resolutions may serve to camouflage or mute the disagreements between richer and poorer states - between, say Algeria and Burundi, or Zimbabwe and Somalia - their interests can no longer be rendered compatible easily. Indeed, their policies may be not only incompatible but rather contradictory - with profound implications for the claim of regionalism - as revealed in their respective and divergent development strategies for the difficult world of the 1980s.

C   AFRICAN DEVELOPMENT IN THE 1980s: DEPENDENT OR SELF-RELIANT?

African unity is increasingly tenuous, therefore, because African states have increasingly divergent positions within the world system; a divergence which Lome does not transcend and may even exacerbate. The majority of primary commodity producers have suffered declining terms of trade as the prices of manufactures and petroleum have increased; over the last decade the LLDCs have hardly grown at all, with several enduring negative growth rates in the second half of the 1970s. By contrast, the NICs have grown at an almost exponential rate, especially those that are also OPEC members (e.g. Algeria and Nigeria). Africa is, therefore, an increasingly unequal continent in which growth, industrialisation and optimism are concentrated in a few NICs, while the majority of countries and peoples suffers minimal growth, continued marginalisation and a pessimistic outlook. In these circumstances, development strategies diverge, as do growth rates, despite collective economic policies in the OAU, Lome and Group of 77 arrangements.

At decolonisation, most African leaders opted for some variant of 'African socialism': economic nationalism which emphasised import substitution and increased exports. With the evident failure of orthodox 'modernisation' theory to produce results and facing the general threat of OECD disinterest - notwithstanding the special relationship of France and francophonie - the ruling class moved towards the espousal of some variant of 'self-reliance'. Such 'defensive radicalism'[7] was intended (a) to head off the pressures resulting from internal and international inequalities and (b) to turn to advantage the ungenerous and increasingly protectionist behaviour of advanced industrialised states. In short, the LLDCs were to satisfy their own BHN before, rather than after, meeting 'international' demands for primary products.

By contrast to this 'disengagement'[8] orientation of the Fourth World, Third World African states have encouraged further incorporation within the world system. Their contrasting experience in the post-war, post-colonial global economy makes them more positive towards orthodox strategies, so the NICs have sought, especially since the mid-1970s, to maximise the benefits from an extroverted, outward-looking orientation. They do not want to disengage from, but seek merely to reform, established patterns of 'interdependence'. Contemporary changes in the character of international capitalism have been beneficial for them; they do not contemplate self-reliance but merely encourage national participation in transnational networks.[9] Hence, their ambivalent attitude towards their role in ACP: leaders or followers, given their privileged position <u>vis-à-vis</u> the EEC.

In short, the LLDCs look inwards, while the NICs look outwards; poorer African states advocate self-reliance, while the richer favour further incorporation. These 'back-to-back' developmental orientations have important implications for regional as well as continental cooperation. The LLDCs tend to favour collective as well as national self-reliance, but the prospects for autonomy through regionalism are reduced when the 'core' of each potential region is more extroverted in policy and in practice: African and EurAfrican regionalism become contradictory at such junctions. The periphery cannot effectively turn around regional institutions towards disengagement, when the semi-periphery seeks to play an intermediary role, involving continued association with metropolitan countries and corporations. In other words, regional integration in Africa is now jeopardised because regional leaders are either disinterested or diverted: successive Lome arrangements provide alternative avenues for pressure and position.

The logic of the semi-periphery has negative implications for successful integration within the periphery except as an extension of ubiquitous EurAfrican connections. Regional powers, like Algeria, Egypt, Ivory Coast, Kenya, Senegal and Zimbabwe, grow not only because of their relatively large extractive, manufacturing or service sectors but also because they have come to dominate regional relations, diplomatic as well as economic. In an area of relative superpower withdrawal, they have had their intermediary role recognised and expanded. So they play effectively the role of regional leader - catalyst and core - but their connections with metropolitan countries and corporations make them linkages in the centre-periphery chain. In other words, their interest in regionalism as the semi-periphery - dominance and growth - may be quite different from that of the periphery - development and self-reliance: the conception of regionalisms within Africa and EurAfrica are quite distinctive and may be dialectical.

This also means that the semi-periphery has an orientation quite different from that of the other major continental organisation - the Economic Commission for Africa (ECA). Yet, in an era when the Pan-African political consensus within the OAU has become elusive - see disputes over Angola, Chad, Sahara, Shaba, Somalia, etc. - the apparent Pan-African economic consensus within the ECA has become broader and more solid. Given projections of increased inequalities, dependence and underdevelopment,[10] the ECA has called for a collective response outside of the EEC-ACP nexus to head off an unpromising future. At a time when the definition and implementation of (political) non-alignment and Pan-Africanism have become diluted, advocacy of (economic) self-reliance has become relatively commonplace. The ECA, in suggesting designs for national and collective self-reliance, is taking the part of the majority of peripheral, Fourth World states rather than advancing the interests of the minority in the semi-periphery. Instead of being permissive about Africa's inheritance of integration within the world system, especially within EurAfrica, the ECA has called for a reconsideration of unequal exchange, a re-evaluation of international economic relations:

> Their significance lies in the role they play in facilitating or inhibiting (a) the establishment of self-reliance, i.e. the substitution of domestic for foreign factor imports, and (b) the promotion of self sustainment, i.e. the substitution of internally generated forces determining the speed and direction of economic growth ...[11]

The ECA has encouraged such self-reliance at national, regional and continental levels, with efforts at the latter level being increased in 1980 through the first OAU-ECA economic summit which was sandwiched between Lome II and III. The Lagos Declaration on Africa's economic future advocated a continental common market by the year 2000 as the only way to avoid forecast inequalities and underdevelopment.[12] But in the more immediate future, the ECA still encourages efforts at regional integration as stepping-stones towards continental cooperation. Despite, or because of, the elusiveness of development in Africa, the ECA is in the vanguard of moves towards more appropriate and innovative development strategies. However, elegant declarations and designs do not by themselves transform a history of incorporation and a projection of impoverishment, especially when the global economy of the 1980s is less accommodating than that of the first two decades of formal political independence; hence the continued attachment to Europe in case some crumbs 'trickle down' from the tables of the rich. Effective economic decolonisation may remain elusive for the rest of the century, despite advocacy of self-reliance, especially in the periphery, even if less so in the semi-periphery, and especially if ambiguities about regionalism persist.

D.   AFRICAN REGIONALISM IN THE 1980s: FROM EURAFRICA TO PAN-AFRICA?

The site of the April 1980 economic summit - Lagos - is also the headquarters of the latest attempt at regional integration - ECOWAS; it was also the centre of ACP strategy in the negotiations for Lome I. Despite the problems of effective collective self-reliance at the regional level in Africa since independence, optimism persists that this largest-ever grouping can succeed and so become one of the foundations for the proposed continental common market. This scenario of regionalism paving the way for continentalism serves to resolve the historic debates over the primacy of regionalism or continentalism, functionalism or federalism that have bedevilled previous attempts at development through integration. Yet the contradiction between Pan-African and EurAfrican integration remains despite increasing disinterest in Europe and growing diversity in Africa.

Paradoxically, ECOWAS was being discussed and designed at the same time as on the other coast the East African Community (EAC) was in a state of disorder and decay. Some ECOWAS institutions were structured with the failure of EAC in mind, but there are limits to which West African political economies can be pushed to avoid a similar tragedy on the West coast. The interests of dominant regional forces - those of indigenous and international capitalisms and of the semi-periphery - cannot be easily disregarded unless regionalism is defined in more radical terms than collective self-reliance. But, given the central role of elements within incumbent ruling classes[13] in espousing regionalist causes, any such redefinition in practice is quite unlikely, unless national and global pressures combine to change the position of such fractions. In short, unless more regimes go beyond the constraints of state capitalism and state socialism towards more genuine forms of socialism, regionalism may still serve established national and transnational class interests rather than advancing the BHN of the poor countries and communities. Despite frequent claims to the contrary, the continuing popularity of Pan-African regionalism may lie in its compatibility with dominant interests.[14] And it is these very interests which are still attracted to EurAfrica too, recognising that some fractions are more Pan-African and others more EurAfrican in orientation.

One reason for the apparent success of regionalism as a declaration in Africa, and conversely for its demise in practical or operational terms, is that it can be defined in a variety of ways.[15] Like 'African unity', it is a widely-agreed goal or ideology; but its conceptualisation or operationalisation is quite variable. John Renninger points to the theoretical roots of this ambiguity:

> African states lack, for the most part, the
> pre-requisites identified in the literature of
> regional integration as being necessary for
> successful integration to take place. But the
> relevance of that literature to underdeveloped
> countries is questionable, and, indeed, it is
> increasingly recognised that the entire body of
> theory is becoming passé. In particular, the
> necessity for developing countries to
> concentrate on the fundamental economic
> transformation of their societies, rather than
> on the expansion of trade through the
> elimination of various types of barriers, means
> that countries forming regional groups must
> pursue quite different policies than would be
> the case for developed countries that have
> followed the laissez-faire approach to
> economic integration.[16]

So the utility of links with, or ideas from, other
regional efforts is questionable. Indeed, genuine
attempts at collective self-reliance in Africa may
not benefit from, say, links with or ideas from such
links, and ideas may be quite contradictory to
authentic or autocentric African regionalism. If one
goal of regionalism is greater autonomy, then inter-
regional North-South relations, as in EEC-ACP
links, are counter-productive.[17] On the other hand,
South-South relations, as in, say, ECOWAS
connections with CARICOM or ASEAN, may be rather
fruitful, even if difficult.[18]
Yet, despite the demise of some schemes for
regional development in Africa and other parts of
the Third World, confidence in regional integration
amongst both indigenes and donors remains
surprisingly strong. In part, residual faith in such
a collective development strategy may be a
reflection of lack of alternatives. It may also
reflect the continued interaction amongst regional
integration efforts, both at the level of exchange
and at the level of conceptualisation.[19] However, no
external model or reference group can ensure the
success of other experiments. Although ECOWAS is
designed to ensure regional integration by stages -
free movement of goods and services, free movement
of capital, free movement of persons, and
cooperation in specific economic fields[20] - it
embodies several of the features that have retarded
or jeopardised cooperation with CARICOM and

elsewhere. In particular, James Sackey points to
the absence of the pre-conditions for regional
trade in West Africa, particularly the dominating
economic presence of Nigeria, and the difficulties
of redistributing income either between or within
member states. He argues that labour mobility will
not resolve this problem by itself: 'In the case of
ECOWAS, the income distribution problem is clearly
not adequately catered for by the Treaty (even at
the conceptual level)'.[21] Like others, Sackey
laments the absence of political as well as economic
will and content in ECOWAS, cautioning that economic
rationality alone is a necessary but not sufficient
condition for successful integration.[22] And
sufficient political will is unlikely to be present
while EurAfrican alternatives exist and until
internal contradictions become antagonistic.

In his analysis of the demise of the East
African Community, Agrippah Mugomba emphasised
divergent national and ideological interests:
different national development plans and
orientations and different foreign policies toward
African unity and liberation. He pointed in
particular to ways in which global and regional
pressures pushed post-uhuru Kenya in the direction
of sub-imperialism and post-Arusha Tanzania in the
direction of self-reliance. Integration in Africa,
according to Mugomba, requires:

> an ideological consensus among the partners,
> the acceptance of a common economic strategy, a
> willingness to tackle the regional problems of
> distribution, and the ability to devise
> effective methods of minimising inequalities.[23]

ECOWAS may claim to be based upon such a consensus,
but general understandings are likely to break down
under the stress of particular events or pressures.

So Renninger is sceptical about the formulation
and implementation of the ECOWAS treaty. He
concludes that it is unlikely to overcome either
dependence or underdevelopment because of diverse
economic and political interests within the region
clustered around the competing EurAfrican nexus:
transnational class linkages and uneven development
work against a more fundamental definition or
interpretation of regional integration. 'Thus,
although ECOWAS can undoubtedly contribute to the
achievement of collective self-reliance in West
African sub-regions, it will not, by itself, lead to
collective self-reliance.'[24] More basic issues of

political economy would have to be addressed for
such regional plans to be designed and effected. But
the post-colonial ruling class has little interest
in going beyond reform towards a more radical
definition of regionalism, especially the ruling
classes within regional centres like Nigeria with
their EurAfrican connections.

ECOWAS for instance, is essentially an orthodox
common market with some developmental content, but
its structural intent is quite limited: it seeks
free trade in goods and peoples rather than the
creation of a more self-reliant regional political
economy, the rhetoric of collective self-reliance
notwithstanding. Although the diversity of interests
and resources - and learning from the demise of
EAC - was reflected in the creation of a Fund for
Co-operation, Compensation and Development, this
Fund is not central to ECOWAS' structure or success.
Moreover, its novel 'collective defence' potential
reflective as it is of the centrality of 'security'
issues as prerequisites for regionalism is an
adjunct to its central purpose rather than integral
to its design; it may also raise questions about the
compatibility of ECOWAS with the OAU, given the
latter's off-on interest in an African High Command.
However, the basic issue confronting regionalism in
Africa is not compatibility with either the EEC or
the OAU, although these remain important issues;
rather, it is compatibility with established
political economies and ruling classes. And, when
these are outward oriented towards extra-
continental integration, intra-continental
connections remain undeveloped and unimportant.

In a more critical vein, Sackey has raised some
of these major concerns about regionalism: their
external support and their regional consequences. On
extra-African advocates, he laments that 'the role
of class interest and the transnational domination
through peripheral organisations, such as the local
merchants, in shaping the ultimate destiny of ECOWAS
appears not to be recognised by authors in the
area'.[25] And on regional class solidarity - as
expressed in plans for regional collective security
- he warns that regionalism may constrain
experimentation in political economy:

> The presence of class interest and political
> opportunism in the formation of ECOWAS would,
> as in the case of CARICOM, mean the endorsement
> of a developmental ideology which favour (sic)
> capitalism as the only solution to the poverty

> of the region. This, in turn, would create a favourable atmosphere for the development and consolidation of the class interests of the rapidly rising national bourgeoisies and petty bourgeoisies within the region. The converse of this development would be the elimination of socialism and the inhibiting of a socialist perspective of natural growth and transformation elsewhere.[26]

With remarkable foresight - he wrote before the Rawlings and Doe coups and before the anti-Pereira putsch in Guinea-Bissau and the abortive uprising in Gambia - Sackey warned progressive forces in West Africa about collective conservatism rather than collective self-reliance or socialism:

> This might take several forms, such as military coup in Guinea or support for further state capitalist development in Guinea-Bissau. The ultimate of these developments is the entrenchment of an authoritarian central state, at the service of capitalism, through the concept of political functionalism.[27]

In which case, regionalism would not only fail to advance either development or disengagement, it would also serve to limit the range of choice of African states: regional political order may be achieved at the cost of regional economic development. This, after all, is the function of regional powers - to maintain regional order. The felt need for this 'interventive' role may grow, as semi-periphery and periphery diverge in the future. Moreover, protectionist pressures in the world system may make development ever more elusive, generating more contradictions and antagonisms. In short, the prospects for regionalism advancing either development or self-reliance in Africa would appear to be less promising for the next (and final) 20-year period than in the previous 20 years, a period characterised by exceptional growth in the global economy. Neo-mercantilism in the north may reinforce the regional dominance of the semi-periphery and serve to marginalise the periphery further. In which case, Pan-African regionalism may seek to contain increased contradictions rather than advance self-reliance. Yet, even the maintenance of the status quo is problematic, given divisive external pressures, especially those within the EurAfrican regionalist nexus. In short, for

different fractions, different forms of regionalism
may come to represent control and connections rather
than autonomy and development.

E.   FUTURE OF UNITY AND DEVELOPMENT IN AFRICA:
      BEYOND EURAFRICA

Given (a) changes in the global and regional
political economies and (b) ambiguities in the
design and direction of regionalisms in Africa,
predictive   scenarios   are   rather   problematic.
However, the distinction in the literature between
orthodox   and   radical   investigations   and
prescriptions can be extended into the mid-term
future. This would at least provide a framework for
evaluating the prospects for and progress of ECOWAS.
Nevertheless, such a task remains hazardous, as
unforeseen eventualities can arise (e.g. dramatic
increases in the prices of energy or money) and
social   relations   ipace   max   are   not   readily
predictable (e.g. the expansion, contraction and
reaction of the indigenous proletariat). Quite
clearly, however, linkages amongst the centre, semi-
periphery and periphery are not static, while the
impact of regionalist schemes on them is likely to
be rather marginal. Nevertheless, the outcome of the
dialectic between semi-periphery and periphery is
of considerable importance to the definition and
orientation of regional communities like ECOWAS.
    At least five central questions can be raised
about the intention and direction of regional
integration in Africa before the year 2000, the
answers to which will depend on whether a more
orthodox or a more radical mode of analysis is
applied. In turn, any projections will be informed
by the different positions and perceptions of these
divergent approaches. All need to be situated in the
context of prevailing and pervasive security and
economic structures.
    First, who are the major advocates of
regionalism? They may be located outside the region
(e.g. multinational corporations and international
organisations versus national bourgeois fractions
or the labour aristocracy within the proletariat).
Which of these social formations is dominant in
designing and establishing regional institutions
will be reflected in regional priorities and
processes. In general, the more national the
bourgeois forces and the more proletarian the
advocates, the greater the prospects for African
self-reliance,   even   if   not   necessarily   for

socialism.[28] Conversely, the more comprador the bourgeois fraction and 'aristocratic' the labour, the greater the prospects for EurAfrican connections.

Secondly, and related to the first point, does regionalism seek to reform or refine the international division of labour? If on the one hand its concern is with increased self-reliance rather than with increased trade, it would seek to reform or transform the regional and global divisions of labour away from the 'peripheral capitalism' of extraction and towards a greater degree of industrialisation. If, on the other hand, its concern is with increased exchange, as in EurAfrica, it will attempt to refine but not reform its position: producing more and selling higher, but not altering its place in the global hierarchy. Clearly some regionalists (inside and outside West Africa) would prefer reform - Pan-African regionalism - while others would support just refinement in the region's place in the international division of labour - EurAfrican regionalism.

Thirdly, depending on which transnational coalition of regionalists prevails and the degree of reform thereby advanced, regional cooperation may be concentrated in different sectors: trade, industry, agriculture, service or labour. Orthodox functionalists tend to concentrate on trade creation and diversion, whereas neo-functionalists emphasise industrialisation, technology and capital-formation. Few regionalists advocate agricultural growth because of assumed lack of complementarity, although in fact regional food production is becoming an imperative (e.g. for both the Sahel and Nigeria[29]). A balanced range of regional sectors may be desirable but that would have to be premised on a balanced set of regional advocates and resources, an unlikely situation. In general, regional schemes lay down a political framework and physical infrastructures for cooperation: who benefits depends on who can best exploit these facilities.

Fourthly, the purposes of regionalism can differ from development to dominance. The peripheral participants would tend to favour the former orientation; semi-peripheral and core actors (state and non-state) the latter, despite their relative disinterest in regionalism because of the global reach of their interests. Clearly, the direction of any regional institution depends on which advocates, functions and sectors are dominant.

In the ECOWAS case, is regionalism (a) to help the majority of poor states and citizens to develop, and/or (b) to help the minority of middling rich (e.g. state and non-state interests in Ivory Coast and Nigeria) to grow, and/or (c) to advance the interests of metropolitan countries and corporations (e.g. those most closely associated with EurAfrica, a collective and contemporary form of 'neo-colonialism' in an essentially post-neocolonial world)?

Finally, what results might be expected from these alternative variants of regionalism? An orthodox, semi-peripheral perspective would favour the development of underdevelopment, because its advocates can benefit thereby. However, a more radical, peripheral position would prefer the reduction of dependence and the encouragement of development through collective self-reliance. But, because the latter position threatens established metropolitan and semi-peripheral interests, its prospects are circumscribed. On the other hand, if protectionism on a world scale leads to trade wars, then regions as well as states[30] may be forced to look inwards rather than outwards, as noted in the final paragraph below.

In any event, the outcome of the orthodox versus radical competition overlaps with the periphery versus semi-periphery tension as well as with Pan- versus Eur-African conception; both of these respective modes of analysis and modes of production are preferred by antagonistic national, regional and global social formations, with their respective transnational coalitions. The future of ECOWAS depends essentially on the outcome of these complex confrontations which, in turn, are functions of changes in 'national' political economies within the world system.

Finally, the environment for regionalism in Africa depends not only on regional, continental and global conditions in general but also on the outcome of the struggle in southern Africa in particular: will uneventful (reformist) or eventful (revolutionary) scenarios materialise there. For, just as political and economic relations among regions have affected the character and potential of ECOWAS (i.e. North-South linkages with EEC and South-South linkages with ASEAN, CARICOM, etc.), so the prospects for regionalism in southern Africa constitute, on the one hand an intriguing model for West Africa and, on the other hand a potential resource base.

In the past, African continental unity has been facilitated by collective opposition to colonialism and racism in southern Africa. In the future, African regional unity may be encouraged by the model and resources of southern Africa, with implications for the ability to resist EurAfrican pressures. The 'pariah' middle power of that region - South Africa - has made a series of largely unsuccessful attempts since World War Two to widen patterns of regional cooperation in the southern part of the continent to enhance its own economic growth and military security. However, the execution of successful wars of liberation in Angola, Mozambique and Zimbabwe has not only increased opposition to South Africa's schemes but has provided the foundation for counter-dominance institutions, despite the latter's relentless pressure for bilateral strategic understandings. The Front Line States, along with Malawi and Botswana, Lesotho and Swaziland (BBLS) have created a Southern African Development Coordination Conference (SADCC) to avoid and resist South Africa's continuing attempts at regional hegemony. This innovative regional proposal is distinctive, not only because it is related to the continuing war effort in Namibia and South Africa, but also because it brings together a group of state socialist regimes.

If SADCC regionalism works, it will constitute a challenge not only to South African 'sub-imperialism'[31] but also to more orthodox patterns of regionalism elsewhere on the continent. The appearance of more radical regimes in southern Africa because of the protracted liberation struggle there has already upset the continental dominance of more conservative (often semi-peripheral) states. The further transformation of these state socialist regimes into a viable radical regional political economy would pose another challenge to more benign forms of regionalism as in ECOWAS, as well as to prevailing actions of EurAfricanism.

In which case, by both example and resources, southern Africa might come to affect the orthodox versus radical political and analytical balances in West Africa. In turn, this would serve to reinforce the pressures towards more progressive and self-reliant Pan-African strategies already apparent because of the protectionist mood in the advanced industrialised states: the problematic character of EurAfrica in a disinterested Europe. The international division of labour between centre, semi-periphery and periphery would be further undermined as mercantilism in the North and disengagement in southern Africa came to produce alternative patterns of exchange and accumulation. Steven Langdon and Lynn Mytelka have put such change in southern Africa into the context of shifts within global and continental political economies:

> Armed conflict in Southern Africa, though, is likely to be no more than the most dramatic form of confrontation between dependence and self-reliance in the 1980s. We expect the contradictions of periphery capitalism in Africa to become more acute in most countries on the continent in the next decade, and we expect the struggles for change in such countries to become more bitter as a result. We are confident, however, that out of such conflict can come more equitable and self-reliant development strategies that benefit the great majority of Africans.[32]

In which case, the future for unity and development at continental and regional levels in Africa may be rather brighter but no less certain than already suggested.

ECOWAS, and other Pan-African regionalist designs on the continent, can only be explained and projected in the context of such pressures - national, regional, continental and global - in the international division of labour. Hence the continuing dialectic with EurAfrican conceptions, unless protectionism and recession so undermine extroverted fractions among Europe's bourgeoisies that the EEC comes to pull away from the ACP rather than vice versa. In a post-neocolonial world, ACP advocates of Lome may yet be abandoned by a combination of (a) introversion and isolation in Europe[33] and (b) Africa's Fourth World, leaving the semi-periphery fractionless between a protectionist centre and a self-reliant periphery.[34] In which case, Pan-African conceptions of regionalism would no longer have to compete with residual EurAfrican definitions,[35] and Pan-Africanism could re-establish its primacy over EurAfricanism; a prerequisite for the redefinition of regionalism as self-reliance.

NOTES

* An earlier version of this chapter is to appear as 'ECOWAS and the Political Economy of Regionalism in Africa' in Julius Okolo and

Stephen Wright (eds.) West African Regional Cooperation (forthcoming).

[1] See Robert Boardman, Panayotis Soldates and Timothy M. Shaw (eds.), The EEC, Africa and Lome III (Washington, University Press of America, 1984, Dalhousie African Studies Series).

[2] T. dos Santos, 'The Crisis of Development Theory and the Problems of Dependence in Latin America', in Henry Bernstein (ed.), Underdevelopment and Development: The Third World Today (Hardmonsworth, Penguin, 1973), p.73.

[3] See Timothy M. Shaw, 'Introduction: The Political Economy of Africa's Futures' and Adebayo Adedeji, 'Development and Economics of Africa's Future to the Year 2000: Alternative Projections and Policies' in Timothy M. Shaw (ed.), Alternative Futures for Africa (Boulder, Westview, 1981), pp.1-16 and 279-304.

[4] See Timothy M. Shaw, 'Discontinuities and Inequalities in African International Politics', International Journal 30 (3), Summer 1975, pp.369-90; and 'The Actors in African International Politics', in Timothy M. Shaw and Kenneth A. Heard (eds.), The Politics of Africa: Dependence and Development (London, Longman, 1979, pp.357-96.

[5] On the Characters and Constraints of Semi-Peripheral Political Economies, see Immanuel Wallerstein, The Capitalist World-Economy (Cambridge: Cambridge University Press, 1979), pp.66-118; and Peter Evans, Dependent Development: The Alliance of Multinational, State and Local Capital in Brazil (Princeton, Princeton University Press, 1979), passim.

[6] For an introduction to and comparison between these two modes of analyses, see Timothy M. Shaw, 'Africa', in Werner J. Feld and Gavin Boyd (eds.), Comparative Regional Systems (Elmsford, Pergamon, 1980), pp.355-97. See also, I. William Zartman, 'The Future of Europe and Africa: Decolonisation or Dependency', Foreign Affairs 34 (2), January 1976, pp.325-43; revised version in Shaw (ed.), Alternative Future for Africa, pp.259-77.

[7] See Claude Ake, Revolutionary Pressures in Africa (London, Zed, 1978), pp.92-144.

[8] See Kal Holsti (ed.), Why Nations Realign: Foreign Policy Restructuring in Post-War World (London, George Allen & Unwin, 1982).

[9] On the Nigerian Case, see Timothy M. Shaw, 'Introduction: Nigeria as Africa's Major Power', in

Timothy M. Shaw and Olajide Aluko (eds.), <u>Nigerian Foreign Policy: Alternative Perceptions and Projections</u> (London, Macmillan, 1983).

[10] See Timothy M. Shaw and Don Munton, 'Africa's Futures: A Comparison of Forecasts' in Shaw (ed.), <u>Alternative Futures for Africa</u>, pp.37-92.

[11] <u>Biennial Report of the Executive Secretary of the United Nations Economic Commission for Africa 1977-1978</u> (Addis Ababa, February 1979, E/CN.14/695) 12.

[12] See ECA <u>Plan of Action for the Implementation of the Monrovia Strategy for the Economic Development of Africa ... to the First Economic Summit of the Assembly of Heads of State and Government of the OAU, Lagos, Nigeria, 28 and 29 April 1980</u> (Addis Ababa, 1980). E/CN.14/781/Add.1), especially pp.1-8.

[13] On the Nigerian debate over whether to advocate or oppose ECOWAS, an issue which is closely related to the whole issue of Nigeria's political economy, development strategy and global position, see Olatunde J. B. Ojo, 'Nigeria and the Formation of ECOWAS', <u>International Organization</u> 34 (4), Autumn 1980, pp.571-604. In turn, this issue is one aspect of the continual bargaining that occurs within the 'triple alliance' of social forces that characterise the semi-periphery; regionalism is a prospect that affects the balance of forces within the 'complex alliance between elite local capital, international capital and state capital' (Peter Evans, <u>Dependent Development: The Alliance of Multinational, State and Local Capital in Brazil</u> [Princeton, Princeton University Press, 1979], II).

[14] i.e. some elements within the triple alliance may favour regional initiatives (both economic and strategic) over global connections whereas other fractions may prefer links with the metropole over connections with the periphery; hence the ambiguity of foreign policy in regional centres such as Ivory Coast, Kenya and Nigeria.

[15] From a more materialist perspective, such variation in definition is a function of different relations to the mode of production as well as of different fractions within the local bourgeoisie.

[16] John P. Renninger, 'The Future of Economic Cooperation Schemes in Africa, with Special Reference to ECOWAS', in Shaw (ed.), <u>Alternative Futures for Africa</u>, p.160.

[17] On the reformation of EurAfrican links in the post-colonial world, see Timothy M. Shaw, 'EEC-ACP Interactions and Images as Redefinitions of

EurAfrica: Exemplary, Exclusive and/or Exploitative?', Journal of Common Market Studies 18 (2), December 1979, pp.135-8.

[18] See Anirudha Gupta, 'South-South Cooperation, India and Africa: "Partners in Development"?' in Timothy M. Shaw and Ralph I. Onwuka (eds.), Africa and World Politics: Independence, Dependence and Interdependence (London, George Allen & Unwin, 1984).

[19] James A. Sackey, 'The Structure and Performance of CARICOM: Lessons for the Development of ECOWAS', Canadian Journal of African Studies 12 (2), 1978, p.263, points to similarities amongst the definitions of terms employed by EEC, CARICOM and ECOWAS.

[20] See Ibid., p.260, and Okon Udokang 'ECOWAS: Theoretical and Practical Problems of Integration', Nigerian Journal of International Studies 2 (I), April 1978, pp.1-20; and Ralph I. Onwuka, 'The ECOWAS Treaty: Inching Towards Implementation', World Today 36 (2), February 1980, pp.52-9.

[21] Sackey, 'The Structure and Performance of CARICOM', p.268. See also, Aguibou Y. Yansane, 'West African Economic Integration: Is ECOWAS the Answer?', Africa Today, 24 (3), July-September 1977 pp.43-59; and Ralph I. Onwuka, 'The Multinational Corporation and Regional Integration in West Africa', in Timothy M. Shaw and Sola Ojo (eds.), Africa and the International Political System (Washington, University Press of America, 1982).

[22] Of course, from a more critical perspective, the political economies of member states may include a variety of interests and goals: success for different national fractions may not equal success in terms of the ECOWAS treaty.

[23] Agrippah T. Mugomba, 'Regional Organisations and African Underdevelopment: The Collapse of the East African Community', Journal of Modern African Studies 16 (2), June 1978, p.267.

[24] Renninger, 'The Future of Economic Cooperation Schemes in Africa', p.170. See also John P. Renninger, Multinational Cooperation for Development in West Africa (Elmsford, N.Y., Pergamon, 1979).

[25] Sackey, 'The Structure and Performance of CARICOM', p.272.

[26] Ibid., p.273.

[27] Ibid., p.273.

[28] This formulation raises interesting questions about the regionalist inclinations of social forces in both the periphery and the semi-

periphery: the subject of another paper, however.

[29] See Barry B. Hughes and Patricia A. Strauch, 'The Future of Development in Nigeria and the Sahel: Projections from the World Integrated Model (WIM)', in Shaw (ed.), Alternative Futures for Africa, pp.179-200.

[30] Evans, (Dependent Development, p.321) comments on this paradox: 'As the alliance between the state and the multinationals has been strengthened in the "semi-periphery" relations between the multinationals and the state in the centre have become more constrained'.

[31] See Timothy M. Shaw 'Kenya and South Africa: 'Sub-Imperialist' States', Orbis 21 (2), Summer 1977, pp. 357-94.

[32] Steven Langdon and Lynn K. Mytelka, 'Africa in the Changing World Economy', in Colin Legum et al., Africa in the 1980s: A Continent in Crisis (New York, McGraw-Hill, 1979. Council on Foreign Relations 1980s Project), p.104.

[33] See Boardman, Soldatos and Shaw (eds.), The EEC, Africa and Lome III.

[34] See Timothy M. Shaw, Towards a Political Economy for Africa: The Dialectics of Dependence (London, Macmillan, 1984).

[35] See David F. Luke and Timothy M. Shaw (eds.), Continental Crisis: The OAU Lagos Plan of Action and Africa's Future (Washington, University Press of America, 1984, Dalhousie African Studies Series).

Jinmi Adisa is a Lecturer in the Department of Political Science, University of Ibadan, Nigeria.

Adigun Agbaje is a Lecturer in the Department of Political Science, University of Ibadan.

Sola Akinrinade is a Lecturer in the Department of History, University of Ife.

S.K.B. Asante is a Professor of Political Science, University of Ghana, Legon.

Dennis Austin is a Professor of Government, Manchester University.

Daniel Bach is a Research Fellow, Centre d'Etude d'Afrique Noire, Bordeaux.

Toyin Falola is a Senior Lecturer in the Department of History, University of Ife.

James Mayall is a Reader in the Department of International Relations at the London School of Economics and Political Science.

James Mulira is a Lecturer in the Department of History, University of Nairobi.

Amadu Sesay is a Senior Lecturer in the Department of International Relations, University of Ife.

Timothy Shaw is a Professor of Political Science, Dalhousie University.

Fola Soremekun is a Senior Lecturer in the Department of History, University of Ife.

Africa
drought in 39, 177
economic development
in 157, 178, 184,
193, 194
foreign aid in, see
specific country
Lagos Plan of Action
206-8, 213, 215,
223
minerals and resources
in 43, 59, 66, 84,
112
regional integration
230, 232, 236, 238
Algeria 12, 84, 142, 147,
148, 171, 226, 228,
230
Angola 12, 42, 45, 47,
48, 49, 80, 144, 147,
148
civil war in 39, 40,
79, 86, 91-3, 96,
108, 139, 158, 168
colonialism in 86-8,
90
Eastern Bloc aid 93,
96
scramble for 25
Soviet Union 94, 105,
107, 110, 113, 154
Anti-Apartheid Movement
(AAM) 66, 119

Belgium 13, 15, 16, 19,
21, 42, 169

Benin 9, 42, 43, 80,
142, 148
Berlin Congress
1878 15
1884/5 19, 21, 39,
49, 150, 152, 184,
185, 222
border disputes 38, 40,
43, 48, 82
Botswana 62, 133
Brandt Commission 59,
201
Britain 3-8, 12-13, 79
Congress of Berlin
(1884) 19
decolonization 53,
139, 140
East Africa 22-4, 36
foreign aid 61, 62
Horn of Africa 24, 25
scramble 22, 32
southern Africa 25,
26, 66, 67, 71
Suez 17, 18, 19, 23,
53, 154
West Africa 17, 18,
41
Burkina Faso (Upper
Volta) 43, 48, 142
Burundi 39, 40, 142

Cameroon 19, 35, 41, 48,
77, 78, 82, 143
Central African Federa-
tion 54, 62, 70, 71
Central African

Republic 80, 81, 82,
    141, 142, 143, 144,
    146, 158, 160
Chad 39, 41, 43, 45, 47,
    48, 76, 77, 78, 80,
    81, 142, 143, 144
China 110, 111, 114, 136,
    138, 156
Christianity and Africa
    1, 2, 6, 7, 9, 10, 11,
    12, 27
Commonwealth 53, 56, 57,
    58, 59, 60, 62, 64,
    65, 129, 139, 140,
    192, 196
Comoro Islands 79, 142
Congo 2, 15, 16, 17, 21,
    77, 79
Congo Brazzaville 80, 142
Cuba
    southern Africa 42,
        43, 80, 97, 108,
        114, 115, 118, 154,
        163, 169, 170, 171

Dahomey 9
Djibuti 44, 45, 49

Economic Commission of
    West African States
    (ECOWAS) 57, 208, 224,
    231, 232, 233, 234,
    235, 237, 239
Egypt 1, 12, 15, 17, 18,
    43, 81, 114, 147, 226,
    230
    relations with Britain
        17, 18, 19, 23, 24
    see Suez under Africa
Equatorial Guinea 44
Ethiopia 39, 42, 43, 47,
    48, 63, 80, 106, 158,
    Italy 24, 25
    civil war 39, 40, 41,
        45
    and Soviet Union 110
European Economic
    Community (EEC) 56,
    57, 65, 78, 83, 99,
    111, 141, 183-5, 189,
    190, 193, 195, 197,

198, 203, 205, 211,
    212, 226, 229, 233
European exploration
    colonialism 7, 35,
        37, 38, 89 passim
    decolonization 35,
        53 passim
    occupation of Africa
        13, 17, 29-31
    reasons for scramble
        5, 9, 13-16, 21,
        56
France 2, 4-6, 12, 14-
    16, 42, 43, 45, 133,
    136, 141, 142, 143,
    145, 146, 171
    Chad 76, 78, 81
        see also Chad
    foreign aid 76, 77,
        83, 84, 141
    Franc zone 76, 77,
        140, 156
    Guinea 75, 77
    Nigeria 76, 77, 78,
        79
    South Africa 79, 80,
        see also South
        Africa
    Suez 17, 23, 154
    West Africa 17, 22
Front Line States 55, 80

Gabon 16, 76, 77, 78,
    79, 80, 141, 142,
    143, 146, 154
Gambia 12, 54, 63
General Agreement on
    Trade and Tariffs
    (GATT) 56, 63
Germany 12, 13, 14, 17,
    32
    scramble 17, 18, 19,
        22, 23, 35
    East Africa 23, 24,
        28, 36
    southern Africa 25,
        26
    South West Africa 36
    foreign aid 61 passim
Ghana (or Gold Coast) 2,
    3, 12, 32, 40, 41,

53, 147
Guinea 25, 77, 148, 154, 159, 164-7
Guinea Bissau 89, 148, 159, 236

Holland 3, 6

India 3, 35, 62, 99
    British India 14, 70
International Monetary Fund (IMF) 42, 210
intervention
    types of 47, 152-5, 159, 160
    OAU responses to 160-72
    by France 79 passim
irredentism 41, 116, 158
Italy 13, 14, 15, 24, 36
Ivory Coast 43, 77, 78, 83, 141, 142, 226, 230

Japan
    foreign aid 61

Kenya 23, 36, 42, 62, 226, 230, 234

Liberia 5, 7, 9, 21, 160
Libya 35, 41, 42, 48, 81, 142, 143, 148, 171
Lome Convention 5, 7, 184-6, 188, 193, 195-7
    Stabex scheme 198-202, 203, 209, 226

Madagascar 77, 142
Malawi 62
Mali 43, 48, 75, 142, 147
Mauritania 79, 142, 144, 146
Mauritius 142
Middle East 2, 35, 47, 135
Morocco 2, 35, 42, 142
Mozambique 12, 39, 47, 80, 148, 170
    and civil war 40, 86, 89, 93, 139
    and scramble 25
    colonialism 86, 87,

88, 90
    and Soviet Policy 105

nationalism 40, 46, 48, 116
New International Economic Order (NIEO) 57, 59, 205, 206
Niger 19, 21, 36, 43, 77, 83, 84, 141, 142, 143
Nigeria 7, 12, 39, 40, 41, 45, 48, 56, 57, 63, 65, 76-9, 82, 147, 169, 226, 228
non-alignment 148
North Atlantic Treaty Organization (NATO) 146, 164
nuclear weapons 156

Organization of African Unity (OAU) 38, 39, 44, 45, 67, 81, 90, 161, 168, 227, 229, 231
    intervention and 80, 164-7
    weaknesses of 174 passim
Organization of Petroleum Exporting Countries(OPEC) 157, 226

Pan-Africanism 43, 105, 146, 163, 171
Portugal 2, 3, 9, 21
    slave trade 4, 6, 87
    southern Africa 12, 139, 148
    West Africa 9, 154

Romans and Africa 1, 2, 35
Rwanda 39, 40, 49, 142

secession 45-8
Senegal 2, 12, 15, 21, 36, 40, 78, 230
Seychelles 142

Index

Sierra Leone 5, 7, 9, 10,
    12, 45, 54, 63
slave trade 1, 3, 4, 5,
    6, 7, 8, 87
Somalia 36, 39, 41, 42,
    48, 106, 107, 110, 148
South Africa 40-2, 47,
    65, 98, 105, 113, 114,
    119, 148
    Angola 96, 98, 108
    apartheid 39, 68, 74,
        140
    arms embargo 67
    British-Boer rivalry
        25, 26
    France 78
    Mozambique 170
    sanctions against 71
    strategic position 14,
        66, 112, 137, 138,
        141
Southern African Develop-
    ment Coordination
    Conference (SADCC) 63,
    72, 208, 224, 240
South West Africa 18, 23,
    42, 68, 80, 97, 113,
    119
Spain 2, 6
Sudan 11, 22, 24, 36,
    39, 40, 42, 45, 47,
    81, 148, 158
Sweden 6, 45

Tanzania 44, 48
Togo 32, 41, 44
trade 7, 8, 9, 11, 12, 56
    colonial trade patterns
        194, 195, 196, 197,
        228
    inter-African 157
Tunisia 15, 142
Turkey 23, 35

Uganda 36, 40, 45, 158
United Nations 41, 66,
    68, 69, 71, 105, 155,
    156
    and apartheid 67, 71,
        81
USA 5, 57, 61, 67, 69,

79, 82, 116, 118,
    145, 147, 148, 149,
    East Africa 42
    foreign aid 61, 63,
        83, 156
    Horn 42
    Morocco 42
USSR 43, 69, 105, 106,
    145, 147, 148, 149,
    159
    foreign aid 105, 109,
        111, 114, 115,
        117, 148, 156
    minerals 133, 136,
        138
    southern Africa 42,
        43, 94, 99, 112,
        154, 163
    Suez 23

Western Sahara 39, 41,
    44

Yaounde 141, 190-2

Zaire 39, 40, 42, 45,
    48, 49, 77, 78, 79,
    80, 82, 108, 112,
    133, 142, 143, 144,
    154, 155, 158, 168,
    169, 171
Zambia 40, 62, 112, 168
    and minerals 133
Zimbabwe 39, 40, 54, 60,
    62, 71, 95, 96, 112,
    113, 226, 230
    and minerals 133, 140

For Product Safety Concerns and Information please contact our EU
representative GPSR@taylorandfrancis.com Taylor & Francis Verlag GmbH,
Kaufingerstraße 24, 80331 München, Germany

Printed and bound by CPI Group (UK) Ltd, Croydon, CR0 4YY
08/05/2025
01864320-0001